The Best of
GRANTLAND RICE

Watts Sports Books

BASEBALL'S GREATEST PLAYERS TODAY
Edited by Jack Orr

THE BEST OF RED SMITH
Selected by Verna Reamer

MORE SPORT, SPORT, SPORT
Selected by John Lowell Pratt

PRO, PRO, PRO
Selected by John Lowell Pratt

THE QUARTERBACKS
Edited by Don Smith

SPORT, SPORT, SPORT
Selected by John Lowell Pratt

The Best of
GRANTLAND RICE

Selected by Dave Camerer

FRANKLIN WATTS, INC.
575 Lexington Avenue • New York 22

Acknowledgments

To A. S. Barnes & Company, Inc. for permission to reprint
chapters from THE TUMULT AND THE SHOUTING by
Grantland Rice. Copyright 1954 by A. S. Barnes & Company, Inc.

To the estate of Grantland Rice for permission
to reprint poems from THE FINAL ANSWER
published by A. S. Barnes & Company, Inc.

To The New York Tribune (New York Herald-Tribune)
for permission to reprint several SPORTLIGHT
columns and newspaper stories. © The New York
Tribune, Inc. (New York Herald-Tribune)

To the Curtis Publishing Company for permission to reprint
NEVER ANOTHER JONES from *The Saturday Evening Post*.

To the Macfadden-Bartell Corporation for permission to reprint
IT TAKES PLENTY TO WIN THE TRIPLE CROWN
from SPORT, May 1947, OPEN LETTER TO A COLLEGE
PRESIDENT from SPORT, May 1950.

To The North American Newspaper Alliance for permission to
reprint the many columns from SPORTLIGHT and the several
news stories which were syndicated by them.

To Crowell-Collier Publishing Co., Inc. for permission to Reprint
THE GRANTLAND RICE ALL-AMERICA TEAM OF 1937
from *Collier's*.

To Jack Wheeler, Grantland Rice's firm friend, who was of great
help in making this book possible.

First Printing
Library of Congress Catalog Card Number: 63-21363
Copyright © 1963 by J. Lowell Pratt & Company, Inc.
Printed in the United States of America

Contents

From *The Saturday Evening Post.*

PART THREE: THE OLD ORDER CHANGES

PART FOUR: THE TYPEWRITER GROWS HEAVIER

* From *The Tumult and the Shouting* by Grantland Rice.
Copyright 1954 by A. S. Barnes & Company, Inc.

The Best of
GRANTLAND RICE

GRANTLAND RICE
BY JAMES MONTGOMERY FLAGG

INTRODUCTION

Following Grantland Rice's death in 1954, Movie Producer Mark Robson, endeavoring to zero in on a strong central core in Rice's life, said that it seemed to him that, along with Lardner, Hemingway and Fitzgerald, Rice lived a kind of charmed, careless life—at times punishing himself by excesses and often times taking terrible chances.

In reply to the question, John Kieran, former sports columnist for the *New York Times* said: "Grant was like Babe Ruth, physically. He had enormous endurance and resistance. I was often amazed at how he could talk, drink and work at the same time for days at a time. He could turn out columns while going through a concrete mixer."

Kieran should know. During Rice's more than 50 years of professional life, Granny's hard rock constitution enabled him to pound out more and better prose and verse than any American author.

In the prologue of his final testament, *The Tumult and the Shouting,* Granny asked the question, "Why this book?"

"It seems to me," he wrote, "that I have already written too many words. I know, better than anyone else, that I should have ceased firing years ago. Well, work, above everything else, is habit forming. From 1901 through the better part of 1954, I have written over 67,000,000 words, including more than 22,000 columns, 7,000 sets of verse, over 1,000 magazine articles plus numberless working scripts for my SPORTLIGHT films. . . ."

In retrospect, any man who could fulfill such a continuous assignment on the treadmill of life, indeed needed a wonderfully healthy and realistic approach to work. But Granny had something more going for him. Where so many of us are replaceable cogs in the big machine, Granny, in himself, was the whole works. What fed that machine was his enthusiasm for people, places and events. However, if enthusiasm was the fuel, something more precious permeated the man and his work.

1

Not long ago, writer Robert F. Kelley touched on that certain something with more accuracy than most. "I'll always remember how, in any group of which Granny was the center, he had a way of picking out the fellow on the fringe," said Bob. "By putting a direct question to him, Granny made the outsider the sudden center of attraction. God, how he warmed people! He was the *kindest* man I ever knew."

Nobody had reason to appreciate Kelley's remarks more than I.

It was about 25 years ago that the sports editor of the *New York World-Telegram* tossed a bone to me, his rawest recruit. There was to be a Football Writers' luncheon at a certain New York hotel with many college and professional coaches there. If I hurried I might dig up my first byline.

Less than a half hour later, I stood outside that particular hotel dining room, nervously checking my buttons, when a man I instantly recognized approached. His gait was a pigeon-toed shuffle. He wore a blue serge suit, white shirt and blue polka dot bow tie. Apparently he sensed my apprehension concerning my first belly whopper into Journalism.

"Dave Camerer," greeted Grantland Rice with a smile and a handshake that would have melted a glacier. "My name is Rice. Meet my pal Frank Graham. We understand you're writing for the *Telegram*. Congratulations! If you're not waiting for somebody, how about sitting with us?"

As I entered that room, flanked by such a pair, John Philip Sousa's band could not have tendered a warmer launching.

Several Saturdays later, along with the *Telegram's* wheelhorse, Dan Daniel, I was assigned to work my first big college football game at the Yale Bowl. Dan would handle the lead and play-by-play while I groped for color notes and filler. Shortly after the kickoff, Dartmouth exploded for a quick touchdown. Forgetting where I was or what I was supposed to be, I was on my feet yelling to

2

beat hell for my old school. Thunderstruck, Daniel glared. "Siddown," he growled. "You're no longer a college kid. You're a newspaperman. Try to act like one."

Several typewriters away, Grantland Rice rose like a veritable Clarence Darrow. "Go to it, Dave!" he shouted. "Wake the dead! . . . First time in twenty years I've heard anybody in this old press box let loose with some college cheer."

There were other times down those hurrying years when to be in the same crowd with Grantland Rice and to share his affection and his enthusiasm made one extra proud to be a sportswriter. Bruce Barton, in his eulogy at Granny's funeral, said, "People felt better in his presence. He made us all feel better—made us feel that somehow we could do more, be more. This was his gift to his friends. . . ."

Incidentally, in Granny's choice of friends, age was absolutely no barrier. His lone overture to age was, "He's over forty . . . or under seventy." The years in between simply didn't count. All he asked was the interest and the enthusiasm. From Ring Lardner, a contemporary, to Gene Fowler who was ten years younger, to Henry McLemore or Red Smith at least twenty-five years younger, he took them as he found them. And when he was rolling in high gear he found them everywhere. In the dugouts . . . under the saddling sheds or in the paddocks of racing plants from coast to coast . . . at the 19th hole . . . at ringside . . . in press boxes and stadiums everywhere. Following a big football game there are writers who give birth to their bylines. Granny worked fast, without fuss or bother. After handing his copy to his wire man, he would make his way to the dressing rooms . . . not to the winning coach for his pearls of wisdom, but nearly always to the loser. Strange, wasn't it, that he should pay his respects to the beaten coach before he congratulated the victor.

Or was it?

Only the brave know what the hunted are—

3

The battered—and the shattered—and the lost—
Who know the meaning of each deep, red scar,
For which they paid the heartache and the cost.
Who've left the depths against unmeasured odds
To ask no quarter from the ruling gods.

Born—live—and die—cradle along to the grave.
The march is on—by bugle and by drum—
Where only those who beat life are the brave—
Who laugh at fate and face what is to come,
Knowing how swiftly all the years go by,
Where dawn and sunset blend in one brief sky.

The first time that I became acutely aware of Granny's advancing years was the Sunday following the 1947 Derby. We flew to New York in a plane that bucked like a bronc over the Alleghenies. Granny had been battling a deep chest cold that, subsequently, brought on pneumonia and another of his bouts with the oxygen tent. That heavy cold, the congestion in his lungs plus the combination of too little rest and too much of everything else during that Derby week had suddenly (it seemed) landed on him like a ton of bricks. As he debarked from that plane at LaGuardia late that Sunday afternoon, I suddenly realized that Granny was pushing seventy—and, for the first time, looked all of it.

For weeks it was touch and go. During that period, one day Granny's condition was discussed with Bill Corum. Strangely, it seemed, Bill suddenly slipped into the past tense.

"Granny gave himself all too cheaply to too many people," he said. "I said as much to him on many occasions but he simply shrugged it off."

Past tense or not, by July, Granny was back at the track bucking the Daily Double with his three racing sidekicks—former coach Greasy Neale, Ed Duffy, the political cartoonist for the *Saturday Evening Post,* and John McNulty, that rarely gifted essayist for *The New Yorker* magazine. Of that Scotch foursome only Neale remains.

4

A short while after Rice's death on July 13, 1954, I mentioned Corum's words to Rube Goldberg, the King Features cartoonist and a Rice contemporary clear back to 1910.

"Bill was right about Grant," said Rube. "He wasted a lot of himself. After all, down the stretch he had all that pneumonia and laryngitis . . . but you'd see him here, there and everywhere—in the press box or at the track, in miserable weather, with his collar turned up and hardly able to talk. Kit [his wife] would try to control him and keep him indoors, but after a day or two he *had* to get out and get going."

Did Rube consider Granny something of a fatalist, at least in his apparent unwillingness to guard his health?

"Death intrigued Grant . . . as it does Gene [Fowler]," replied Rube. "He was a hundred per cent fatalist and he and Lardner and Fowler enjoyed kicking death around with a light, sardonic humor. Dying to them was either a grand adventure or a joke. Grant and that bunch relished discussing and kidding it, gently. In Grant's case, I think it got him away from responsibilities and worries like the state of the cockeyed world, the market, war and the rest. One day over their martinis he and Fowler cooked up The Happy Morticians Club, of which they fancied themselves charter members. They'd laugh like hell about the cut rate embalming clothes they'd furnish, such as half-derbies, half-shoes, shirts, suits and the rest because this would involve only wasting half as much on the stiff."

In August of 1953, after Ben Hogan had won the British Open, the Texan was tendered a testimonial lunch at Toots Shor's. That particular noon I wandered into Toots' saloon and up to the second floor, scene of the party. The hour was early. There, alone at the bar, stood Granny. He was fingering his favorite drink, a dusty martini,"powder dry and bitter cold," and discussing some aspect of life with the bartender. He was glad to see me.

"This should be a nice affair," he said. "I only hope I don't louse it up. They've got me down as toastmaster . . .

5

but I feel like an interloper. After all, I wasn't over there with Ben. I didn't see a shot."

"Don't worry," I said. "With the shots you've covered, you can do it by memory." It made me feel good just to be able, for a change, to afford Granny a bit of comfort. A third arrival on the scene had barely accepted his drink when he turned to Granny and put the old question to him.

"About your autobiography, Granny. When will you tackle it?"

Rice smiled. "You want a direct answer?"

"Certainly."

"Probably never. I'm so far past the point of no return, it's all I can do to recall when I started and where I've been."

Concerning this volume, *The Best of Grantland Rice,* a great deal of himself appeared in that semi-autobiography *The Tumult and the Shouting,* which, as he stated, he didn't intend to write—but did. However, a great deal more of Granny at his uncompromising best— including excerpts from *The Tumult*—has been incorported in this volume. Under-the-gun columns that he hammered out from press boxes around the world . . . some of The Sportlight columns, on good days and dull ones, that he wrote in his New York apartment or from his summer place at Easthampton, New York . . . a big slice of his verse (he never called it poetry), much of which has little to do with sport, as such, but more concerned with the peaks and the valleys of Life. From the mountain of magazine features he turned out, many bear the Grantland Rice hallmark. In one of these, Granny pays tribute to the override of speed and stamina which a Thoroughbred needs to win The Triple Crown. He never realized it, of course, but Granny had more of both than any champion—horse or human—he word-painted.

DAVE CAMERER

March, 1963

PART I

A Sportswriter Come of Age

In 1910, after nearly 10 years of covering nearly every conceivable newspaper beat in the cities of Atlanta and Nashville, plus a short trek in Cleveland, Grant Rice invaded New York. At his bride's urging, Rice, than 30, accepted a ten dollar a week cut to go with the New York Evening Mail.

"Rice," said John Stoddard, the Mail's *owner, "I've been reading your verse. I never knew a sportswriter worth fifty dollars a week, but in your case I'll risk it."*

Less than 20 years later, Granny's verse and prose— much of it under his Sportlight heading, was syndicated to more than 250 papers throughout the country. Income from columns, plus allied interests in magazines, films, etc., grossed him well over $100,000 a year.

Perhaps the big difference between the material that trademarked Rice and that of his contemporaries was simply that Granny was satisfied to celebrate and glorify his subjects rather than stick sophisticated needles into them. In later years it was said that Rice was the founder and the headmaster of the "Gee Whiz" School of Sportswriting. He had his answer to that.

"It seems to me that the champions I write about," he said in the Prologue to The Tumult, *"have something to say to all of us, especially in these uncertain times which the editorial writers call 'The Age of Anxiety.' They all had tremendous confidence and belief in them-*

*selves . . . . qualities which are relatively rare today . . .
and sometimes openly ridiculed as naïve or worse."*

*More than once he told me that Enthusiasm coupled
with Purpose was the best Daily Double he'd ever played.*

MY FIRST BIG STORY, TY COBB

Those two writers, Ty Cobb and Ted Williams, recently have been waging a public vendetta. You may recall that Cobb said that the old timers were much better ball players. Ted countered by saying the moderns outranked the former stars and that he could name many men better than the players of Cobb's day. "All except Cobb and Ruth," wrote Williams. "They stand alone."

I have no particular argument about all this except that John McGraw and Ed Barrow, with the angles after devoting their entire lives to baseball, picked Honus Wagner as the greatest "all around" player. From that "all around" stand, they could be right. Wagner could play more positions better than either Cobb or Ruth.

It was in 1895 that I saw my first professional ball game at Nashville. George Stallings brought his black-uniformed Augusta team to town. That was 60 years ago. Since then I've seen the entire parade go by.

I've occasionally compared the youngsters with the oldsters—for what it's worth, which isn't much. Any more than Cobb's and Williams' appraisals are worth much—except as a bit of synthetic excitement.

Connie Mack, years ago, told me, "Grantland, you can't judge or measure the ball players of one era by those of another. From 1900 to 1920, baseball was an entirely different game from the game we now know. Until 1920, it was Ty Cobb's type of game—belonging more to speed, skill and agility than to power. They played with a dead ball, so it was a day of base running. Came the Golden Twenties and we had Ruth and the livelier ball, and we watched speed give way to power. You simply can't match two entirely different games which call for dis-

9

similar skills. An outfield composed of Cobb, Speaker and Ruth, even with Ruth, lacks the combined power of DiMaggio, Musial and Williams."

So it is quite possible that Williams' modern outfield is more useful in today's game than the old trio, as great as they were. Incidentally, I agree with Ted that Cobb was wrong in his estimate of the moderns. Any era that gives us DiMaggio, Williams, Musial, Slaughter, Rosen, Kell, Campanella, Robinson, Rizzuto, Berra, Roberts, Reynolds, Lopat, Gordon, Doerr, Schoendienst, Feller, Kiner, Mantle, Greenberg, Dickey, Cochrane, Gehringer, Raschi, Rolfe, Reese, Hodges—we can go on and on—is right up there with the all-time best. Defensively, Musial and DiMaggio were better outfielders than Cobb or Ruth; neither was the defensive equal of Tris Speaker. Williams doesn't rank too high on the defensive side. You might call him adequate, but he is no Jim Piersall, Willie Mays or Duke Snider, currently climbing fences for the Red Sox, Giants and Dodgers. Few are or have been.

Which brings me to Cobb, a man apart. The shrewdest athlete, and perhaps the shrewdest man I ever knew, Ty played a trick on me that stood up for more than 40 years.

It was a late afternoon in February, 1904. The paper had just been sent to press and, as a "veteran" reporter of 24, I was involved in a poker game in the *Atlanta Journal* office.

A messenger boy came in with a postal from a news tipster. I took the postal and read the following, fresh from Royston, a town in Georgia:

"Tyrus Raymond Cobb, the dashing young star from Royston, has just started spring training with Anniston. He is a terrific hitter and faster than a deer. At the age of 18 he is undoubtedly a phenom."

I tore up the card, returned to the poker game and later sent the following to Royston:

"After this, the mails are fast enough for Cobb."

It was a sad mistake. I should have asked the *Journal* to get out an extra. For this same Tyrus Raymond Cobb was on his way . . . on his way to make more than 4,100

10

big league base hits . . . to steal nearly 900 bases . . . to break almost every record in the books except the home-run mark.

It might be recalled that today good ball players are justly proud of the fact they have made 2,000 base hits . . . like such great hitters as Enos (Country) Slaughter and Johnny Mize. Think what it took to run up more than twice that number and move into the 4,000-hit territory!

In addition to being the greatest competitor I've ever known, Cobb was the most ambitious kid that ever entered sport. And he appeared to have a lot of fans who believed in him. During that 1904 season Cobb played with both Anniston (Alabama) and Augusta (Georgia) in the Southeastern and South Atlantic Leagues. That spring I was deluged with letters and postcards from wherever Cobb was playing. The messages were meaty.

"Keep your eye on Ty Cobb. He is one of the finest hitters I have ever seen." . . . "Watch Cobb of Anniston. He is sure to be a sensation." . . . "Have you seen Ty Cobb play ball yet? He is the fastest mover I've seen in baseball." These and dozens like them were signed Brown, Smith, Jackson, Holmes . . . and they showered in from all points of both circuits.

Under pressure I finally wrote a column that a new wonder had arrived, "the darling of the fans"—my first big story but I didn't realize it at the time. A few days later I journeyed to Augusta's ball park to see my discovery. At 18, Cobb was something to look at. He was around 5 feet 11, weighed 155 and had the legs of a deer —legs destined to carry him for 24 years of hard campaigning.

I went down to the dugout and talked to the lad, six years younger than I, before the game.

"I've been hearing about you," I said. "My name is Rice. I write baseball for the *Journal*."

"Is that so?" he replied. "I've heard of you, too."

During those early years, I found Cobb to be an extremely peculiar soul—brooding and bubbling with violence, combative all the way, a streak, incidentally, he never lost. Although our greatest American essayist, Ralph Waldo Emerson, may not have known it, he was writing to a vision of Cobb when he penned his immortal challenge on Self-Reliance. Always the non-conformist, except when it involved team play on the diamond, Cobb's frequent and violent explosions with his teammates as well as the enemy were the rule. From the first, Cobb's life was a constant war, and Ty lived in a hostile camp.

Cobb moved to Detroit in 1905. A year or so later, when pitcher Bob Willett moved in with him, his Detroit teammates ordered Willett to move out.

"Having to live alone," Cobb told me, "I spent all my time thinking baseball—of plays I could make . . . of tricks I could try. Baseball was one hundred per cent of my life."

From the start Cobb never lost an opportunity to study his craft. I recall that in 1904, working on a tip, I got Abe Powell, Atlanta's manager, to sign a long, loose-jointed fireballer known as Happy Harry Hale, from Happy Hollow, Tennessee.

Cobb was then with Augusta. I made considerable copy of Happy Harry's debut. On the day he was to pitch, Cobb got permission to come to Atlanta to study the unveiling of the young phenom.

Built like a tuning fork, Harry Hale was 6 feet 6—and all up. He couldn't have weighed more than 140, soaking wet. For four innings that day, with his long, lean arm and his tall, lean body, Hale's fast ball mowed 'em down. At the end of the fourth he was breezing along with a potential no-hitter.

Then in the fifth some dastard in human form bunted. Happy Harry had never seen a bunt. By the time he'd unraveled his frame, the runner was on first. Another safe bunt! When the third man bunted, Hale crashed in, arms and legs akimbo, tried to scoop up the ball and spiked his own hand. That was the finish of Happy Harry Hale and sportswriter Rice's discovery.

Three years later, in 1907, in Washington, a country

12

pitcher from Weiser, Idaho, was mowing down Detroit—along with Cobb. For three innings they couldn't dent him. Cobb remembered the episode of Harry Hale. He told his manager, Hughie Jennings. The Tigers started bunting on the young smokeballer named Walter Johnson, who, like Hale, couldn't field bunts at the time. That was also Johnson's end—that day. But it never worked again.

"I'd sometimes figure out a play—or a weakness—and then have to wait a month or a year before the chance came to use it," reflected Cobb.

Incidentally, while returning on the train next morning to Augusta, following Harry Hale's losing battle to the bunt, young Cobb fell into conversation with a large fat boy from Milledgeville, Georgia. His name was Babe Hardy, later famous as a member of the comedy team, Laurel and Hardy. Cobb told Hardy he was with the Augusta team.

"Are you the bat boy?" Hardy asked.

"Bat boy?" blurted Cobb. "You come to the game today; I'll show you."

Babe took in the game. "It was something at that," reflected Hardy one day 40 years later on the Hal Roach lot. "Cobb hammered a single, two doubles, a triple and a home run—and stole two bases."

"You're not the only one he fooled," I replied, mentioning the postcard from Royston, Georgia, I'd snubbed back in 1904. It had hardly occurred to me then that in addition to his 4,191 hits and 892 stolen bases—including 96 during the 1915 season—Cobb would also lead the American League for 12 out of 13 consecutive years and average a .367 mark for 24 seasons. During those years Cobb outshone the likes of Joe Jackson, Napoleon Lajoie, Sam Crawford, Tris Speaker, Elmer Flick, Eddie Collins—fellows who lived to hit. There was also a young fellow named George Sisler, who hit .420 in 1922. In those days they threw the .350 hitters back.

Almost from the start, Cobb figured out every baseball record that he might break. During those evenings alone he studied the record book. Home runs were fated to be

13

Ruth's domain, but Cobb trampled most of the others. He scored 2,244 runs. Lord, how he concentrated on runs! He scored more than once from first on a single.

Durability? In 1922, 18 years after he broke in at the age of 19, Cobb batted .401. That, to me, is the most incredible mark of the list—surpassing even the .323 he hit in his 24th and final year. He batted over .300 for 23 consecutive years, his first year, 1905, being the lone season he failed.

I doubt that many minutes passed during Cobb's entire major-league span when he wasn't ready to take full advantage of any chance that might develop . . . including the psychological.

An example of Cobb, the psychological tail-twister, involved Shoeless Joe Jackson of the old Chicago Black Sox. Jackson got the Shoeless Joe tag when he played with some little, dinky league in East Tennessee before joining Connie Mack's Athletics in 1908. A farm boy from South Carolina with no spikes of his own when he first joined the club, Jackson played the outfield barefooted. The field, a former dump, was cluttered with sharp stones and broken glass. After the fourth inning of a particular game, Jackson came in shaking his head, slammed down his glove and blurted, "I quit."

"What's the matter, Joe?" asked his manager. "That outfield too tough on your feet?"

"It ain't the feet," complained Jackson. "It's just that all that busted glass is fuzzin' up the ball so's I can't peg it good."

The rhythmed beauty of Jackson's black bat was hitting over .400 down the home stretch of the 1911 season. Joe was leading Cobb by several fat percentage points. Detroit was playing Cleveland. During batting practice the always amiable Jackson greeted Cobb.

"Hello, Ty," said Jackson.

"Get away from me!" blurted Cobb.

"Why, what's eatin' on you?" replied Jackson, hurt and wide-eyed.

"Stay away from me," hissed Cobb.

14

A brooding Jackson went hitless during those first three games while Cobb fattened his average. On the last of the four-day series, Cobb, seeing Jackson in batting drill, was peaches and cream.

"Why, hello Joe . . . and how's everything?" beamed Ty.

Jackson never did know quite how or why Cobb pulled the rug from under him. Cobb did. He would have given his own grandmother the "treatment" if she had been leading him. Cobb finished the season with a .420 BA; Jackson with a .408.

On August 16, 1920, when Yankee pitcher Carl Mays killed Cleveland's brilliant infielder, Ray Chapman, with a pitched ball, Cobb was drawn into the headlines. The accident occurred in the fifth inning, with bases empty, when Mays let a fast ball get away from him. The ball struck the plate—crowning Chapman so squarely over the left temple that it dribbled down the third base line where Aaron Ward, thinking it a bunt, pounced on it and rifled to first baseman Wally Pipp. Standing motionless an instant, Chapman then collapsed. He regained consciousness in the clubhouse long enough to say, "Tell Mays not to worry," then died during the night.

Detroit, meanwhile, was playing in Boston. The morning papers featured Cobb's "statement" that Mays had beaned Chapman on purpose. The Detroit team arrived in New York on Friday, an off day, prior to a weekend series with the Yanks. That morning Ty called me at home and asked me to come down to the Commodore Hotel.

I found Cobb in bed with a temperature of 102. Both thighs were a mass of adhesive and torn flesh, testimony to some rough base stealing. He was up to his chin in morning papers—all blasting him for that interview back in Boston.

"The first thing you need is a doctor," I said.

"Never mind the doctor," Ty replied. "I've got to be at that game tomorrow and face the wolves. Your New York papers are sure steaming things up. But this, Grant, I

15

want you to know! I never gave out any interview! I knew nothing of what happened until long after that game."

On Saturday, 33,000 stormed the Polo Grounds—the Stadium wasn't completed until 1923. Cobb didn't take batting practice, in fact didn't appear on the field until ten minutes before the game. When he did show, the crowd stood up and booed. Making the long walk from the center-field clubhouse, Cobb stopped near home plate, stared at the crowd and bowed toward the press box, then situated himself behind home plate in the lower grandstand. In effect, he was saying, "There's your story, gentlemen. They are responsible for it."

Detroit won that game, Cobb getting one single, stealing one base and scoring one run—the difference. My interview with Cobb stating he had not blamed Mays was put on the wires. Sunday's fans gave Ty a warm ovation. He replied by getting five hits in six times at bat—including four singles and a double as the Tigers cakewalked.

With nearly a quarter of a million balls being pitched during a big league season alone, helmets or not, the miracle remains that there are not more killings, especially with night baseball in such vogue.

One day in 1928 I sat in Philadelphia's dugout at the Yankee Stadium talking with Cobb. He had come to Connie Mack from Detroit after putting in 22 years with the Tigers. Now, in his last year, at the age of 42, Ty was in a reflective mood. Vain of his skill to the very end, Cobb was slowing up . . . and he knew it.

"Speed is a great asset; but it's greater when it's combined with quickness—and there's a big difference," he said. "I'm about as fast as ever—once I get in motion. But my 'flexes are fading. I'm starting much slower. I don't get the jump any more. I can see the ball as good as ever, but I don't get that quick start from the plate like I used to. If I could, I'd be a .350 hitter right to the end!"

Cobb played in 95 games that year. He hit .323.

One night—it must have been in 1935, a half dozen years after Cobb had quit baseball—we were together in

16

the Detroit Athletic Club. "Nig" Clarke, the old Cleveland catcher, came by. We were jabbering about the old days when I happened to mention Clarke's rapid tag and immediate throwing of his glove aside, signifying the third out.

Clarke laughed. "I missed many a runner who was called out," he said. "I missed you at least ten times at the plate, Ty—times when you were called out."

Cobb was on Nig with one wild charge. "You cost me ten runs! Runs I earned!" roared Ty. It was all I could do to pull him off and calm him down. Clarke left. Ty was burning a half hour later.

The first player I can recall who sensed the great change that hit baseball in 1920 was Cobb and he was blunt about it.

"Well, the old game is gone," he said one day in 1924 as we watched Babe Ruth rocket batting-practice pitches into the new Yankee Stadium bleachers. "We have another game, a newer game now. In this game, power has replaced speed and skill. Base running is about dead. They've all just about quit stealing . . . now they wait for somebody to drive 'em home."

Cobb pointed to Ruth, who was being watched by the players from both clubs.

"Babe Ruth has changed baseball," he continued. "I guess more people would rather see Babe hit one over the fence than see me steal second. I feel bad about it for it isn't the game I like to see or play. The old game was one of skill—skill and speed. And quick thinking. This game is all power. But there'll never be another power-man like this fellow.

"The Babe was a really fine pitcher . . . with control, speed, a hook and the guts up there," continued Cobb. "But he can blast that ball harder than anyone who ever lived. Just watch the ball next year . . . they'll start juicing it up like a tennis ball because Ruth has made the home run fashionable.

"But they'll ruin more sluggers than they'll make. A lot of these kids, in place of learning the true science of

17

hitting or baserunning, are trying to knock every pitch over the fence."

Ty reflected for a moment. "There'll be a few of these youngsters who'll make good with the big blast. But most of 'em won't."

Cobb was right. Just as Connie Mack was right! Ty might have considered the change when he authored that magazine blast against the modern players.

Cobb always resented the idea that he was a rough, or spiking, base runner. I won't forget the day that Hal Sims, the bridge expert—and a sharper mind never cogged —tried to nettle Cobb about his base running.

It was in 1939, during the winter. I was taking my annual sojourn in California which, for years, has been an excuse for a wonderful reunion for Kit and me with our daughter Florence. Cobb was living out there and I arranged a friendly foursome at Pebble Beach with Cobb, Sims, Mysterious Montague, the fellow who shoots par with a rake and a shovel, and me. It was a four-ball match, with Cobb and me playing Sims and Montague, perhaps the strongest fellow I ever knew.

Sims was in good form . . . and when he was in good form, there was no better, or worse, needler. At breakfast, before teeing off that foggy morning, Sims settled his bulk over a third cup of black coffee, looked at Cobb and said, "Ty, I've always admired you. As a ball player you were in a world apart. But tell me this if you will. Why did you have to spike so many men?"

Cobb colored up like an old gobbler, the cords jumping up the back of his neck. He was furious, but managed to contain himself.

We teed off. Normally a pretty fair player, Cobb, still writhing, lunged at the ball as if to kill it. We lost the first seven holes.

Sims, as happy as he was tremendous, was playing lovely golf. Montague, of course, could spot us all ten strokes each and murder us; but awaiting the explosion, his mind wasn't on the game. I, meanwhile, was trying

18

to soothe Cobb. It was like throwing water on burning oil.

On the eighth tee, Cobb pushed his drive almost out of bounds and hit a provisional. However, both balls had landed in a bunker, so naturally Ty played his first ball. He came out all right and managed a bogie 5. Sims was keeping the card.

"What did you have, Ty?" asked Hal, as we headed for the ninth.

"A five," said Cobb.

"A five?" questioned Hal.

Cobb exploded. Grabbing Sims' arm in his vise-like grip, he snarled, "Listen, no one questions my word or score!"

Montague shot between the two over-age destroyers. Holding each at arm's length, Monty advised both to act their age or he'd bash their heads together.

Hal was visibly upset by Cobb's charge. Cobb, however, settled down and from that moment shot fine golf coming in. Sims couldn't hit a shot.

That evening, Cobb returned to Sims' insinuation that he, Cobb, had been a dirty base runner.

"I only recall intentionally spiking one man in twenty-four years," he told me during dinner. "He was Frank Baker, who was squarely in the path in a Philadelphia game—in 1913 it was. There was no other way to reach the base. From the start, I concentrated on a new form of sliding. This was to send my toe for the bag. I only gave them my toe to tag! It was exactly the opposite of crashing in, hurling spikes or body at the baseman. I don't know how many hours I worked on my type of sliding—a slide that avoided the tagger. Why, I couldn't have been a rough base runner under my system even if I'd wanted to.

"I'll admit I used to run wild, but I did it for a purpose," he continued. "I wanted the other team to think I was a crazy base runner . . . to establish mental hazards . . . one way to keep up the tension. But I actually didn't do much crazy, more particularly, dirty base running!"

As great as any of Cobb's features was his stamina. He

19

had that at 18—he still had it at 58. As a youngster and as a veteran ball player, Cobb hunted all winter and played ball all spring, summer and fall. As a result, he was able to play 3,033 big-league games and appear at bat 11,429 times.

I recall one spring, I'm sure it was 1911, the year after I'd left Nashville to come to New York, that Cobb was a holdout. He'd been with Detroit five years—a veteran. The stories drifting back from spring camp questioned Cobb's fitness, when and if he decided to report. I didn't hold much stock in them. Cobb never had to work into condition . . . he was always in condition. Knowing he was ready, he merely didn't care to report so soon. He got his raise and reported one week before the season opened. That was the year Cobb rapped out 248 base hits for an average of .420 while stealing 83 bases. His legs must have been the most remarkable pair ever known to man—even Paavo Nurmi.

The annals of sport don't record Cobb the polo player, but he did take a crack at that sport too. It was during the early 1930's; he was out of baseball but the old competitive fires were still burning.

One day, at Aiken, South Carolina, Cobb watched a polo game. Something about the speed and fury of men on horseback galloping down each other's throats appealed to him. In short order he was riding, and pretty well, but after he'd got in a few licks of polo he wanted to change the rules. Instead of three men to a side he wanted to play it one against one! Nobody wanted any part of him —including the ponies.

"That Mistah Cobb's a madman on a horse," an old colored groom told me one day. "He don't ride *over* you! He rides *through* you!"

That short interim with the horses marked Cobb's entrance and exit from polo.

Cobb never played football. At 17 he was in baseball to stay. But many times I sat with Zuppke, Warner, Jock Sutherland or Rockne and watched them marvel at Cobb. To a man they thought he would have made a great end

. . . with his speed, size, hands and overpowering will to win, he would have been a Tartar.

Those who claim to know Cobb insist he's one of the coldest men ever. Flint hard, perhaps, but not so cold—at least in my book. One spring day in 1947, Ty and I were motoring north from Augusta where we'd taken in the Masters Golf tournament. As we drove into Greenville, South Carolina, Ty said, "Grant, I've got an old friend in this town. Let's find him."

Driving up to the next cop he asked where he might find Joe Jackson. Informed he worked in a small liquor store on such and such street, we found it and went in. Behind the counter was Jackson. Waiting his turn, Ty stepped up, looked the old boy in the eye and said, "How's business?"

"Just fine, sir," replied Jackson, turning his back to rearrange a shelf.

"Don't you know me, you old buzzard?" said Cobb.

Jackson wheeled around. "Christ, yes, I know you!" grinned Joe. "I just didn't think you knew me after all these years. I didn't want to embarrass you or nothin'."

It was a nice reunion—with three old gaffers fanning about the days that used to be. Jackson died four years later, in December, 1951. Cobb's paying Jackson a visit must have been the high point in the waning limbo years of one of baseball's natural "greats" . . . a "fall guy" in that 1919 Black Sox scandal.

Not long ago, Gene Fowler, Henry McLemore and I were being driven by Cobb from the San Francisco airport to his home at Menlo Park. Gene and I were in the back seat, Henry up front with Cobb. Ty handles a car like he ran the base paths . . . full steam ahead. Also, he has a way of turning his head to talk to you while driving that makes me uncomfortable.

"Grant," he said, suddenly stopping near the end of the runway while a giant transport buzzed us, "do you remember the card you received back in 1904 . . . about the phenom from Royston?"

"I sure do, Ty," I replied.

21

"And do you remember a flock of postcards from all over Alabama and Georgia, telling you what a hot shot I was . . . all signed with different names?"

"I certainly do . . . why?"

"I sent you the card and all those notices," chuckled Cobb.

"It's taken you a few years to get around to telling me," I said. "Why did you do it?"

"Because I was in a hurry," replied Cobb. "We were both youngsters on the way up. I didn't know it then but I was trying to put you onto your first big scoop!"

Self-confidence is the hallmark of a champion . . . any champion. Not only had Cobb had that amazing cheek and flair at 18—more important, he knew how to use it, something few can handle at any stage of life.

Babe Ruth's record of 60 home runs in one year may be broken, although personally I hope it stands for eternity. It has almost been equaled twice.

But it is a sure thing that Cobb's mark of 4,191 base hits will never be approached. And it's just as certain that no ball player during our sojourn on earth will bat over .300 for 23 consecutive big-league years!

Cobb had too much of the physical and mental strung together, too much of the eternal will to win plus the physical sinews to carry him along. He had too much co-ordination, too many perfect reflexes ever to be equaled on a ball field.

Ty Cobb, the Georgia Peach, had too much of everything.

THE YALE-HARVARD GAME—1916

(N. Y. *Tribune*, November 26, 1916)

Yale won.

These two words mean more in New Haven tonight than all the classic diction of Presidential notes that are commonly reported to have kept this country out of the greatest carnage in history.

Yale won. Only those of the 78,000 who heard the wild Yale yell and who saw the spectacular fervor of the Eli snake dance as the Crimson flag came down at sunset can quite appreciate the full significance of these two simple words, as unadorned as Harvard's bankroll was before the clock struck 5.

For seven years, adrift in the wilderness, Yale had been struggling in vain for a Harvard defeat. For nine years, since 1907, the Yale assault had been thrown back from the Harvard goal line. Today Yale wiped away both counts when Jim Neville crashed two yards through tackle for a touchdown in the second quarter, with only a minute left to play.

This clean, hard drive to victory beat Harvard, 6 to 3, and beyond this it made the name of Tad Jones one of the greatest in Yale's entire football history. For it was the spirit of Tad Jones that triumphed at last over the Haughton system, the system that had baffled and bewildered and overwhelmed Yale for four of the most melancholy years the Blue had ever known.

The spirit that Jones instilled was this: "You can crowd a Bulldog just so far; then pick out the nearest tree." And, what is more to the point, Jones had the rare pleasure of proving this scientific point before the greatest crowd that ever saw a football game in this country

23

that Columbus saw first. Seventy-seven thousand four hundred and fifty-four people paid over $150,000 to see what a young fellow by the name of Jones could offer against the magic and the craft of the great Haughton, who had been beating one Yale team after another with such ease and dispatch that it had become a fixed habit that seemed to know no law of change.

This great deluge of humanity smothered and blotted out the town, and once packed into the big Bowl it lost all form of life and color and became merely a huge mass that outranged the vision from any one spot.

It was only when Robinson kicked Harvard's field goal in the first quarter and later on when Eddie Casey ran seventy-five yards across Yale's line, only to be called back for Harvard holding, that the Crimson section of this mass became suddenly alive with human beings. While these two episodes were under way the Blue section was still a silent, drab-looking mass, devoid of everything but gloom.

But a few minutes later on the Crimson section sank back into a formless conglomeration of dismay when Le Gore's fumble flopped over the lines into the waiting arms of Ty Gates and the great Yale tackle ran twenty-one yards to Harvard's 12-yard line before he was dragged to the ground.

This was the play that wrecked the Haughton system for the day, that ended Harvard's long reign over Yale and lifted the Blue at last to the old-fashioned place above the Crimson banner.

Harvard, at the moment, was leading 3 to 0. Just a moment before Comerford's long shot for a goal from placement had struck one of the uprights and bounded back.

In a flash, so it seemed at that stage, the action of the play had been pointing to a climax. It was here that Yale, with an attack led by Le Gore, started her drive.

From Harvard's 38-yard line Le Gore started another rush. The pass struck his arms and then, in some way not

24

to be explained, flopped forward over the two surging lines in a 7-yard, drooping curve.

In the first glimpse of things the Yale stands, seeing only the fumble, groaned in their despair. But the groan rippled out into a vocal cataclysm of cheering when Ty Gates, one of the day's big heroes, snatched the ball off his shoe tops and rushed twenty-one yards farther on, to within twelve yards of Harvard's goal.

Here at last was the chance that Yale had waited for and dreamed of since Roome dived over the Harvard goal line back in 1907.

Quite a number of things have happened since 1907— quite a number. But among them was no Yale touchdown against Harvard.

From the Crimson mass the old cry of "Hold 'em, Harvard—hold 'em!" answered Yale's call for a Bulldog score.

Such is the force of habit that, even here, Harvard had not thought of any successful Yale assault upon a position that had been impregnable for so long.

But when Le Gore and Neville hammered their way still further on for eight yards in two savage assaults, Harvard's impressive confidence in her defense began to wane.

A moment later Neville made it first down for Yale on Harvard's 2½-yard line; and here, with four assaults left to carry the ball across, the Yale stands went into one of those frenzies that only a football fan knows.

The wild and woolly uproar, starting in the Blue wing, soon rolled around the field when the Crimson section began to gather in the full valor of the Harvard defense. For, with their feet braced upon their own goal line, Harvard's forwards here put up a battle that should be forever memorable in Harvard play.

On the first play Le Gore, the panther, came smashing in, only to crumble and buckle up as he struck the fighting wall still in the way. La Roche then shifted and called upon Neville to carry the ball.

25

But Neville, too, was battered back and down, without gaining the span of his shoe.

Once more La Roche shifted back to Le Gore—and this time, for a change, he sent the Yale star on a dash outside of tackle.

For one flash there was an opening ahead; but, as Le Gore came through, Coolidge, the fine Harvard end, collared his man with such force that once more the Yale assault was driven back. Coolidge struck Le Gore with such force that the hard-running back was literally driven into the ground.

Small wonder at this point that the greater volume of cheering came from Harvard's side. After all, tradition is tradition, and habit is habit. "They shall not pass" had been written too many times against the Yale attack.

But Yale still had one chance left. This time La Roche decided to switch once more to Neville. He called the play through Gates, the man who had first given Yale her chance; and Gates and Neville made good together.

The hole which the Yale tackle opened was not impressively wide, but it was wide enough for Neville to fight his way safely across for the touchdown that Yale was beginning to believe had long since became extinct.

Comerford failed at goal; but that slip was a minor detail. Yale had come from behind; Yale had scored a touchdown; Yale was now leading, and the rest of it was less than nothing!

Yale's victory today was the most impressive victory, the most buoyant, that a Yale team ever won.

Yale had come to the end of a campaign reeking with trouble, a campaign started under a new system and facing one of the hardest schedules of the year. While Harvard had rested and prepared for this final game, Yale had been forced to face Colgate, Brown and Princeton without rest.

Yet such was the spirit and soundness of play instilled by Tad Jones, and such was the efficiency of Trainer Johnny Mack, that the supposedly battered Yale eleven

26

not only outplayed Harvard in most of the essentials of the game, but finished with only one substitution, and finished fighting a harder, more aggressive battle than ever through the closing quarter.

It was a freak of fate and a queer break of the battle that the scores made by Harvard and Yale both came, indirectly, from Yale fumbles. If this isn't a world's record, it ought to be.

Harvard's chance to score arrived in the first quarter, when La Roche fumbled Horween's long punt on Yale's 27-yard line. Casey, on a fake pass, got six yards, and Robinson then dropped back to drop-kick from the 29-yard line for three points and first blood.

Yale's chance to score resulted, as related above, from Yale's own fumble on a rushing play.

But, leaving all this out in the cold, Yale undoubtedly played the better, harder game and deserved to win.

Yale deserved her victory because she utterly crushed and conquered the Harvard attack. The old deception in Haughton's plays failed to deceive. Harvard shifts and fakes were met by Yale charges, directed with a driving smash to the right spot.

The old strategy of luring the blind Bulldog charge to one side and then rushing through failed to work. Harvard had had her day of bewildering and baffling Yale. This time Yale was in the road, and when her two great ends, Moseley and Comerford, left off, the line, with Gates, Black and others, was there with an unbroken front.

Harvard tried all she had.

Casey rushed and Horween bucked. Robinson plunged and Thacher smashed. But, save for a few futile gains, Harvard's attack was all dressed up with no place to go—but down.

The story of Yale's defense is this—Harvard made but three first downs all day, and out of eleven forward passes only one gained ground. The others were battered down or intercepted by the Yale backfield.

Rolled back and repulsed, Harvard nevertheless fought on to the end. Harvard, in fact, fought a notable fight;

27

for she was facing a charging, aggressive eleven with greater physical strength.

The Crimson courage was worthily maintained against one of the hardest breaks that ever decided a game. This came in the second quarter, just after Le Gore had punted to Harvard's 25-yard line.

On the first play Casey, taking the ball, swung out around Yale's left end, whirled to the side lines, cut quickly in, and then, fighting off four Yale tacklers who seemed to have him surrounded, ran seventy-five yards across the field and over Yale's line.

No more spectacular play has ever graced a Yale-Harvard battle. As Casey eluded the last Blue tackler and raced on into the open, another old-fashioned Crimson triumph seemed to be the order of the day.

But Harvard was here penalized for holding. In place of seventy-five yards and a touchdown, the Crimson lost fifteen yards, and Horween had to punt from his own 10-yard line.

The moral effect of this terrific upset would have been sufficient to break the morale of any but a good, game bunch. Right after this spectacular effort, which went to seed in the morass of Harvard woe, one of the most vital plays of the day developed.

After Horween had punted, Le Gore returned the kick with a long, twisting punt down the field. As the ball bounded along it flipped away from Robinson, and was then anybody's ball as it rolled and bobbled along the ground within eight yards of Harvard's line.

There were two men left for the chase. One was a Yale end; the other was Horween. In the dash for the ball both dived at almost the same moment, but the stocky Crimson fullback beat his rival to the spot by an eyelash, saving another touchdown.

Forced to kick here, Horween punted to La Roche, who called for a fair catch on Harvard's 44-yard line.

With the wind at his back Comerford tried for a goal from placement. The ball started low, gathered momentum

28

and, drifting on with the wind, was on its way two feet across the bar when it struck one of the uprights and bounded back into the field.

These points are outlined to show there was a fairly even break in the fortunes of war; and that, at the end, the team that played the better, harder football finished out in front.

As the game started, a cold, whipping wind began to drive its late November chill into the great crowd. The latter looked to be packed too closely, however, to suffer from exposure.

It was only a few minutes after Harvard had won the toss and Comerford had kicked off that the immense crowd suddenly began to sense a decided change in Yale affairs. Yale was on the aggressive from the start, with Captain Black again leading his men on; and these aggressive Yale tactics soon had Harvard in trouble.

On one of the first few plays Horween was forced to kick from back of his goal line. To show his courage, the Crimson fullback drove the ball seventy yards down the field for the longest punt of the day. Horween's kicking was consistently good, but here, in the time of impending trouble, when a slip would have meant disaster, he gave the best he had and about ten yards more. If this isn't kicking in a pinch, Johnny Evers never invented the system.

Right after this magnificent punt a Yale mistake gave Harvard her first chance. Standing on his 25-yard line, Le Gore punted but thirteen yards against the wind, giving Harvard the ball on her rival's 38-yard line. But on the first play a Harvard penalty wrecked the chance for a score, putting her back fifteen yards farther down the field.

These first two Harvard penalties, the one just named and the one called against Casey, were damaging beyond repair. They cost the Crimson seven sure points, and possibly ten. They upset the entire game from a Harvard viewpoint, turning a safe margin of victory into a defeat.

But penalties happen to be the wages of transgression;

29

and Harvard must have known, with a number of others, that the way of the transgressor isn't soft.

When La Roche fumbled and Robinson kicked a field goal Harvard's scoring machine had completed its day's work. The redoubtable system had at last crashed into a snag.

From that point on it was Yale's game and Yale's day. And as the game drew out and Haughton sent his fresh reserve sides to the field Yale's veterans, battered as they were from so many hard games in a row, met each shift with a harder drive and a keener punch.

In the final quarter Yale gained almost two yards to Harvard's one, showing the amazing stamina and condition of the Blue machine. In this last period the Crimson attack, with its rushing game, cut to pieces and battered to a pulp, fell back on the last desperate hope of the beaten —the forward pass.

Eight times here Harvard tried the passing game, only to have seven of her attempts broken up or intercepted. But the one success came near reversing the score.

With the ball in Harvard territory, Murray passed to Casey, who ran to the left, whirled and, with a southpaw peg, shot the ball far down the field to Coolidge.

The first Harvard end caught the ball on Yale's 37-yard line. He had an open field beyond, but just as he got under headway Le Gore, with a great diving tackle, brought Coolidge to earth, saving an almost sure touchdown.

This play should be ranked with the best of the day. Even then Harvard was in striking distance for a goal but an intercepted forward pass killed her final chance.

As the game ended over 5,000 Yale men rushed upon the field for the first snake dance in many Crimson moons. As hats and coats were thrown across both crossbars a flash of red fire was started from each post—for Yale had waited too long not to celebrate with all she had.

In the midst of this jubilee another crowd rushed for Tad Jones and Cupid Black, who had given so much to bring Yale back upon the football map.

30

and physical, of this Yale eleven lifts him high tonight among the great coaches of the game. No man ever de-

The showing made by Jones in the development, mental served success more than Jones deserves the acclaim that both Yale and Harvard men are giving him around this bedlammed citadel right now.

For Yale today the first feature was the wonderful work of Ty Gates, the Yale tackle, and the brilliant showing of Moseley and Comerford, her two ends. These three were the stars of the afternoon, with Gates leading them all.

This man was all over the lot. He was a ball-playing centipede, with a dozen arms and two dozen eyes; and it is no great wonder that Yale thinks as much of her Ty as Georgia does of hers.

In addition to these three, the brilliant rushing of Le Gore, the steady plunging of Neville and the good work of Captain Black belong. But for that matter Yale, with only one change in her original line-up, finds it hard to pick out any one or two above the crowd.

They all looked 100 per cent efficient to Eli at 4:50 o'clock.

Harvard's leading feature was the good rushing of Casey, the fine punting of Horween and the effective work of Coolidge and Harte, who gave Yale's great pair an even fight.

The end play stands out as one of the most distinct features of the game, for it held consistency mixed with brilliancy that has seldom been equaled in any one game.

Yale won because she had the greater drive, the greater physical power, and, in a way, the greater determination to get there first.

Yale won because she had made up her mind not to be beaten, and because for the first time in a long while she had a defense alert enough to break up Harvard's shifting, deceptive attack.

But the final answer to her victory comes in the fact that she brought Tad Jones to New Haven to bring Yale back to old-fashioned ways—and Tad made good.

31

The answer here, with a hard luck team is this: Yale 10, Princeton 0. Yale 6, Harvard 3.

There may be nothing much to the patrician in the name of "Tad Jones," but to Yale it looks good enough to eat.

THE FINAL ANSWER

This is the word I bring you, from jungle and from town,
From city street where weary feet are seeking vague
    renown,
From cotton fields to northern snows, or where the west
    winds cry,
This is the word I bring you: "Keep strong, or else
    you die."

They speak of battle's finish—they talk of peace to come.
They cheer for songs supplanting the bugle and the drum.
They think of dreams in clover, beneath a cloudless sky,
Remember what I tell you: "Keep strong, or else you die."

Peace on this war-torn planet? I want it understood
I like a cheerful neighbor—but give me hardihood.
Give me the fiber needed to face what lies ahead,
To make good for the living, to make up for the dead.

The easy road is over, for in this swarming hive
Those who can take a beating are those who will survive.
We've ripped a pleasant planet, it's too late now to sigh.
Remember what I've told you: "Keep strong, or else
    you die."

THE DEMPSEY-WILLARD FIGHT—1919

(N.Y. *Tribune*, July 5, 1919)

TOLEDO, July 4—Jack Dempsey proved to be the greatest fighting tornado, in a boxing way, the game has ever known, when in nine minutes of actual combat today, he crushed Jess Willard into a shapeless mass of gore and battered flesh.

One minute and 58 seconds after the two men had squared away, Dempsey hooked a three-quarter left to the point of Willard's jaw, and the champion sat down heavily with a dazed and foolish look, a simple half-smile crowning a mouth that twitched with pain and bewilderment.

At the count of six, Willard rose slowly to his feet. Less than ten seconds later another of Dempsey's terrific hooks lifted the human mountain from his tottering base, and once again he crashed to the sun-baked canvas with a thud that rolled forth the echo of his doom.

Seven times in that first round Dempsey tore in and lifted the reeling, battered champion off his feet. Six times Willard slowly lifted his weary, broken frame back into position to receive once more a right or left hook that snapped his bloody head to the back of his wilting spine.

Never in all the history of the ring, dating back to days beyond all memory, has any champion ever received the murderous punishment which 245-pound Jess Willard soaked up in that first round and the two rounds that followed.

While Dempsey gave one of the greatest exhibitions of mighty hitting anyone here has ever seen, Willard, in a different way, gave one of the greatest exhibitions of raw and unadulterated gameness. He absorbed enough punishment to kill two ordinary men and only his tremendous

33

vitality and the hack of the bell carried him beyond the first round.

About ten seconds before the bell closed the first round, Willard reeled over toward the right corner, away from Dempsey, and there the Colorado slugger, putting everything he had into a right hook, dropped the champion for the seventh time.

As Willard flopped on this occasion nothing but the bell could have saved him. He sat there dazed, bewildered and helpless—his big, bleeding mouth wide open, his glassy bloodshot eyes staring wearily and witlessly out into space, as a 114-degree sun beat down upon his head that was rank with perspiration and blood.

The big crowd, seeing Willard's utter helplessness, failed to hear the bell in the wild uproar that followed. Dempsey started to climb through the ropes as Willard was dragged to his corner, as one might drag a sack of oats. There was no expression to his face except that witless, faraway look that might belong to a simpleton who had just crawled out from under a rock crusher, wondering what it was all about.

While the uproar was at its height Dempsey was hurriedly called back to the ring and the bloody, pitiless drama went on to the second act.

Twenty seconds after the second round opened Willard was a terrible wreck to behold. His right eye was completely closed, a big blue moon with a fringe of crimson protruding far beyond his face, with a gray, twitching slit where his eye once had been.

Dempsey fought with all the necessary brutality of his craft. With the championship now in plain sight, with the goal of his dreams just at the end of another hook, with all the world before him at twenty-four—lifted from a tramp two years ago to a millionaire's income just ahead—he hooked those salvos of rights and lefts, shifting from Willard's mutilated face to his quivering body, with only a few pauses between his deadly blows.

After the first round Willard came back as a game man comes to meet his fate, as sure and as certain as death

34

and the grave. Here and there he handed a few weak, faltering punches that failed to even check Dempsey's rush; but in the main he spent his time glaring helplessly at his opponent out of his one undamaged eye and groping feebly to rest his great bulk upon the lighter man, not to wear him down, but to find a moment's rest from the vast and utter weariness that was beginning to soak through his giant frame, deadening his nerve cells and moving slowly but steadily to his brain.

At the end of the second round there was a question again as to whether Willard would answer the bell. But once again he lifted his bulk to reeling, tottering legs and stood to receive the rush of his successor who, without a moment's delay, started the fountain of gore spurting again as Willard wearily turned his head to spit out clots of blood upon the canvas.

It was easy to see in the middle of the third round that the conqueror of Jack Johnson would never answer another bell. For, in the meanwhile, the right side of his face had swollen to unbelievable proportions. The flesh there had been so badly cut and jabbed and mashed by Dempsey's terrific hitting force that purple blotches began to intermingle with the red.

If you could imagine a thick hamburger steak, painted blue and purple and crimson, plastered to the side of a man's face, you might get some idea of how Willard looked in the middle of that third round. If a six-inch shell had exploded against his right jaw it could hardly have changed his features more.

No dreams came to him of a vanishing title. He knew no anguish of fading glory. With glassy, rolling eye and a foolish, twisted face he reeled along his way to oblivion.

The endless punishment he had received had first deadened his nerve cells and shut off all the electricity that runs the human system. This deadening growth had moved to his brain, so that in the closing minutes of the fight he had no sign of intelligence left. He stood or reeled without any sign of comprehension displayed over his face—if you'd care to call something a face that some time

35

before had lost all resemblance to anything human or to anything even belonging to the wild.

The wonder is that his vast system had enough vitality to carry that much punishment and still stay up. For after the first round Dempsey scored no further knockdowns, unless two are so registered where Willard crumpled against the ropes and hung there like a side of beef on display in a butcher shop. No other man could have taken that much punishment and lived.

If there was any pity in the prize ring (which there isn't) it might have found expression here where this man once known as the physical marvel of the ring—this man who five minutes before had stood with a bold and confident look as champion of the world, trained to the day, as fit as he could ever hope to be—now stood as an open target for an opponent nearly fifty pounds lighter and six inches shorter in stature—a target that rocked and swayed under the blistering sun while 50,000 looked on and waited for the coming end.

As time was called for the third round there was no need of Walter Monahan's sponge to announce that Jess had closed his engagement as champion of the world and that Jack Dempsey now wore the crown that had belonged in turn to Sullivan, Corbett, Fitzsimmons, Jeffries, Johnson and Willard.

And Dempsey had proved to be the most spectacular champion of them all.

It had taken Corbett twenty-one rounds to knock out Sullivan. It had taken Fitzsimmons fourteen rounds to drop Corbett. Jeffries had needed eleven rounds to crush Fitz. Johnson traveled fifteen rounds to blot out Jeff, and Johnson lasted twenty-six rounds against Willard. But Dempsey, with the crushing force and the blazing speed, in those punishing hooks, delivered with either fist, needed no such leeway.

Only a matter of a few seconds saved Willard a one-round knockout for, if the bell had known a second's delay, Dempsey would have drawn another one-round verdict to add to his amazing list of one-round affairs.

36

How Willard ever stayed on his feet after the fusilade of that first round will ever remain one of the mysteries of the game. Doughboys have taken a .45 bullet into their bodies and still rushed forward for one last trench knife blow.

You may recall how Fuzzy-Wuzzy, in Kipling's verse, soaked up British fire and still broke a British square. But here was a man who through the last six minutes of the battle stood up to take upon his unprotected jaw an almost countless flurry of punches from a man who had already shown he was the hardest hitter the fighting game has ever known.

It was unbelievable. From less than ten feet away we looked on and refused to credit the vision of our eyes. It looked as if every punch must tear away his head, but in place of this the fountain continued to gush, the features continued to swell, the raw meat continued to pop open in deep slits as the red surf rolled from his shaking pulp-smashed frontispiece.

If Willard had not been in wonderful shape he would have been killed. He surely would never have answered the bell for the second round.

Dempsey left the ring unmarked. He had planted his nerve-killing blow before Willard had ever found opportunity to test the hitting power of his long, tremendous arms. Where was the famous uppercut? No one will ever know, for before the Kansan had a chance to test either, his motive power was paralyzed and he needed every ounce of vitality left to keep him on his feet.

And how this Dempsey can hit! No wonder Carl Morris and Fred Fulton and so many others crumpled up before his blows. When he hit Willard it was exactly the same as if some strong man had swung upon the ex-champion with a heavy hammer. He felt as if raw steel had broken through his skull. He fell before a man who must be able to hit harder than any man who ever lived.

And so, as Willard at thirty-eight passed out, Dempsey at twenty-four becomes champion of the world. The champion boxer—not the champion fighter. For it would

37

be an insult to every doughboy that took his heavy pack through the mules' train to front line trenches to go over the top at dawn to refer to Dempsey as a fighting man. If he had been a fighting man he would have been in khaki when at twenty-two he had no other responsibilities in the world except to protect his own hide.

So let us have no illusions about our new heavyweight champion. He is a marvel in the ring, the greatest boxing or the greatest hitting machine even the old-timers here have ever seen.

But he isn't the world's champion fighter. Not by a margin of 50,000,000 men who either stood, or were ready to stand the test of cold steel and exploding shell for anything from six cents to a dollar a day.

It would be an insult to every young American who sleeps today from Flanders to Lorraine, from the Somme to the Argonne, to crown Dempsey with any laurels of fighting courage.

He missed the big chance of his life to prove his own manhood before his own soul—but beyond that he stands today as the ring marvel of the century, a puncher who will be unbeatable as long as he desires to stay off the primrose way and maintain the wonderful vitality of a wonderful human system.

THE SPORTLIGHT

(N. Y. *Tribune*, August 1, 1919)

To a Pair of Demobilized Boots
(Lifted from their nook in the den to
help round out a fishing jaunt.)

You have gathered dust from the long white roads
   That wind through the drifts of France;
You have known the mire of an Argonne trail
   In the wake of an old advance;
You have known the hike of a blasted pike
   As you floundered along the way,
As heavy as sin when the dawn brings in
   The light of another day.

You've slogged your way through the bally mud
   Where only the dust remained
Of an old French town that caught the blast
   Where the Hun shells whirled and rained;
Floundering on through the slime and wreck—
   And sometimes stepping high—
Where the roofless walls of Avicourt
   Stared up to a sullen sky.

And you've quivered a bit—I'll say it now—
   Around two shaking feet,
Two feet as cold as the Arctic snow,
   Or a January sleet;
And more than once you have wished to be
   Or hold your ancient sway
Along some friendly lane at home
   Three thousand miles away.

And now, uncleaned, with ghostly mud
  Long dried upon your hide,
Forgotten even by the gods
  You rest upon your side;
And I wonder if ever there comes to you,
  Here in your Harlem den,
The call to rise for another hike
  And take to the road again?

Where the bugle calls at the edge of dawn
  As reveille draws near—
Where the ghostly pine trees sway again
  In the haunts of Camp Sevier?
Just one more oldtime slogging tramp
  Beyond the city walls,
By battered roads and shattered towns
  Where the Great Adventure calls?

And So It Goes

Five years ago this August Norman Brookes was giving fervid battle to McLoughlin the Comet.

Quite a few things of at least normal note have happened since that date. Brookes was no raw kid, even then. He was supposed to be out near the end of the athletic road. Since that time his great pal Wilding has gone to the Star Inn that adorns the game's Valhalla, and Brookes himself has known the service of a long campaign. Yet here he is again in still another August, planning to pick up where he left off five years ago. It is much as if there was a notation on the theatrical programme to this effect: "Five years elapse between the first and second act." Up goes the curtain again and here are the same old actors waiting to take their turn at Forest Hills—Brookes, Williams, Johnston, McLoughlin, Murray—all except Wilding. But he will not be forgotten when the championship swings under way.

Considerable Month

August will be something of an interval in a sporting

40

way. There will be no heavyweight championship to stir the mob into a frenzy, which is just as well. In this respect August is lucky. The Fourth of July won't look the same for quite a spell.

But in addition to the lawn tennis championship, to be fought out mainly by demobilized soldiers and sailors, there will be the general onslaught on Chick Evans's title at Oakmont, where the fusilade will get under way around August 18.

Chick this season will face tougher competition than he drew at Marion, where Ouimet and Travers were absent. These two will be on the card with Bob Gardner, Kirkby, Bobby Jones, Walker, Whitney and others known to the golfing line-up.

In addition to which August is a great month to sift the wheat from the chaff in a baseball way. This is the month where the first loud, noisy, resonant cracking process usually arrives. So all in all the next thirty-one days will carry their share of thrills, despite the fact that Messrs. Dempsey and Willard will not entertain us again with their costly wares.

THE SPORTLIGHT

(N. Y. *Tribune*, July 21, 1920)

One night in France Colonel Kennedy of the First Division Field Artillery was discussing the needed ingredients in war.

"Courage," he said, "is, of course, a big factor. So is speed in action. But after all, give me fortitude and stamina among my men and I'll take the chance with everything else."

There are occasions when too much attention is paid to courage in its more flashy forms and to speed in sport.

In the first of the cup races *Resolute* had the speed— but not the stamina of construction to finish.

This is a frequent occurrence in many forms of sport. It comes with the pitcher who can go for five innings at top speed, but who can't last beyond the sixth canto.

It comes in tennis and in golf. But it is only when speed is hooked to stamina that the real champion survives.

AT THE TOP

There is, in this connection, the case of Everett Scott, of the Boston Red Sox.

Scott is no big mess of brawn and fiber. He is rather slenderly built, along lines that tend more to litheness than to latitude.

Yet in this day and time, when ball players are constantly breaking up, developing sore arms or sore legs or spiked thighs or something else, Scott has set one of the most remarkable records ever known.

He has already played in over six hundred consecutive ball games without missing a battle. He has smashed all records ever known.

Scott has speed enough, but he will go down in history as the stamina kid. He has the great quality of being able to last—the necessary iron in his system to go for year after year without ever caving under for a day.

His amazing record now leaves him as one of the big baseball heroes of the year—not one of the spectacular type to appeal to the populace, but one who is deserving far beyond the meager praise he has drawn.

Speed may never help to develop a race to any large extent, but stamina remains as one of the great qualities any individual or any nation can ever know.

ANOTHER CASE

Man o' War has speed. Everyone knew the great three-year-old could whirl along at a dizzy clip.

But when he picked up 126 pounds against a rival of class and was forced to break a world's record for a mile and a furlong he proved again that his stamina was in no sense second to his speed.

Tilden had the stamina to go through in the British tennis championship, where Johnson in this case failed.

Stamina was one of the main factors which carried Dave Herron and Bobby Jones along to the championship finals in golf at Oakmont last August—a thirty-six-hole grind over a course 6,700 yards in length, under a blazing sun.

Mere skill is no longer sufficient in any of these championships. There must be also sufficient physical endurance to stand the strain—to remain in control of one's nervous system.

No man is at his best when poisoned with fatigue. His game under this condition is sure to break badly.

The laurel belongs not only to the one who has the speed and the skill, but also to the one who has the needed stamina to go all the way through with his speed and his skill intact.

It is for the general good of the breed that this condition should exist. Proper training is as much a matter of

43

any championship as knack or ability. The brittle contender is merely lucky when he happens to come safely through.

It Goes for a Team

This goes for an entire club as well as for an individual. Stamina plus lack of brittleness is frequently the deciding factor in a pennant race.

A ball club with a long string of injured or ailing athletes ordinarily doesn't deserve to win.

Scott has proved that a ball player in condition can play over six hundred games, lasting over four years, without missing a contest.

If the Brooklyn club has the stamina to last it has a great chance this season to win a national league pennant. In other respects it has the material, especially the pitching, and certainly the manager—no greater than Pat Moran, but one of the best.

In the American League battle between Cleveland and New York it is now largely a matter of which club keeps on going without caving in—a matter of mental and physical stamina in the testing days of the big race. For, after all, it is the hard drive from early August that usually tells the story.

* * *

"You can't expect," writes a fan, "that opposing pitchers are going to lay one over for Ruth to hammer out of the lot." Urban Shocker didn't feel that way about it when he whiffed the Babe three times in one game. Not so as the Babe could notice it. There's just a trifle difference between "laying one over" and the intentional pass two feet out of range.

44

PART II

The Golden Twenties

In his eulogy at Rice's funeral on July 16, 1953, Bruce Barton said that Grant came into the world at a fortunate time for us all. While the harsh rule of the Puritan tradition had begun to be relaxed . . . . life still meant, to the great majority of Americans, only work—hard work, long hours—the harder and longer, the more commendable.

"This austere tradition," said Barton, "Grant helped mightily to break down. He was the evangelist of fun, the bringer of good news about games . . . . He made the playing fields respectable. Never by preaching or propaganda, but by the sheer contagion of his joy in living, he made us want to play. And in so doing he made us a people of better health and happiness in peace; of greater strength in adversity. This was his gift to his country; few men have made a greater one."

That Granny happened to reach his professional peak as a writer during the Golden Twenties, is one of those fortunate things. If Walter Hagen made the professional golfer "respected" on both side of the Atlantic, Rice by his own thoroughbred gait—both in writing and in living—unconsciously conferred an aura of something fine and decent on the business of writing sports! And if he made giants of those he chronicled, they at least gave him the muscle and flare with which to work.

"I see them walk by in a dream—Dempsey and Cobb
    and Ruth,

45

Tunney and Sande and Jones—Johnson and Matty
and Young—
Alex and Tilden and Thorpe—was there a flash
of youth
That gave us a list like this, when our first tributes
were sung?

Man o' War waits for the break—Shoeless Joe
Jackson's at bat.
John McGraw barks from the line—Hagen is tak-
ing his swing.
Gehrig is watching the pitch—Greb is outclawing
a cat—
Milburn and Hitchcock rise up—taking the ball on
the wing.

Where the old dreams move along—shadows that
drift to and fro—
Moving on back through the years—I've seen a
pretty good show."

JACK DEMPSEY,

THE MAN FROM MAUMEE BAY

In sport, you'll find there are great defensive stars and brilliant offensive competitors. Among the great offensive athletes I've studied I must include Ty Cobb, Bill Tilden, Babe Ruth, Harry Greb and Jesse Owens. But I found the greatest attacking, or pure offensive, star one June day in 1919 in Toledo, off the hot and steamy shores of Maumee Bay.

His name was Jack Dempsey. I had been in France during 1917 and 1918, so had seen no prize fights in that period. When I first met Dempsey, he was burnt purple. He had trained down to 180 pounds in getting ready for Jess Willard, the 250-pound giant. Dempsey was then 24 years old. He was keen and lithe, almost as fast as Cobb. It was his speed, speed of hand as well as foot, that made him such a dangerous opponent.

Dempsey was the oddest mixture of humanity I've known. In the ring he was a killer—a superhuman wild man. His teeth were frequently bared and his complete intent was an opponent's destruction. He was a fighter—one who used every trick to wreck the other fighter.

Yet, outside the ring, Jack is one of the gentlest men I know. I've seen him in his restaurant at times when some customer, with more enthusiasm than good sense, would grab his vest or part of his shirt—strictly for a souvenir—with no kickback from Jack. I've known the man closely for more than 30 years and I've never seen him in a rough argument or as anything except courteous and considerate.

Looking at Dempsey and Willard in 1919, it was hard to give Dempsey a chance. Dempsey, slightly over 6 feet, weighed 180. Willard, at 6 feet 6, weighed 250 at least.

Willard looked on Dempsey as a little boy. The night

47

before the fight Bob Edgren and I called on Jess. He thought the fight was a joke.

"... outweigh him seventy pounds," Willard said. "He'll come tearing into me ... I'll have my left out ... and then I'll hit him with a right uppercut. That'll be the end."

Next day when the first round opened. Dempsey circled Willard some 25 or 30 seconds. He was a tiger circling an ox. Finally Willard couldn't wait any longer. He jabbed at Dempsey with his left, and the roof fell in. Jack ducked under Willard's left, threw a right to the body. At the same time he nailed Willard on the right side of the head with a smashing left.

"I knew it was all over then," Jack said later. "I saw his cheek bone cave in."

Jack rubbed his own wire-stubbled jaw reflectively. "Funny thing about this fight," he continued, "was that Kearns [Dempsey's manager Jack Kearns] claimed he had bet ten thousand dollars to one hundred thousand dollars I'd knock out Willard in the first round. That's what I did. The referee had raised my right hand, awarding me the fight. Willard's head was hanging over the lower rope. He was practically unconscious from several knockdowns. I left the ring. The fight was over ... or it should have been. I must have been twenty-five yards from the ring when they called me back. That was the biggest shock I ever got ... when I was told the bell had rung three seconds too soon. Suppose it had? My hand had been raised and I had been given the fight by the referee."

Willard, bleeding like a half-butchered ox, was unable to answer the bell for the fourth round.

"I sure recall my end of that purse," recalled Dempsey. "For three rounds I collected twenty-seven thousand five hundred dollars, my first big payday. Willard did all right too. His share, win, lose or draw, was one hundred thousand dollars."

Lining up Georges Carpentier for the Dempsey vs. Carpentier fight, at Boyle's Thirty Acres, Jersey City, for July 1921, was a shrewd piece of work by Tex Rickard.

48

Tex "sensed" more and better gate-building tricks in one minute than today's promoters can dream up in a year. I realize that television has taken a lot of the steam off the need for a "live" gate—what with TV rights selling for great chunks of cash. But the fact remains that Rickard, yes, and Mike Jacobs, had the kind of promotional touch that would have them storming the gates today instead of taking in the fight through a camera.

Carpentier, with a gaudy if superficial war record, had returned to Paris in one piece—and hungry. He was a pretty fair light-heavyweight, but they couldn't have ballooned the Frenchman into a bona fide heavyweight, except in the papers, with two sandbags for added ballast. At any rate, Rickard—knowing the public's love of a hero and villain tangle—cast Dempsey, the scowling, wire-bearded "draft dodger" as the villain, with apple-cheeked Carpentier, the amiable, personable soldier boy, as the hero. Pictures of Dempsey, riveting battleships in patent leather shoes—all at Kearns' behest—flooded the sports pages, along with those of Carpentier, practically winning the war singlehanded.

That fight was the first to be broadcast—with Graham McNamee describing the action—and it had the whole nation taking sides for or against Dempsey.

Carpentier landed in America several weeks before the match. He had never seen Dempsey. He was a Frenchman on a holiday, a good-will emissary.

Dempsey trained at Atlantic City; as for Carpentier, I'm still not certain that he did train. He was never on exhibition to the press—never on a scale; about the only time we'd see him was on a rubbing table or sauntering into a restaurant.

The story of that fight—badly overplayed, but eaten to the last adjective by the public—was actually ordained days beforehand. But the culmination of Carpentier's mental and physical unpreparedness was seen near his dressing room just before the fight at Boyle's Thirty Acres—not by me, but by Kit and Sophie Treadwell McGeehan,

W.O.'s wife and a fine reporter in her own right. It happened this way and here it is in Kit's words.

"Sophie McGeehan was covering the color story for her paper," reports Kit. "A lot of New York's carriage trade was there and that was part of the story. Well, it had started to rain before the bout. I spotted a little exit to somewhere and we decided to get in out of the rain. We were in this little room, sitting on a rubbing table and complimenting ourselves on our abode when a cop entered and said to us, 'Ladies, where do you think you are?'' We told him we were out of the rain. 'You've got to leave. You're in the Frenchman's dressing room!' replied the officer.

"At that moment down the corridor came Carpentier. Dressed, he was as white as a sheet . . . thin . . . and, Oh Lord, but he looked frightened. And several steps behind, wearing trunks and a heavy red sweater, and unshaven, came Dempsey—big, tough and bristling. He dwarfed the cops guarding him.

"I looked at Sophie who, of course, was staring. Studying the contrast between the two men, she said, 'That poor French boy. Why he'll be murdered!' We returned to our seats and waited for the Angel of Doom to claim Carpentier."

It was all over in four rounds, but had Dempsey wanted to put the slug on Carpentier, I think he could have nailed him in the first round. From ringside, all French ships at sea received this cabled flash: "Your Frog flattened in fourth"—for a new "high" in international diplomacy.

I recall another "visitor" who came to America to strike-it-rich against Dempsey—Luis Angel Firpo. When hurt, Firpo truly lived up to his "Wild Bull of the Pampas" monicker; but in recline, after a meal, he looked more like a great bum in the park.

My first glimpse of the South American was two weeks before the fight—at the Polo Grounds, September 14, 1923. His camp was at Atlantic City. When I arrived early one morning Firpo was tackling a light breakfast: a huge steak smothered with lamb chops. After finishing, he walked over to a couch and lay there like a python who'd just swallowed a calf. He seemed dopey and indolent. I compared his camp to Dempsey's at Saratoga. There the order of the day was mayhem, with the massive George Godfrey as Jack's number 1 sparring partner at $1,500 per week, and I wondered at the fight that was about to be perpetrated on the unsuspecting public. Fifty-dollar ringside seats were being gobbled up for $100 each. Firpo had a couple of two-bit sparring partners whom he outweighed by a ton and belabored at will. He sure didn't spend much on that camp, except on food.

At ringside my typewriter was next to Jack Lawrence's. During the final prelim bout, we were discussing the main.

"They're two big guys," said Lawrence. "If somebody goes through the ropes I hope it's Dempsey. At least he's lighter than that truck Firpo."

Just before the bout started, I moved down four seats, next to Bob Edgren of the old New York *Evening World*. Well, for the record, Lawrence got his wish. It was Dempsey who came hurtling through the ropes in that madhouse first round. He landed, back first, on top of Lawrence, who had put up his hands to protect himself. But nobody, including Lawrence, had to help Dempsey back through those ropes. He was all for helping himself—but fast!

Dempsey never cared to talk about that fight at any length. To him it was his closest call.

"Rickard asked me to carry Firpo for four or five rounds . . . to give the customers a run for their money," Jack said. "I told Tex to go to hell, that Firpo was too strong and hit too hard to play with. I told Rickard I'd put Firpo away in the first round—if I could.

"You know, before the fight you had told me that Bill Brennan had said Firpo threw rocks at you . . . that he had a rubber arm . . . that he'd sock you from a good way off. Well, in the first round I got in a little too close and Firpo's first shot—a full right—caught me on the chin. I almost went down but kept punching. I was dazed. You wrote, and others did the same, that I hit him when he was getting up. At that time I wasn't fighting for any

51

championship or any million dollars. I was fighting to keep from being killed. I would have hit him at any place I found him.

"The wallop that sent me through the ropes was a half punch and half shove," continued Dempsey. "It was nothing like that opening right hand he nailed me with earlier."

"What was your first thought as you went flying through the air out of the ring?" I asked.

"To get back up and in as quickly as I could," he said. "I might say that no one at ringside tried to help me. They put up their hands to break my fall. It was all instinctive."

I don't think there was ever a moment in any fight that Dempsey thought in terms of defense. He had a method of weaving and moving about that was partly defense but it always led to attack or headlong assault.

Dempsey was not a bad boxer. He wasn't as good in this respect as Tunney, Corbett and Louis were; but he was none too easy to hit with a good punch. He knew most of the tricks.

Dempsey was head and shoulders over Rocky Marciano as a boxer. He had to be to go 15 rounds with Tom Gibbons when Gibbons was hungry and able. That brings up the Dempsey-Gibbons title match at Shelby, Montana, in some ways Dempsey's most demanding fight. As a promoter's dream, the Shelby fight—that and the Sharkey-Stribling fight in 1929 at Miami Beach—were both pure phantasmagoria.

Mike Collins, a fight manager of sorts out of St. Paul, had a string of fighters barnstorming through Montana in 1923, working any town where there were a few dollars to be made. Collins met Loy Molumby, head of Montana's American Legion, and in a short time they were cruising all over the state in a flimsy old airplane . . . shooting off horse pistols and calling for wine. In the course of their meanderings they ran into a man named Johnson, who, among other things, was Mayor of Shelby and president of the local bank.

With the talk flaring around fights and fighters, somebody had the glorious idea of staging a heavyweight

52

championship fight right there in Shelby! It would cause a land boom, make it a city overnight. Collins called his pal, Eddie Kane, Gibbons' manager back in St. Paul, and propositioned him.

"Listen, Mike," replied Kane. "You get Dempsey out there . . . anywhere . . . and Gibbons will fight him for nothing. All you got to do is pay Dempsey. What do you think of that?"

That, they liked. Next they wired Jack Kearns, Dempsey's manager, offering him $300,000 "to defend his title against Tom Gibbons at Shelby on July 4th."

Kearns wired back: "Send $100,000 now . . . $100,000 in a month and $100,000 before Dempsey steps into the ring and it's a deal."

The first $100,000 came easily enough, and seeing they meant business Kearns and Dempsey headed west and set up training quarters at Great Falls, Montana, about 70 miles south of Shelby. Eddie Kane went direct to Shelby and set up Gibbons' training camp there.

Late in June, I boarded a Pullman in Chicago with a crowd of other writers—Broun, Runyon, Bide Dudley and Hugh Fullerton were there—and we were off by way of the Great Northern, to the wild and woolly West, by God! Great Falls, we discovered, was a fair sized town. Visiting Dempsey at his camp among the cottonwoods, I found him in high humor. I recall it was June 24th, his twenty-eighth birthday. His dad was there and so was his cousin, Don Chafin, a rawboned husky from West Virginia, and a paid-up life member of the famed Hatfield clan. The camp mascot was a cub timber wolf. Jack was giving himself daily facials with some sort of bear grease that had toughened his face to the general texture of a boar's hide. It was Jack's first title defense in two years but he looked to be in great shape. Even walking, he seemed to slither along, snakelike, his muscles glinting in the sun.

I don't recall just what I expected from Shelby, the fight site, but I wasn't impressed. A town of perhaps 2,000, it was little more than a crossroad in the middle of a desert. There were few houses and a building or two

53

that passed for hotels. Press headquarters and living accommodations were in one of the Pullman cars shoved over on a siding.

Gibbons, meanwhile, was training hard and looking forward to what I thought was certain annihilation. His wife and two children were with him. It was a case of Papa Bear, Momma and the kids, all up there in a stark little house on the crest of a barren little hill with not so much as a shrub as far as the naked eye could see.

I remember Hughey Fullerton spotting a Blackfoot brave in war regalia, including paints and eagle feathers. Trying out an Indian dialect, Hughey asked him, "Who Big Chief like? Dempsey or Gibbons?"

Much to Fullerton's astonishment, Big Chief replied, "Sir, I happen to like Dempsey. Gibbons has the skill as a boxer. Dempsey has the power. Power usually prevails over skill." He was a Carlisle graduate brandishing an English course.

Mayor Johnson, Molumby and friends were beginning to realize the facts of life . . . and were having a rough time scraping up that second $100,000 installment—with still a third to come. Kearns, meanwhile, remained adamant. After Johnson all but hocked his bank, Kearns had $200,000.

"You've got to pay Dempsey every cent, or you won't see Dempsey at all!" was the ribald chant on Shelby's Main Street.

Included in my Sportlight column were occasional pearls under the subhead, "Campfire Songs from Shelby."

In the wide open spaces where men are men
The slogan today is, "Never again!"

In the wide open spaces, loud rings the fuss,
"Germany's lucky compared to us."

In the wide open spaces, they cry bereft,
"Yes, we have only bananas left."

54

I arrived back at Dempsey's camp about four days before the bell rang. Dempsey was enthusiastic. "Grant," he said, "we're really shootin' today. . . . Think you'll enjoy it."

George Godfrey again was Dempsey's Number One sparring partner. Had he come along ten years later, this Negro might well have been a world's champion.

Godfrey was under instructions to do his best. He weighed about 230; Jack about 190. From the bell, the two tore at each other. Godfrey threw a full right, a real bomb that grazed Jack's chin, bringing blood. Jack retaliated with a left hook that knocked Godfrey down into such a heap he broke two ribs. So much for the shooting. "Big Ben" Wray, a 7-foot 2-inch "cowboy" had lasted 28 seconds with Dempsey a fortnight earlier. Jack's left hook broke Wray's right jaw . . . all of which left Wray, his head in a plaster cast, taking nourishment through a straw. I recall the doc removed two teeth to admit the feeding tube.

Meanwhile, owing to Kearn's vacillations about the purse, special trains, alerted to bring in crowds from San Francisco and Chicago, had been forced to cancel. The night before the fight, slated for Independence Day afternoon, was the most harrowing in Shelby's history. Still claiming the last possible ounce of flesh, Kearns "officially" called off the fight seven times. Endeavoring to keep fresh, up-to-the-minute bulletins pumping over the wires, Broun, Runyon and the rest of us had long since gone nuts.

At the 12th hour, Kearns again reversed his field, decided to gamble on the gate "take" and declared the fight was on. In a matter of minutes Shelby's main drag erupted into a madhouse. Cowpokes, their spike heels kicking up the alkali dust, bought drinks for millionaires and the millionaires mingled with Blackfoot Indians, many of them in full tribal gear. Drifters, motorists from Louisiana, society ladies and wild dames. Hollywood stars and sheep herders—they were all there, along with Mrs. Raymond T. Baker, the former Mrs. Alfred Gwynne Vanderbilt, and

One-Eyed Connolly. I recall Mrs. Baker's private Pullman car, The Palm Beach, reclined on a nearby siding and I spotted Mae Murray peering at the revelry from the sanctuary of her own private car. Against a background of blaring bands, the snake dance lasted clear through the night. Yes, it was prohibition, but that night everybody packed a bottle.

And looking down on it all from his little family shack on a bare hill sat Tom Gibbons, like Teufelsdröckh, the attic watcher in *Sartor Resartus,* and had his share of philosophical cogitations. I thought about Tom. More, I thought of his sweet wife. Her man, a family man 34 years old, was about to face Dempsey, "The Killer," and for nary a thin dime!

The fight was scaled at $50 ringside and the huge wooden bowl erected for the bloodletting was built to hold some 50,000 customers. But the final count was a trickle over 7,000 when the Main finally went on.

Dempsey and Gibbons went 15 rounds like two featherweights. I've never witnessed as much sheer speed in a heavyweight bout. At the finish, the decision was clearly Dempsey's, but Gibbons, a wildcat that steaming afternoon, remained dangerous all the way. Dempsey resorted to every boxing trick he knew and as the bout unfolded, he knew plenty: But he couldn't nail a scowling, stabbing Gibbons, who fought the fight of his life . . . for nothing.

"He never hurt me, really, after the first round," Gibbons said. "But Lord, how that fellow can hit! It was in the first round. Dempsey shot a straight right punch. . . . I saw it but couldn't duck it, entirely, and took it on the top of my forehead. That's the thickest part of a man's skull . . . but Grant, I didn't come out of a daze until the fourth round.

"I'd like to fight him again, for money," concluded Gibbons. "But don't let anybody ever tell you Dempsey can't box. He knows all the tricks."

I was having breakfast with Jack and Max Baer one February morning back in 1931 at the Warwick Hotel. The day before, Jack had refereed the Baer-Tommy

Loughran fight at Madison Square Garden. Max had been decisioned in ten rounds.

"I've been looking at left jabs all night," Max said. "Lefts . . . lefts . . . lefts . . . that's all I've seen!"

"The funny part," said Dempsey, "is that you could have stopped that 'Lefty' in the first round."

"How?" Baer said.

"Take off your coat," replied Jack to big Maxie, 6 feet 3 and 220 pounds. Max shucked off his coat and faced Dempsey. "Now lead with a left, just as Loughran did," said Jack. Max led . . . and there was an immediate yelp. "You broke my arm," Max howled as he backed away, holding it.

As Baer led with his left, Dempsey had dropped his huge right fist across the right biceps with paralyzing force. The left arm became useless for thirty minutes.

"I'll show you another punch," Jack said. He spun Baer and then socked him.

"You can't do that," Max said. "It's illegal."

"They'll only warn you the first time," Dempsey said.

Jack Dempsey was and remains the most restless man I ever knew. When he was in his middle twenties, he couldn't sit still for two minutes. He was all over the room, always in motion. After he quit fighting to settle down, he settled down all over the map. Buenos Aires one week, Toronto, Canada, the next and on to Boston or Dallas or San Francisco—refereeing wrestling matches and prize fights or representing some company in an advertising drive. He also took a flier with various circuses . . . and he loved the work. In one circus he had a chimp that always waited for him. He'd give the chimp a cigar and a bottle of Coke. The monk would drink the bottle, smoke the cigar and jam the cigar in the bottle for a stopper. He was Jack's pal.

Even today, the sight of a restless Dempsey cooped up in some hotel room reminds me of a caged tiger. I've always loved animals, particularly wild animals. In other years, I don't know how many hours Gene Fowler and I spent studying the tigers, elephants, lions and big snakes

57

at zoos in New York, Chicago, St. Louis—or even the 'gator farms in Florida. During the late 1930's I envisioned a short-lived plan for transporting pairs of jungle beasts to Florida and turning 'em all loose in the Everglades. I believe they would have thrived. When the Florida dream fizzled, I was for doing the same general thing with the Brazilian jungles and had the late Martin Johnson enthused over it—until World War II knocked that out the window. I still think my plan had more merit than that, or any war.

The tiger, particularly, contains more grace and less waste motion in one flick of his paw than most of us possess in our entire physical makeup. For pure animal grace, the sight of Sam Snead murdering a tee shot; Babe Ruth swinging from his heels; yes, and Jack Dempsey raining savage destruction on a foe—these remain for me the acme of tigerish reflexes in human form.

Some years ago while in Sarasota, Florida, on the spring baseball beat, I spent a morning on the Ringling Brothers' circus lot. In a short time I was back with the menagerie watching my old friend, the tiger, prowl his caged beat. Studying him, I compared the fellow to Dempsey. These lines began to take shape on that March morning with the thermometer pushing the eighties.

To a Caged Tiger

I've watched you stalking back and forth, the hurt look
    in your eyes,
Seeing, far off, the jungle grass, the blazing Indian skies,
The matted snarl of underbrush that sweeps the covered
    loam,
The hidden places that you knew, and looked upon, as
    home.

There you could move on silent paw to track your luck-
    less prey—
There you could find the jungle thrill that knows the
    right of way;

58

Part of the ancient plan that came with life's first flame
    of sun,
Lord of the kingdom that you ruled, where might and
    right were one.

I've watched you in your steel-bound cage, but you are
    not alone,
O, hapless captive with your dreams that seek the outer
    zone;
Don't look with envy on the lot of those who cross
    your view,
The world today is chain or cage, for all except a few.

For we who watch your restless step can understand
    your dreams
Of far-off shores and jungle grass and sunlit, singing
    streams,
Chained to a desk, or out of work, drab captives of
    some fate
That shuts the Great Adventure out, beyond the city's
    gate.

Tiger—the Indian sun is hot—the jungles' echoes call—
Tiger—I know just how you feel—with chain and cage
    and wall—
On restless feet you'll dream your dreams—and stay
    within your cage—
With restless heart I'll dream with you—and write another
    page.

I once asked Dempsey why college athletes never made
good fighters. "Football is just as rough," I said. "They
star in those games. But seldom in boxing where the big
money is."

"They're too smart," Dempsey said. "The fight game
is the toughest game on earth. When I was a young fellow
I was knocked down plenty. I wanted to stay down. I
couldn't. I had to collect that two dollars for winning—
or go hungry. I had to get up. I was one of those hungry

fighters. You could hit me on the chin with a sledge hammer for five dollars. When you haven't eaten for two days you'll understand.

"Few college fellers ever get that low. I had one early fight when I was knocked down eleven times before I got up to win. You think I'd have taken that beating if I had had as much as twenty-five bucks with me? No chance."

He would have.

And speaking of money, when he finally earned it there's no telling how much of it he gave away. One week it amounted to $1,700, just handouts to bums. He was and is one of the most liberal of men.

Dempsey has two lovely daughters—Barbara and Joan, both now married. He has watched over and guarded them like four mothers. His care of them has been complete.

Gene Fowler, the writer, knew Dempsey back in Denver as a kid. "He never liked to fight then," Gene said. "He was the nicest kid in the neighborhood. He has been one of the greatest fellows I've known. Whatever a real gentleman is—that's Dempsey."

Jack had steel fists and an iron jaw. Some experts have written that Marciano punches harder or with more explosive force than Dempsey. Gene Tunney says this statement is ridiculous. Marciano has at least one asset that matches Dempsey. Dempsey could take it—to a full degree. So can Marciano.

"There are two things that count in ring success," Dempsey once told me. "The big punch and the ability to take a big punch. Any real champion must have both."

I recall at Chicago in '27 . . . in the fourth round I think it was. Tunney had Dempsey in trouble. He looked groggy. "Why didn't you follow up that right hand?" I asked Tunney later.

"Because I know Dempsey," Tunney replied. "He can recover quicker than any man I ever fought. He's dangerous with a five-second interval."

Two months before his return match with Tunney, Dempsey fought Jack Sharkey in the Yankee Stadium.

It was the night of July 21, 1927 . . . and this, Dempsey hoped, would be a tight tuneup for the revenge bout with Tunney.

That night Sharkey, at twenty-five, was as good a fighter as he ever would be. And when he was right, Josef Paul Zukauskas (Sharkey's square name) was plenty good. Dempsey, at thirty-two, was something else again. Stories from Dempsey's camp at Saratoga reported Jack was soaking his left arm—the one that sired the hooks that smashed Willard, Carpentier and Firpo—in nightly applications of hot salves. The betting odds established Sharkey as the favorite.

Sharkey, in fine trim, was becoming cockier by the minute. One day while he was being rubbed down after work, Sharkey asked me to drop into his room.

"Come in here a minute," beckoned Sharkey. "You know," he said when the door was closed, "I could'a had this fight with Tunney. . . . Rickard offered it to me."

"Why didn't you take it?" I replied. "By the looks of you, it might have been a short cut to the title."

"Tunney can wait," said Sharkey. "I know I can lick Dempsey, and by beating him I figure it'll be a better buildup for Tunney."

Nearly 80,000, shelling out more than $1,000,000, made another Rickard promotion pay off that night. Names from the entertainment world dotted ringside. I recall bumping into Byrd and Chamberlin, trans-Atlantic heroes of that year, en route to working press.

Instead of charging his foe in customary fashion at the opening bell, Dempsey suddenly played it cute waiting for Sharkey to make the first move. Sharkey did—almost tearing Jack's head off with a left and right.

"I must have hit him five punches in quick succession," said Sharkey later. "What a sucker I was. The old champ is staggering. All I need is one more punch. But I remembered how they cheered Dempsey and booed me when we were introduced. So with Dempsey groggy, I turned to the mob and yelled, 'Here's your bum champion! How do you like him?'

"When I returned back to Dempsey he had recovered enough to clinch and save himself. That's how I lost the fight."

When hurt, Dempsey, at twenty or thirty-two, would have used a tire iron on his tormentor if one happened to be at hand. But that reaction was inexplicably slow to ignite against Sharkey. Had the once hungry but now opulent Dempsey gone soft—and cautious? For six rounds Sharkey knocked Jack all over that ring. Instead of jabbing and moving, jabbing and moving—the way he'd defeated Jimmy Maloney and many others—Sharkey, despite orders from his corner, threw caution overboard and punched flatfooted, shooting for a knockout. An over-confident Billy Conn tried the same thing in his first fight against Joe Louis in the Polo Grounds 14 years later. As the bell ended the sixth round, a battered, bloody Dempsey whipped two shots to Sharkey's face. As referee O'Sullivan pried the men apart, the crowd jeered Sharkey and cheered Dempsey.

Dempsey opened the seventh with two sharp rights to Sharkey's belly—right on the belt line. Stunned and hurt, Sharkey, instead of covering up and riding out the storm, looked appealingly at the referee. O'Sullivan warned Dempsey, but the suddenly rejuvenated Manassa Mauler tore into Sharkey's belly again with palpably low shots. Sharkey again turned to the referee, gesturing pain. Wham! That dreaded left hook landed flush on Sharkey's jaw. Down he went, in a distended heap, half crawling and clutching his groin—his head groveling the canvas. O'Sullivan, himself dazed for a moment, seemed to be deliberating whether to start counting or award the fight to Sharkey on a foul. He finally picked up the count from the timekeeper, Kid McPartland. At ten, little Joe Humphrey climbed between the ropes and raised Dempsey's hand. Bedlam broke loose with straw hats sailing into the ring and cries of "Foul!" and "Quitter!" booming through the Stadium. Hammering away at my morning lead, I wasn't sure whether I was working a heavyweight fight or a riot.

Two months later in Chicago's Soldiers Field, nearly 105,000 paid $2,658,660 to see an all but washed up Dempsey try to regain his crown from Gene Tunney.

I mentioned Dempsey's fight at Shelby, and the Sharkey-Stribling fight at Miami Beach six years later, as two historic nightmares. Dempsey, unwittingly, played an important role in the Florida venture.

The Jack Sharkey vs. Young Stribling fight at Miami Beach in February of '29 foreshadowed the dead-ahead depression. Carl Fisher, the "inventor" of Miami Beach, had fellow Hoosier and publicist Steve Hannagan and his partners Joe Copps and Larry Smits booming Miami Beach. This fight was blueprinted as a heady publicity adjunct.

Once the preliminaries were under way, a ruptured appendix killed Tex Rickard. He was a good friend of mine. Money was never his main interest—it was just stuff to move around. He loved publicity and wanted to be known as the greatest promoter of all time. That was all. In this he was and will remain safe. He was the greatest.

When Rickard died, Bill Carey, one of the head men of Madison Square Garden, was handed a tube of sunburn cream and rushed into the breach. As a portion of Rickard's "property," Dempsey was pressed into service as Rickard's stand-in. Dempsey was to get $50,000 or $100,000 for promoting the fight.

Bill Carey—a gentleman and everybody's pal—was perhaps the greatest booster professional ice hockey ever had in New York. As a fight promoter, however, Bill knew as much as an elephant knows about contract bridge . . . or a kangaroo knows about golf. He began spending money so fast and with such a lavish hand that Dempsey soon saw there would be nothing left for him. So—Jack agreed to work for nothing. "I was afraid I would have to pick up the check," he remarked.

All correspondents, plus droves who didn't know a typewriter from a milk can, were admitted—free—to the day and night revels. Carey had leased Fisher's mansion right on the beach at the head of Lincoln Road and, as I recall, several writers were wounded in the rush for rooms overlooking the Atlantic Ocean. Four hotels, including the Drake as base of operations, were utilized to handle 435 newsmen from all over the world. For nearly seven solid weeks it resembled New Year's Eve in Babylon—and I don't mean Long Island.

Meanwhile, Dempsey, now working for nothing to save a little money, was engulfed. So were all others trying to steer affairs back to sanity. The tidal wave was on, beyond control. Everybody within fifty miles of The Beach became one of Carey's freeloaders. Headquarters for the press gang became headquarters for everything—with the beach itself serving as the front lawn. I recall Harry Grayson got an old ex-manager pal, Gus Wilson, then running a restaurant-bar in New York, to act as maitre d'hôtel for the press. It was prohibition, of course. But with Gus, if you ordered a gin fizz, you got a gin fizz! Beer costing Carey one dollar a bottle was used to water the geranium plants. How many cases of champagne, gin, bourbon and scotch were consumed I don't know. But I do know that Nat Fleischer, in charge of auditing, signed a check for $32,100 for booze alone. That was one of the thirstiest mobs ever. There must have been two drunks to every square yard of beach. And the majority of the crowd had no connection whatsoever with the fight.

I went to Miami three weeks early. The New York *Tribune,* for whom I was operating, told me not to cover the fight. They thought it a phony—no good. However, I had promised Harry Staton, the manager of the Tribune Syndicate, that I would cover his 50 or more papers. I was writing two separate columns—one for those who wanted the fight covered, another for the *Tribune.* Meanwhile, the rest of the sports-writing fraternity was beating out copy—of sorts.

A week before the fight, it was apparent that they were going to take in more than $400,000 on a sellout and still lose big money. Meanwhile, Lionel Levy, the young architect who had built Madison Square Garden, was putting the final touches on his open-air wooden arena in Flamingo Park.

Back in New York, Bill McGeehan, the *Tribune* sports editor—and one of the best ever—decided to come down and investigate. Bill had been roasting Carey daily in his column. When he arrived, Bill expected Carey to have him tossed out. I introduced them, "Mr. Carey, Mr. McGeehan."

Carey beamed his welcome through his milk-bottle lenses. "And by the way, Mr. McGeehan," he said, "what business are you in?" That was the only time I ever saw McGeehan stopped cold. He fled the camp. He refused to write a word. Harry Cross then followed to "cover" McGeehan. In a few more days that brilliant if at times baffling youngster, Don Skene, arrived to cover both the boss and Cross. Following Bill's precepts, both refused to write a word. At the eleventh hour the New York desk suddenly wired all four of us to file 1,000 words or more. McGeehan, Cross and Skene—wherever he was—filed nothing. I wavered and weakened after a plea from Staton, my boss.

During that final week, Al Capone, from his island home, decided to make character . . . and threw a demure cocktail party for all visiting writers. I didn't attend but Scarface was strictly Emily Post. Capone managed to spread his peculiar good will the night of the fight by scattering $100 bills among the ushers. They got paid even if Dempsey didn't.

The actual fight should have made big money— $200,000 anyway. It lost. During all the buildup I'd had a room at the Flamingo Hotel—at the straight daily rate. I could look over the situation with a clear conscience, but that didn't help Carey and the Madison Square Garden Corporation. Sharkey won when he might well have lost. Later Jack told me, "Stribling hit me with a full right over the heart. It hurt a lot. I fell in to grab him. He beat me to it by grabbing me first and holding on until I was ready to go on. Had our positions been reversed, I could—in fact, I would—have murdered him."

65

Stribling could have been a great fighter. He wasn't. He was a fine boxer . . . a good puncher . . . fast and strong. But he was the oddest ring fighter I ever knew. He was dead game—out of the ring. He was seldom as game in the ring during a tough fight. Yet he would drive a shaky aircraft in front of a hurricane . . . or a motorcycle through a heavy wall. I have seen him do it. He was killed on that motorcycle.

PREDESTINED

I am the ghost that follows men—I give each one his
    break,
For life is largely accident, no matter what they say—
I lift and lower at my will—I give and then I take—
And laugh to see the experts squirm and figure out the
    play.

In some I plant the yellow streak, which they must hold
    from birth;
To some I bring a fighting heart, which holds the world
    at bay;
To millions I bring tragedy—to millions I bring mirth,
But only those I give the breaks can have the right of way.

I let an able artist starve—I take a dolt of brawn
And give him fame and wealth to spare—the laurel on
    his brow—
And I have followed this set plan from time's first streak
    of dawn,
And I will keep this schedule up a million years from now.

JONES WINS U. S. OPEN GOLF TITLE

(N. Y. *Tribune*, July 16, 1923)

The red badge of courage always belongs upon the breast of the fighter who can break and then come back with a stouter heart than he ever had before.

This crimson decoration of valor came to Robert Tyre Jones, of Atlanta, twenty-one-year-old amateur, when he rode at last yesterday to the crest of the open golf championship of the United States on one of the boldest and greatest iron shots ever played in the game that goes back through 500 years of competitive history.

They couldn't keep the youngster out forever, but the final shot that beat Bobby Cruickshank, the brilliant, hard-fighting Scot of Shackamaxon, by two strokes was easily the greatest effort in Bobby Jones' career.

You must get the entire setting to appreciate the full value of the masterpiece. Only the day before, young Jones had come to this same hole with the championship gathered to his arms at last, after four years of futile strife. Even a 5 here would have won the big crown of the game. Under the heavy strain he gave way upon the last rim of victory, missed two shots and took a 6. Only those who know Jones can understand how he brooded over this big smash on Inwood's home green.

It was upon this same eighteenth hole that Cruickshank had gathered immortal fame with the par-breaking 3 that tied the count. Yesterday they came to the same tee still deadlocked, with the open championship hanging on a single hole. Each contestant at this point had taken seventy-two strokes for the seventeen holes already finished. There was the feeling of drama in the heavy air, drama of even greater proportions than the day before. For as the big gallery swung in long, compact lines from the tee to the green 425 yards away, all present seemed to understand that it was the hole which had broken Jones and made Cruickshank.

Certainly Jones and Cruickshank must have felt the deep, inner psychology that beats with driving force upon the raw soul at such a moment. It is a psychology that all golfers know. With the gallery finally adjusted, Cruickshank, the first to play, hooked to the rough at the left of the course. Jones followed with a longer ball, but when it stopped rolling it was resting in the rough to the right. Cruickshank then played out safely, having no chance to carry the faraway strip of water that guarded the final strip of green beneath the fluttering flag.

Jones then faced the toughest decision of his career. Cruickshank, with his safe shot down the middle, had apparently a certain 5 in sight. Jones needed a full driving iron from the rough to get home across the water, 200 yards away. If he made the carry and kept the ball straight he was at last at the end of his greatest dream—the new open champion of his country. If he failed he could get no better than a 6, with the title in Cruickshank's hands. And this was the same hole that had cost him his nearly won glory the day before.

His hesitation was slight. For just a moment he sized up the situation, took out his straight-faced driving iron and tore into the ball with everything he had. For just a half breath there was deep silence in the crowd. And then the first roar began as the white ball, sailing clean and true against the gray, shadowed sky, picked out a straight line for the pin and finally dropped just eight feet beyond the cup.

He had matched Cruickshank's brilliant shot of the day before, had matched it in both skill and courage, and when the ball stopped spinning just beyond the pin the hysterical clamor that swept across Jamaica Bay was tribute to something more than a brilliant stroke. It was tribute to a heart stout enough to trample psychology and imagination into the dust and come through at the big moment upon the same shot that had yielded bitterness and disaster only the day before.

This eighteenth hole at Inwood should be the site for the next national dramatic theater of America. No other hole in all golf history has ever shown a greater amount of pulse-stirring drama within two days. Psychologically, Jones's iron shot was even greater than Cruickshank's from the day before, one of the great shots of all time.

This was the shot that made Bobby Jones the new open golf champion of the United States, successor to Gene Sarazen, who beat him out by just one stroke at Skokie a year ago. For Cruickshank, facing only a thin shred of hope after a great fight, tried too desperately to get his 150-yard approach stone dead and caught a trap just hole high to the left of the green. When he finally came out and took his 6 he reached across at once to congratulate Jones, who still had an eight-foot putt for his 3.

"Not yet," said Jones, "not yet." Too many things had happened to him in this bizarre game since he first came out of Georgia seven years ago, at the age of fourteen, to cause his first sensation at Philadelphia. Too many sudden and unexpected turns had cropped up around the rim of victory for him to take anything for granted even now. Taking no chances of any mistake, he tapped the ball stone dead to the cup for a sure 4 in place of going for his 3. Just at this moment Luke Ross, Bobby's caddy from Cleveland, came up to tell his story.

"He's a chance from the bottom of his shoes to the top of his head," said Luke. "On that last iron he was lying closely, with the ball in the dirt, from a place I never thought anyone could smash the ball across that water 190 yards away. But he took just one second to say, 'Give me an iron,' and he took just one second to play the greatest golf shot any man ever saw before. It was a No. 2 iron that he used, with a pretty straight face to carry through the wind. I wasn't quite sure what would happen until I saw the look on his face, with his jaw set and his eyes almost blazing, and then I knew we were home.

"Yes," added Luke, "I knew we were home when I saw that look. Honestly, I think he'd 'a' knocked Jack

Dempsey out with a punch if he had been in the way of this championship, just at that spot."

Jones made his first big bid for fame when he reached the final round of the amateur championship at Oakmont, Pittsburgh, in 1919, where Dave Herron's phenomenal golf beat him back. He finished among the first seven at Inverness in 1920, well within the first ten at Columbia in 1921, and then second at Skokie, tied with Black, at 289. Beyond any question he deserves the title as the greatest golfer of his day. For the last four open championships, the only four in which he has played, his grand total is now fourteen strokes better than Walter Hagen's, in second place.

Any golfer who can lead Hagen fourteen strokes after 288 holes of open championship play, with a still greater margin on Sarazen, Hutchison, Barnes and others, must take his place at the top of the long and winding caravanserie of stars. It is a record no other golfer on either side of the water, professional or amateur, has ever known, a record that even Harry Vardon never quite reached in any four-year stretch of play.

The remarkable features of yesterday's great match at Inwood is the way the two surviving contestants got under headway after Saturday's gruelling, nerve-wracking finish. They were flanked and pressed by a tearing, rushing crowd that was seldom silent, where loud cries of "Down in front!" came popping without cessation, often as a stroke was being played. Yet they began brilliantly and continued the nervy duel to the last green with no sign of cracking on either part.

It was Jones who got the jump on Cruickshank when the latter, at the first hole, sliced his tee shot to the rough. But with a great iron shot at the second and a great 18-foot putt at the long third, Cruickshank took the lead with two birdies in a row. A fine approach from the rough gave Jones another birdie at the long fourth and again squared the match. But at the fifth Cruickshank sank another 20-footer, to take the lead again.

Here were four consecutive birdies, four in a row, on

70

four of the hardest golf holes in the world. That shows how the two game chickens were meeting the test of nerve and skill. When Jones missed a shot putt for his 3 at the 175-yard sixth, Cruickshank was then two strokes ahead and apparently on his way to victory.

But Jones rapped a great iron shot to the tricky 220-yard seventh green for his 3, and when Cruickshank missed a five-footer there, his first mistake on the green, the doughty Scot was only a stroke ahead. The big turning point of the match came at the eighth hole, if one can name a single turning point in this flashy series of episodes.

Cruickshank here struck a great iron shot to within six feet of the pin. Jones was short of the green, with a ridge to pitch across. The Georgian chipped up in steady fashion to within four feet of the cup. Cruickshank, now facing another nagging putt, again missed. To miss two putts of five or six feet in succession after one has been romping on the greens is no steadying factor.

For the first time Cruickshank, usually a master on the greens, was a bit doubtful in regard to his putting blade. He was one stroke ahead where he might have been three had those two putts dropped. This missed putt was a big factor in the battle, for immediately after, Cruickshank again missed short putts at the ninth and the tenth when he was less than four feet from the cup.

One can always miss a putt. Two in a row gets under your skin. And when Cruickshank missed again at the tenth, after both had been in trouble, Jones at last was one stroke ahead.

After halving the eleventh in 5's, Jones played a master shot at the short twelfth. For just a breath, he seemed to have an ace! His mashie niblick pitch here struck six feet from the cup, trickled just by the pin and stopped only eighteen inches away from a sure 2. Cruickshank followed with a good pitch nine feet away but missed the putt. Jones was now leading by two big strokes that, subsequently, he was to lose at the 14th and 15th.

The 15th came near being another turning point. Jones

71

was but one stroke to the good and Cruickshank's iron to the 175-yard green caught the sand. Jones' iron shot trickled half-way down the slope of the bank.

Cruickshank was well out, thirty feet beyond the pin. His approach putt was four feet short. Jones here played the worst shot he played all day. Still undetermined whether to pitch boldly, to be sure and get out or cut the ball a bit fine, he looked up as he attempted the pitch and the ball rolled back down the bank after traveling only three feet up the slope. So here he lost another stroke and the match was square again with three great holes to play.

Jones took the lead once more at the 430-yard sixteenth with a long, straight iron shot where Cruickshank was bunkered. So he was just a stroke ahead when both reached the trap to the right of the green on their seconds for the seventeenth hole. Jones played out safely, short of the pin. Cruickshank, with amazing courage and skill, went for the pin, crashed in with his niblick and dropped the ball just six feet from the cup. It was one of the nerviest shots played all day, as the pin was near the back of the green with a steep bank just beyond. When Cruickshank sank his six-footer for a 4 they were all even again.

Of these seventeen holes played in 72 strokes, only 3 had been halved. On the other fourteen there had been a win for one side or the other. It was give and take, nip and tuck, ding and dong, fifty-fifty. So the issue came to the eighteenth hole again where the day before Cruickshank had picked up 3 strokes on Jones on the final round.

The story of this finish has already been told. It was the story of the iron shot that lifted Jones up in company with Francis Ouimet, Jerry Travers and Chick Evans, the three amateurs who in 1913, 1915 and 1916 had won the open crown. Jones now rounds out the big four of amateur golf, but his average is far beyond that of any rival. In his only four open championships he has taken just 1,187 strokes, an average of 73½ for sixteen rounds over four hard courses. After all, time and duration of battle are the real tests. That 73½ average of Jones for four years, fourteen strokes below Hagen in second place, is the real mark of his golf greatness.

It is full proof that one of the greatest of all golfers is up where he belongs—full proof that unkempt fate can't block forever the stout heart that doesn't give up.

In behalf of Cruickshank it should be said that he played golf worthy of a crown. He saw his lead cut away, where putts refused to drop after he had been putting brilliantly. He came back twice near the finish to overtake this rival, the last time at the seventeenth green. And only one of the greatest shots of the year finally drove him back, the same type of shot that gave Shackamaxon Bobby his extra day's chance for the open coronet. He gave a great exhibition of golf, especially in the way of fine courage and iron play. He had a tendency to cut his wooden shots, where on almost every hole he was from ten to thirty yards back of his long hitting rival, who slashed away at the ball with all he had.

Cruickshank has nothing to deplore in his defeat. He lost to a great golfer after playing great golf himself. He fought out a worthy battle up to a finishing stroke that no man could have held in check, that iron wallop from the dirt and rough of the eighteenth hole, 200 yards dead straight upon the pin.

So after all his stress and turmoil Bobby Jones at last is sitting on the throne of the old game. To finish one stroke out one year and then win the next is an achievement in this day and time that will last for many years, unless Jones himself comes back next summer to add new sprigs to his laurel wreath. It was not only the winning of the game, but the triumph he achieved over himself on that final fairway that made him look all the greater in victory. All he had to say at the finish was this: "I don't care what happens now." And by this he meant that having once broken through he was satisfied to let fate take its swing in the future.

He had come through at last, come through in a way no one who saw the Inwood test will ever forget.

THE SPORTLIGHT

(N. Y. *Tribune*, July, 1924)

THOUGHTS WHILE BIRD WATCHING

Lives of caddies oft remind us
How to help the weary dubs,
And in starting, leave behind us
Six or seven useless clubs.

*　　*　　*

The substitute for work usually assays about one-tenth of the original.

*　　*　　*

Patience is no heroic ingredient, but it happens to be the cornerstone in the foundation of skill.

*　　*　　*

There are certain small faults that offset great virtues, There are certain great faults that are forgotten in small virtues.

*　　*　　*

Many a losing entry has had every attribute except the belief he was going to win.

*　　*　　*

The main idea is to hit through the object . . . not to hit AT it. This applies especially to boxing, baseball and golf. You can't hit *through* a jawbone or the stomach but when this principle is applied, the recipient usually thinks you have, as he rests on the resin and hears far off the musical twitter and chirping of the larks that sing in poppyland.

74

MIND *vs.* MATTER

Which is superior in the tussle?
Brain or brawn? Mind or muscle?
Which of the lot plays the leading role?
Bulging biceps—heart or soul?
I can tell you this amid all the chatter,
All of the talk and all of the clatter—
"Mind is always superior to matter—
When there's nothing the matter."

* * *

Almost any average citizen who isn't a quitter can handle failure. But not so many can handle success. Failure isn't so bad if it doesn't attack the heart. Success is all right if it doesn't go to the head. But it generally does. Not always, but too often.

* * *

We have just received another pamphlet entitled "How to Play the Mashie." You can't get the full details of that operation into an encyclopedia, much less a pamphlet.

* * *

Our first book on golf will probably be written around the two-foot putt. If you can't hole those the rest of the game is practically a useless maneuver.

* * *

LIMERICK OF THE LINKS

There was a dub golfer named Babbitt,
Who sliced with each club as he'd grab it;
   Until he, half wild,
   Killed his wife and his child
By slicing their throats from sheer habit.

75

THE BIG FELLOW, BABE RUTH

The first time I saw Babe Ruth was in April 1919. Ruth was taking his turn in batting practice at Tampa, Florida, the spring-training camp of the champion Boston Red Sox. Since covering my first World Series in 1905, I'd seen a lot of swingers. But never a swinger like this!

Babe blasted one pitch clear out of the park into a ploughed field. I gauged that trip as about 500 feet—not bad, even without a publicity man around to check the distance with a tape measure. While Ruth hit, I watched, and Ed Barrow, the Red Sox manager, talked.

"Ruth was our main holdout," said Barrow. "He's been signed to a three-year contract. At twenty-four, this fellow can become the greatest thing that's happened to baseball. He's a fine southpaw pitcher—he can become a great one. But the day I can use him in the outfield and take advantage of his bat every day—well, they'll have to build the parks bigger, just for Ruth."

After bombing about ten shots, Ruth circled the bases, mincing along with short, pigeon-toed steps—a base-circling trot destined to become as celebrated as Man O' War's gallop. When Ruth came over to mop his face in a towel, Barrow introduced us.

"You sound like you got a cold," said Ruth.

"I have, sort of," I replied.

Taking an enormous red onion out of his hip pocket, Ruth thrust it into my hand. "Here, gnaw on this," he said. "Raw onions are cold-killers." While Ruth talked I gnawed, with tears streaming from my eyes.

From the start, Ruth and I hit it off. Absolutely honest, the Babe from first to last said exactly what he thought. The Chicago White Sox, he felt, had a smart, hustling club, and Boston would need the breaks to stick close.

76

"Babe," I said, "I was watching your swing. You swing like no pitcher I ever saw."

"I may be a pitcher, but first off I'm a hitter," said Babe. "I copied my swing after Joe Jackson's. His is the perfectest. Joe aims his right shoulder square at the pitcher, with his feet about twenty inches apart. But I close my stance to about eight and a half inches or less. I find I pivot better with it closed. Once committed . . . once my swing starts, though, I can't change it or pull up. It's all or nothing at all."

Throughout a career that spanned twenty years, Ruth never changed the basic fundamentals of that gorgeous, gargantuan arc—a swing that captured the imgination of the crowd nearly as much as the man behind it. To watch Ruth go down, swinging from the heels, often sprawling from the sheer violence of his cut, was almost as exciting as seeing him blast one out of the park.

Of all the sluggers that the advent of the lively ball has spawned, Babe was the only one I ever knew who never shortened or choked his grip when the count reached two strikes. He gripped his bat with the knob of the handle "palmed" in his right hand. So perfect was his wrist snap—and the other reflexes that go into the perfectly timed swing—that he could wait on the pitch until the last split second and "pick" the ball practically out of the catcher's mitt. Ted Williams is about the only other long ball hitter I know who has this amazing faculty.

The Babe liked plenty of lumber in his war clubs. Many of his bludgeons weighed 42 ounces—about a half-pound more than the average bat.

That spring the Red Sox and McGraw's Giants played a four-out-of-seven exhibition series at Tampa. In '18 the Giants had finished second, behind Chicago, and in '19 John J. felt he had a hustling club that was really going places. A Giant rookie that spring was Jim Thorpe, the big, amiable Carlisle Indian. McGraw said Thorpe couldn't hit a curve ball, but I still feel the main reason he got rid of Jim was that Thorpe was turning his team inside out—in friendly wrestling matches.

77

I hung around for several games to watch Ruth hit and play left field. The New York writers were pop-eyed; the Boston boys had already oiled up their best adjectives for him. In the first game he hit the longest ball I ever saw— some six miles over the right center-field fence and into the infield of an adjacent race track.

Bill McGeehan, of the New York *Tribune,* who didn't impress easily, wrote: *The ball sailed so high that when it came down it was coated with ice . . . a drive that would have rattled off the clubhouse roof at the Polo Grounds.*

My own notes include this gem: *No less than 134 automobiles chugged through the gate and surrounded the playing field in a gleaming cordon. This gave Ruth a shining target to shoot at, but the Babe still prefers the old-fashioned fence—over which today's winning smash traveled like a runaway comet.*

That Giant series put the exclamation mark on Ruth, the home-run hitter, and practically wrote his finis as a pitcher. That was O.K. with Babe. Ruth, the outfielder, no longer would have to muscle his way in.

"It was sorta rough at that," he commented years later. "I came up as a southpaw pitcher—and pitchers aren't supposed to hit—or to clutter up the batter's box *trying* to hit during practice. I saw no reason why I shouldn't take my licks. I'd get them, usually, but there were times I'd go to my locker next day and find my bats sawed in half."

That '19 season was one week old when I opened my column with this verse:

SON OF SWAT—BABE RUTH

When you can lean upon the ball
    And lay the seasoned ash against it,
The ball park is a trifle small,
    No matter how far out they've fenced it.
Past master of the four-base clout,
    You stand and take your wallop proudly—

78

A pretty handy bloke about,
  I'll say you are . . . and say it loudly.

I've seen a few I thought could hit,
  Who fed the crowd on four-base rations;
But you, Babe, are the Only It—
  The rest are merely imitations.
I've seen them swing with all they've got
  And tear into it for a mop-up;
But what they deem a lusty swat
  To you is but a futile pop-up.

Somewhere amid another throng,
  Where Fate at times became unruly,
I've heard Big Bertha sing her song
  Without an encore from yours truly.
Yes, she had something—so to speak—
  A range you couldn't get away with,
But when you nail one on the beak
  They need another ball to play with.

Boston finished in sixth place as Chicago's brilliant
team roared in, despite the fact that Ruth hit 29 homers.
In January 1920, when owner Harry Frazee of the Red
Sox was heavily in debt, he sold Ruth to Jake Ruppert's
third-place New York Yankees for $125,000 outright,
plus a $350,000 loan. The transaction remains baseball's
all-time bargain.

A word anent baseball's only scandal, the '19 World
Series between Cincinnati and the Chicago White Sox,
who overnight became known as the Black Sox. Installed
as heavy Series favorites for the best of nine games—a
short-lived concession to post-war fervor—eight Chicago
players sold out to the gamblers. I covered that Series
with Ring Lardner, Jack Wheeler, Runyon and the rest
of the New York crowd.

Chicago was at least 5 to 3 to win it all and could
easily have been an even more lopsided favorite. Their
pitching staff featured Ed (Knuckles) Cicotte, who had

won 29 games that year; Claude (Lefty) Williams, 23 and 11; and Dickie Kerr, practically an also-ran with a 13-8 record.

"Champ" Pickens, organizer of the Blue and Grey football game at Montgomery, Alabama, years later, was in our party. The eve of the first game in Cincinnati, "Champ" walked into my room and said, "I've just been offered five to four on Cincinnati by a professional gambler."

"How much of it did you take?" I asked.

"Take, hell! This Series is fixed," replied Pickens, tossing his ticket on the bed. "You can have it—I'm going to the race track."

Cicotte was knocked out of the box in the first game, the Reds winning 9 to 1.

Williams opened the second game against the Reds' "Slim" Salee, and it was a pitching duel for three innings. Williams "blew" in the fourth, giving three bases on balls and three runs, the Reds winning that one 4 to 2.

I was sitting next to Lardner when Ring started pounding his typewriter furiously. He kept humming, "I'm Forever Blowing Bubbles." His bitter parody of that song, dedicated to Williams, opened with, "I'm forever blowing ball games. . . ."

Kerr, never implicated in the "fix," won two games, his first a 3-hit shutout, but there just weren't enough Kerrs to go around. I felt as though I'd been kicked in the stomach. The investigation lasted through the '20 season, the guilty ones being banned from organized ball for life.

And so it remained for this great, overgrown kid, Ruth, to lead baseball out of the wilderness and back into the aura of respectability. It was at the Princess Martha Hotel in St. Petersburg in 1930, after Ruth had signed a contract calling for $80,000 a year for two years, that Colonel Ruppert commented, "Who are we kidding? I could pay 'Root' two hundred thousand dollars a year and he wouldn't be overpaid."

In 1920, the year following the Black Sox scandal, baseball needed a Superman, a man who could capture the imagination of the public—who could restore America's faith in baseball. Babe fit the bill. The public wanted to see the ball smashed out of the park—where there couldn't be any question of inside baseball—and the game's leaders moved to help. The ball was given a shot of rabbit juice, and in '20 Babe's big bat boomed for 54 homers. He alone realigned the game on the order of the long hit—the big inning. Lifting the Yankees aboard his shoulders, Ruth immediately became the heartwood of what was to become "Murderers' Row." In '20 the Yanks, again third, outdrew the Giants—in the Polo Grounds, to McGraw's chagrin. In '21, '22 and '23 the Giants and Yanks tangled in the World Series—'23 being the year Ruppert's team moved from the Polo Grounds into their own million-dollar home across the Harlem River, "The House That Ruth Built."

Concerning Ruth "the kid," he seldom mentioned his childhood. Actually Babe recalled little about it himself. He was in St. Mary's Industrial Home at Baltimore from the time he was seven or eight until he was seventeen, when Jack Dunn, the old Orioles manager, took him from Brother Gilbert and signed him to a contract calling for $600 for the 1914 season.

Johnny Evers, keystone of Chicago's immortal Tinker-to-Evers-to-Chance combine, once told me an anecdote that Ruth told him.

When Babe was about seven, it seems he tapped the family till. "I took one dollar," said Babe, "and bought ice cream cones for all the kids on the block. When my old man asked me what I'd done I told him. He dragged me down cellar and beat me with a horsewhip. I tapped that till again—just to show him he couldn't break me. Then I landed in the Home, thank God!"

Some years ago, Tom Meany, writing a book on Babe's life, ran into a tout who sold his daily tips, in printed form, at the New York tracks, and who had spent his childhood with Babe at "The Home."

"You know," he said, "either Babe's gone soft or I've gone nuts. But I hafta laugh when I hear that place mentioned as 'The Home.' All I know is that there was guys with guns on the walls. . . ."

Small wonder, then, that for a youngster who had known only the roughest kind of treatment, life as a baseball hero was a case of Christmas every day.

Down the years I've always had a fondness for the horses—the kind that run. And in my wanderings I've come across a lot of tracks in many climes. But I've never been burned as badly as Babe was during the winter of 1925—the year of his giant bellyache—when he visited Charles Stoneham's Oriental Park at Havana and tried beating the ponies. John McGraw was also down there that winter having a go at 'em. In less than two weeks Ruth blew between thirty and fifty thousand dollars. That cured him. College football also intrigued him—but for only one game as a betting medium.

"I bet five thousand dollars on them Harvards," he told me. "But the Yales win it. I'm off that football business, too."

In March of 1933—my third year with the Bell Syndicate—I headed South for spring training, stopping en route at Bob Woodruff's shooting preserve in south Georgia. When it came time for me to pull out, Woodruff gave me his car, chauffeur and a luggage compartment loaded with game.

"I'll throw a Florida dinner in your honor," I said. "We'll feast on Woodruff's eighteen-carat birds, basted with Coca-Cola."

"If you do," replied Woodruff, "I wish you'd invite Walter Lippmann and his wife. They're down near Bradenton, and they're good friends of mine."

The dinner—to which Babe was also invited—was a huge success, until the dignified Mrs. Lippmann asked Babe to describe the home run he "called" in the '32 Series against the Cubs, a four-straight rout for the Yankees.

"It's like this," boomed Babe, bigger than a freshly laundered barn in white gabardine and puffing on a huge cigar. "The Cubs had (censored) my old teammate Mark

82

Koenig by cutting him for only a measly, (censored) half share of the Series money.

"Well, I'm riding the (censored) out of the Cubs, telling 'em they're the cheapest pack of (censored) crumbums in the world. We've won the first two and now we're in Chicago for the third game. Root is the Cub's pitcher. I pack one into the stands in the first inning off him, but in the fifth it's tied four to four when I'm up with nobody on. The Chicago fans are giving me hell.

"Root's still in there. He breezes the first two pitches by—both strikes! The mob's tearing down Wrigley Field. I shake my fist after that first strike. After the second, I point my bat at these bellerin' bleachers—right where I aim to park the ball. Root throws it, and I hit that (censored) ball on the nose—right over the (censored) fence for two (censored) runs.

" 'How do you like those apples, you (censored, censored, censored),' I yell at Root as I head towards first. By the time I reach home I'm almost fallin' down I'm laughin' so (censored) hard—and that's how it happened."

The Babe's baccalaureate finished, a battered Mrs. Lippmann mumbled that they'd have to be leaving. A minute later the Walter Lippmanns were history.

"Why did you use that language?" I asked Babe.

"What the hell, Grant," snorted Babe. "You heard her ask me what happened. So I told her!"

As a golfer, Ruth was a long but not a terrific hitter. I was with him at Clearwater, Florida, when he bet Babe Didrikson $50 a tee shot. She outdrove Ruth by at least 20 yards—for $200—before he was convinced. But nobody ever enjoyed the game—or cussed it and himself—more than Ruth. His special meat was match play, man-to-man competition.

One morning in '33, Babe and I had a date to play with Dizzy Dean at Bellair, in Clearwater. Having recently started the game, Diz was pretty wild with his woods and long irons.

"I got a bushel of bets riding with Dean today," bel-

83

lowed Babe. "I'm giving him strokes on ten different bets—from one to ten shots—and I expect to collect on 'em all."

"Diz may be wild, but not that wild," I warned.

As we reached the club, Babe spotted Pat Dean, Dizzy's handsome bride.

"Pat," said Babe, "come on out with us this morning. The walk will do you good."

Puzzled, but appreciative of Babe's invitation, Pat accepted. Diz said nothing. He hit a good drive, then smothered two shots. After another sloppy shot by Diz on the second hole, Pat commented, "Dear, you're ducking!"

"Ducking, hell!" exploded Dean. "Who asked you on this rabbit shoot anyhow?"

Followed the fireworks. Ruth howled. Pat stalked off. Dean couldn't hit a shot the rest of the round. The Babe never collected an easier hatful.

McCarthy's Yanks were headed north in 1934, Babe's last year aboard. At Atlanta, always an important exhibition stop, Ruth suddenly developed a huge hankering for chicken Georgia style. I called Bob Woodruff and in the course of our conversation mentioned Babe's fresh craving for chicken.

"I'll send my car over," said Bob "Take it and look over these spots." He named a number of attractive places, and Bob Jones added a few more. Clare Ruth, Babe and I covered the list and ultimately chose a small hideaway several miles from town. The proprietor promised he'd prepare four of Georgia's finest hens for Babe's dinner. As we were leaving, Babe admired the front lawn, swarming with spring flowers. He plucked one and handed it to Clare.

"They're pretty daisies," he remarked.

"No, dear, they're daffodils," commented Mrs. R.

"They're still daisies to me," replied Babe. Any flower, from a dandelion to a white orchid, was simply a "daisy" to Babe.

Ruth showered after the sixth inning. Returning to our little hacienda, we were greeted by the beaming proprietor, flanked by a retinue of darky waiters, shining and pop-eyed.

"The chickens—they are prepared," said our host proudly.

"Chickens hell!" exclaimed Ruth. "I want beef steak!"

He got it.

The following day Babe visited his friend Bob Jones. Bob III, now manager of the Coca-Cola plant in Pittsfield, Massachusetts, was then a youngster. We were fanning a highball in Bobby's living room when young Bob roared in with the neighborhood kids in his wake.

"That's him!" cried Bobby III. Babe grabbed an old bat from one of the youngsters, found it was cracked and tore it apart.

"Bobby," said Babe, "I want your old man to buy you a *good* bat. Make him promise."

Had Santa Claus visited 32-50 Northside Drive that day, he would have had to wait his turn.

Babe's love of kids was sincere. In many ways he was a big kid himself. I was in his room for dinner on the eve of the World Series in Chicago in 1932. (He always ate in his room before games because he would have been mobbed by fans and autograph hustlers in the hotel dining room.)

"I've got to go for a short trip, Grant," he said.

"Where are you going on the night before a World Series?" I asked.

"I'll tell you, but if you print it I'll shoot you. I'm going to take a baseball to a sick kid on the other side of town. I promised his mother and father I'd come. He's pretty sick."

The place was twenty or thirty miles away—over an hour to get there and another to get back. No publicity.

Babe was known by more motorcycle cops than any athlete who ever lived. They enjoyed giving Ruth an escort to the Stadium or helping him to get away after a game. They were usually there, like the Travelers' Aid, whenever the Babe needed a lift home to Riverside Drive after a late party.

85

One morning Babe asked me to pick him up for our golf game at Leewood, in Tuckahoe. "Sure," I replied, "but what happened to your car?"

"I lost it," said Babe.

"Lost it?" I said. "You had it last night."

"That was last night," replied Babe. "I wrecked it somewhere in Westchester and left it."

So he had. The cops had driven him home.

Another time, when Babe was roaring along by dawn's early light, the law stopped him, checked on his condition and suggested he be driven home.

"Why you (censored)!" roared Babe, and punched the cop on the nose.

"Now I *know* you're drunk," said the cop. "Move over! I'm drivin' you home."

I was with Babe one evening when he turned down a one-way street—the wrong way. "This is a one-way street," said the cop.

"I'm only drivin' one way!" yelled Ruth.

"Oh, hello, Babe! I didn't know it was you," replied the cop. "Go anywhere you please—but take it easy!"

And so it went.

I once had Babe on a national radio hookup, with Graham McNamee in charge. A short script had been prepared for Ruth to read—pretty much on split-second timing. He worked it over and was practically letter-perfect. Came the big break, with orchestra lending background music. At the last minute, Babe's carefully rehearsed script became scrambled. Before I could throw a halter on him, he was off and running. McNamee was frantic; the orchestra leader was frantic; the producer was frantic—as Ruth rambled on.

At one point the Babe was supposed to refer to the Duke of Wellington's historic remark that the Battle of Waterloo had been won on the playing fields of Eton. Babe managed to come out with this gem:

"As Duke Ellington once said, the Battle of Waterloo was won on the playing fields of Elkton."

Later I asked Babe how he could louse up one short statement so completely.

"About that Wellington guy I wouldn't know," he replied. "Ellington, yes. As for that Eton business—well, I married my first wife in Elkton (Maryland), and I always hated the god-damn place. It musta stuck."

The network got a load of Ruth at his purest that night. But it certainly wasn't NBC's conception of a tight program.

One evening Babe and I were having a few drinks in the grill room of the Chatham Hotel. Suddenly he looked at his watch. "Jesus!" he cried. "I gotta run!" In a flash he'd grabbed his cap and coat and was flagging a cab. Alarmed, I asked what the trouble was.

"Trouble?" yelled Ruth. "Why, 'Gangbusters' is on!"

Moe Berg, the eminent linguist, Princetonian and major-league catcher, once said: "Ruth isn't a man; he's an institution." Ruth was a man who loved crowds. And the crowds always swarmed to see Babe hit. The Yankees from 1926 to '34 were a terrific aggregation, each man big in his own right. But it was Babe the crowds came to see. Each Yankee exhibition-game contract carried this clause in heavy type: "It is understood and agreed that Babe Ruth will play." He seldom missed a curtain call.

I've seen the great ones, from Cobb through Williams, but Ruth was the only ball player I have known who could turn out capacity crowds ever time. He did this in every city the Yankees played. When the Yankee Stadium was dedicated in April 1923, more than 74,000 people turned up—to see the Yankees, sure, but more important, to see Ruth cavort around "The House that Babe Built."

He was the greatest single magnet sport has ever known. Jack Dempsey was top man in his game. But Jack fought in defense of his title only six times in seven years. Babe played each day, six months a year, for nearly 15 years. He lured packed stands in the big cities and he drew them out in the bush. I know, for I followed him from 1919 to his final game in 1935. Big league, bush league, the great cities, small hamlets—at the ball park or train depot—always capacity.

I've ridden in cars with Babe in cities all over the map. Everywhere, the mobs would wave or call his name, and Babe would answer, "How're you, Mom!" . . . "Hello, Pop!" "How can they miss this silly mug?" he used to ask.

Whether it was playing baseball or golf, hunting, fishing or sitting around a room drinking and punching the bag, I can recall no one who got as much joy out of sheer living as the Babe.

Friendship—pure, warm, unadulterated friendship with no holds barred, ever—is the key to the Babe Ruth I most treasure. For the thirty years I knew Babe—until cancer killed him in 1948—I never saw Ruth really sore at anybody. Oh, I've seen him lose his temper—at himself —on a golf course, when he'd bury his club in a bunker after missing a shot or lash his putter after a missed putt. (Once he wrapped the clubhead around his leg so hard he thought he'd broken his ankle and roared like a hopped-up elephant.) But Ruth, the man-boy, was the complete embodiment of everything uninhibited. He couldn't possibly fail—that was Ruth's credo. And when he found that baseball, particularly the Yankees, had no managerial berth for him, he was deeply hurt. But in remarks or actions, the Babe was kindly—so kindly.

Ruth established many records, most of them Homeric, and no pun intended. It will be a long time before any slugger breaks his all-time home run mark of 714. And, at the risk of sounding disloyal to the game, I hope it's an eternity before some youngster, teeing off on today's jet ball, smashes Babe's mark of 60 homers in one season: This I hope for Babe, wherever he is, kicking his heels around on some king-sized cloud.

EARL SANDE RIDES AGAINST
ENGLISH DERBY WINNER

(N. Y. *Tribune*, October 21, 1923)

Back of the flying heels of Zev, America's three-year-old champion, Papyrus, the English Derby winner, saw five open lengths of golden October daylight as sixty thousand spectators roared their acclaim at Belmont Park yesterday afternoon. Papyrus never had a chance. For nearly a mile Earl Sande, the great American jockey, let Steve Donoghue trail only a length behind with hope still flaming in his soul, but when Sande reached the last quarter and let Zev run, the English entry was swept from his feet, wind blown, floundering and weary as the wide gap opened on the way to the wire.

When the great crowd, banked in serried masses on both side of the track, saw Papyrus only a length away as the two contenders passed the mile post there was a sudden flurry of excitement, with an increasing thunder of cheering at the prospect of a mighty battle, head and head, down the stretch.

But the expected battle never took place. Instead of coming on to challenge the flying leader, Papyrus, reaching the last turn home, began to fade from the picture, outclassed in both speed and endurance despite the fact that Zev never ran a fast furlong from start to finish, as he ended his parading march in the slow time of 2:35 2/5, more than seven seconds back of Man o' War's great record for the same route.

It was not so much the fact that Zev raced with hurricane speed, for he did not. The big shock came when Papyrus, after ordinary speed three-fourths of the way, had nothing left to meet Zev's dash for the wire.

It was a day and a setting built for a thrill that never came. October turned on its rarest weather of blue and gold, with a balmy wind from the south. The crowd was the greatest that ever saw a race on this side of the water. Clubhouse, grandstand and lawn were packed with massed lines up and down the length of the inner enclosure.

Every detail was built for the one great moment down the stretch when the two champion three-year-olds of the two greatest racing countries were to fight it out, eye to eye, on by the wire.

Even the betting had indicated a thrilling fight. Zev was installed favorite at 9 to 10, with Papyrus at even money. But the wise old horsemen who saw the smooth plating on the feet of the English horse and considered the still soft track said in advance that Papyrus was doomed.

Zev, caulked toe and heel with Papyrus smooth shod, had a tremendous advantage. "Man o' War," remarked one old-timer, "couldn't beat a steeplechaser under that handicap." Still that choice was up to trainer Jarvis, who stuck to the English fashion which may work well enough upon turf.

This detail, however, did not percolate into the crowd. The massed populace only saw a golden day, a blue sky, a track in fair shape and two international champions all set for the expected whirlwind that soon died into a zephyr when Zev began to run.

At the start Papyrus had almost a length advantage, dashing forward as Sande took his time in getting under way. Papyrus held this lead for fifty yards. For fifty yards he saw only open daylight ahead. And then a dark brown shadow fell across his flank and there was no longer open daylight but another horse out beyond him, another horse of almost the same color, the same height and the same weight. Perhaps Papyrus thought his shadow was falling to the fore. Yet Zev wore blinkers and that should have been the tipoff.

Just a length to the good, Sande settled down to an even pace with no attempt at speed. Once in a while he opened up another half length, only to fall back as if to see how Donoghue and Papyrus were getting along There was certainly no attempt here on Sande's part to run away and leave the two visitors alone in a strange land.

On three occasions, between the first half and the mile, Sande took a length and a half lead, only to ease up and let the invaders move almost alongside. And then, passing the mile post, Sande and Zev moved ahead again to ease up and fall back no longer.

For many days Papyrus had been trailing Bar Gold, his training mate and sparring partner, always beating him at the finish. Papyrus through this training turn had become accustomed to seeing Bar Gold in the lead, only to have him overhauled down the stretch. But coming to the final quarter Papyrus might have been heard muttering beneath his labored breath, "Someone has double crossed me. I don't believe this is Bar Gold I am chasing today. In fact, I am certain it isn't Bar Gold."

The big drive, the hurricane finish, the sweeping pace expected from the English horse down the stretch never came off. As Zev moved steadily along, the gap of golden October daylight grew wider and wider. It ran from one length to two, from two lengths to three, from three lengths on to four and five with Papyrus growing feebler in his faint challenge at each stretch. And as a matter of calm and unbiased record there was no challenge at all. Papyrus was all out, an earnest performer of beautiful mold, doing the best he could, but completely outclassed.

It had been supposed that Zev's great speed would give him an early advantage and that he would need this advantage to stave off the English challenger through the last quarter. So when Zev had only a length to spare at the end of the mile it was only natural to suppose that he was in for a merry party down the somewhat muddy stretch. But the merry party turned out to be an old-fashioned cake walk with no great competition in sight.

Zev was moving further and further away as he reached the wire, with Papyrus losing ground at every worn and weary stride. Even against the ordinary time of 2:35 2/5 for the winner the conquered horse had no run left in his heaving system on the way home. That mile and a half, near the finish, must have looked to him longer than the span of the Atlantic which he had crossed to find defeat.

Granny never had too high a regard for politicians as such . . . and perhaps his quiet look at international greed took in the world politicians, too.

THE SPORTLIGHT

(Armistice Day—1924)

N.Y. Herald Tribune

DISARMAMENT

I wonder what they think of, when gray ghosts get
    together,
The ones who fought to end all war and found the wooden
    cross?
Whose bodies hold the ground they won, unmindful of
    the weather,
Where rain and sun to them are one, beyond the touch
    of loss?

I wonder what their vote would be when, just as dusk
    is falling,
Their ghostly dreams go back again to lanes they knew
    of old?
Or out the path they hear again remembered voices
    calling
From those who come their way no more as time goes
    by untold?

Perhaps it doesn't matter now where, safe beyond all
    sorrow,
They hold their brave and simple rest bereft of haunting
    care,

Out where their ghosts can only see a golden, far tomorrow,
That waits beyond the twilight road where only dreamers
fare.

Perhaps. But if they had the chance to see remembered
faces,
To hear old voices calling them through autumn's hazy
suns,
Or walk unbroken through the years amid old-fashioned
places,
I wonder if their vote would be in favor of the guns?

THE FOUR HORSEMEN

(N. Y. *Herald Tribune*, October 19, 1924)

POLO GROUNDS, NEW YORK, Oct. 19, 1924—Outlined against a blue-gray October sky, the Four Horsemen rode again. In dramatic lore they are known as Famine, Pestilence, Destruction and Death. These are only aliases. Their real names are Stuhldreher, Miller, Crowley and Layden. They formed the crest of the South Bend cyclone before which another fighting Army football team was swept over the precipice at the Polo Grounds yesterday afternoon as 55,000 spectators peered down on the bewildering panorama spread on the green plain below.

A cyclone can't be snared. It may be surrounded, but somewhere it breaks through to keep on going. When the cyclone starts from South Bend, where the candle lights still gleam through the Indiana sycamores, those in the way must take to storm cellars at top speed. Yesterday the cyclone struck again as Notre Dame beat the Army, 13 to 7, with a set of backfield stars that ripped and crashed through a strong Army defense with more speed and power than the warring cadets could meet.

Notre Dame won its ninth game in twelve Army starts through the driving power of one of the greatest backfields that ever churned up the turf of any gridiron in any football age. Brilliant backfields may come and go, but in Stuhldreher, Miller, Crowley and Layden, covered by a fast and charging line, Notre Dame can take its place in front of the field.

Coach McEwan sent one of his finest teams into action, an aggressive organization that fought to the last play around the first rim of darkness, but when Rockne rushed his Four Horsemen to the track they rode down everything in sight. It was in vain that 1400 gray-clad cadets

94

pleaded for the Army line to hold. The Army line was giving all it had, but when a tank tears in with the speed of a motorcycle, what chance has flesh and blood to hold? The Army had its share of stars in action, such stars as Garbisch, Farwick, Wilson, Wood, Ellinger and many others, but they were up against four whirlwind backs who picked up at top speed from the first step as they swept through scant openings to slip on by the secondary defense. The Army had great backs in Wilson and Wood, but the Army had no such quartet, who seemed to carry the mixed blood of the tiger and the antelope.

Rockne's light and tottering line was just about as tottering as the Rock of Gibraltar. It was something more than a match for the Army's great set of forwards, who had earned their fame before. Yet it was not until the second period that the first big thrill of the afternoon set the great crowd into a cheering whirl and brought about the wild flutter of flags that are thrown to the wind in exciting moments. At the game's start Rockne sent in almost entirely a second string cast. The Army got the jump and began to play most of the football. It was the Army attack that made three first downs before Notre Dame had caught its stride. The South Bend cyclone opened like a zephyr.

And then, in the wake of a sudden cheer, out rushed Stuhldreher, Miller, Crowley and Layden, the four star backs who helped to beat Army a year ago. Things were to be a trifle different now. After a short opening flurry in the second period, Wood, of the Army, kicked out of bounds on Notre Dame's 20-yard line. There was no sign of a tornado starting. But it happened to be at just this spot that Stuhldreher decided to put on his attack and begin the long and dusty hike.

On the first play the fleet Crowley peeled off fifteen yards and the cloud from the west was now beginning to show signs of lightning and thunder. The fleet, powerful Layden got six yards more and then Don Miller added ten. A forward pass from Stuhldreher to Crowley added twelve yards, and a moment later Don Miller ran twenty

95

yards around Army's right wing. He was on his way to glory when Wilson, hurtling across the right of way, nailed him on the 10-yard line and threw him out of bounds. Crowley, Miller and Layden—Miller, Layden and Crowley—one or another, ripping and crashing through, as the Army defense threw everything it had in the way to stop this wild charge that had now come seventy yards. Crowley and Layden added five yards more and then, on a split play, Layden went ten yards across the line as if he had just been fired from the black mouth of a howitzer.

In that second period Notre Dame made eight first downs to the Army's none, which shows the unwavering power of the Western attack that hammered relentlessly and remorselessly without easing up for a second's breath. The Western line was going its full share, led by the crippled Walsh with a broken hand.

But there always was Miller or Crowley or Layden, directed through the right spot by the cool and crafty judgment of Stuhldreher, who picked his plays with the finest possible generalship. The South Bend cyclone had now roared eighty-five yards to a touchdown through one of the strongest defensive teams in the game. The cyclone had struck with too much speed and power to be stopped. It was the preponderance of Western speed that swept the Army back.

The next period was much like the second. The trouble began when the alert Layden intercepted an Army pass on the 48-yard line. Stuhldreher was ready for another march.

Once again the cheering cadets began to call for a rallying stand. They are never overwhelmed by any shadow of defeat as long as there is a minute of fighting left. But silence fell over the cadet sector for just a second as Crowley ran around the Army's right wing for 15 yards, where Wilson hauled him down on the 33-yard line. Walsh, the Western captain, was hurt in the play but soon resumed. Miller got 7 and Layden got 8 and then, with the ball on the Army's 20-yard line, the cadet defense rallied and threw Miller in his tracks. But the halt was only for the moment. On the next play Crowley swung out and around the Army's left wing, cut in and then crashed over the line for Notre Dame's second touchdown.

On two other occasions the Notre Dame attack almost scored. Yeomans saved one touchdown by intercepting a pass on his 5-yard line as he ran back 35 yards before he was nailed by two tacklers. It was a great play in the nick of time. On the next drive Miller and Layden in two hurricane dashes took the ball 42 yards to the Army's 14-yard line, where the still game Army defense stopped four plunges on the 9-yard line and took the ball.

Up to this point the Army had been outplayed by a crushing margin. Notre Dame had put under way four long marches and two of these had yielded touchdowns. Even the stout and experienced Army line was meeting more than it could hold. Notre Dame's brilliant backs had been provided with the finest possible interference, usually led by Stuhldreher, who cut down tackler after tackler by diving at some rival's flying knees. Against the Notre Dame line each Army attack had been smothered almost before it got under way. Even the great Wilson, the star from Penn State, one of the great backfield runners of his day and time, rarely had a chance to make any headway through a massed wall of tacklers who were blocking every open route.

The sudden change came late in the third quarter, when Wilson, raging like a wild man, suddenly shot through a tackle opening to run 34 yards before he was finally collared and thrown with a jolt. A few minutes later Wood, one of the best of all the punters, kicked out of bounds on Notre Dame's 5-yard line. Here was the chance. Layden was forced to kick from behind his own goal. The punt soared up the field as Yeomans called for a free kick on the 35-yard line. As he caught the ball he was nailed and spilled by a Western tackler, and the penalty gave the Army 15 yards, with the ball on Notre Dame's 20-yard line.

At this point Harding was rushed to quarter in place of Yeomans, who had been one of the leading Army stars. On the first three plays the Army reached the 12-yard line, but it was on fourth down, with two yards to go. Harding's next play was the feature of the game.

As the ball was passed, he faked a play to Wood, diving through the line, held the oval for just a half breath, then, tucking the same under his arm, swung out around Notre Dame's right end. The brilliant fake worked to perfection. The entire Notre Dame defense had charged forward in a surging mass to check the line attack and Harding, with open territory, sailed on for a touchdown. He traveled those last 12 yards after the manner of food shot from guns. He was over the line before the Westerners knew what had taken place. It was a fine bit of strategy, brilliantly carried out by every member of the cast.

The cadet sector had a chance to rip open the chilly atmosphere at last, and most of the 55,000 present joined in the tribute to football art. But that was Army's last chance to score. From that point on it was seesaw, up and down, back and forth, with the rivals fighting bitterly for every inch of ground. It was harder now to make a foot than it had been to make ten yards. Even the all-star South Bend cast could no longer continue to romp for any set distances, as Army tacklers, inspired by the touchdown, charged harder and faster than they had charged before.

The Army brought a fine football team into action, but it was beaten by a faster and smoother team. Rockne's supposedly light, green line was about as heavy as Army's, and every whit as aggressive. What is even more important, it was faster on its feet, faster in getting around.

It was Western speed and perfect interference that once more brought about Army doom. The Army line couldn't get through fast enough to break up the attacking plays; and, once started, the bewildering speed and power of the Western backs slashed along for 8, 10 and 15 yards on play after play. And always in front of these offensive drives could be found the whirling form of Stuhldreher,

98

taking the first man out of the play as cleanly as though he had used a hand grenade at close range. This Notre Dame interference was a marvelous thing to look upon.

It formed quickly and came along in unbroken order, always at terrific speed, carried by backs who were as hard to drag down as African buffaloes. On receiving the kick-off, Notre Dame's interference formed something after the manner of the ancient flying wedge, and they drove back up the field with the runner covered from 25 and 30 yards at almost every chance. And when a back such as Harry Wilson finds few chances to get started, you can figure upon the defensive strength that is barricading the road. Wilson is one of the hardest backs in the game to suppress, but he found few chances yesterday to show his broken field ability. You can't run through a broken field until you get there.

One strong feature of the Army play was its headlong battle against heavy odds. Even when Notre Dame had scored two touchdowns and was well on its way to a third, the Army fought on with fine spirit until the touchdown chance came at last. And when the chance came Coach McEwan had the play ready for the final march across the line. The Army has a better team than it had last year. So has Notre Dame. We doubt that any team in the country could have beaten Rockne's array yesterday afternoon, East or West. It was a great football team brilliantly directed, a team of speed, power and team play. The Army has no cause for gloom over its showing. It played first-class football against more speed than it could match.

Those who have tackled a cyclone can understand.

KNUTE ROCKNE

Coach Jesse Harper of Notre Dame took the real forward pass east in 1913. He brought it to West Point where Army and Notre Dame met that year for the first time. Harper gave the ball to quarterback Gus Dorais, who threw it to his broken-nosed roommate, Knute Rockne. Rockne caught it and Army was slaughtered 35-13. I didn't meet Rockne on that trip. I met him some years later when I returned to the Point after he became head coach at Notre Dame.

Ring Lardner, a keen Notre Dame and midwestern rooter, went with me on that trip to the Point in the fall of 1920. We ran into John J. McEwan, the big Army assistant coach. John J. was loaded with confidence. One of Army's all-time centers, John coached the Cadet line. Army's strong squad was headed by the flying Walter French, who earned his spurs—and an appointment to West Point—at Rutgers.

"I understand," said Lardner, "that Rockne is coming in again with that kid named Gipp."

"Who the hell is Gipp?" snorted McEwan.

"You'll find out at ten minutes to two tomorrow," replied Lardner.

McEwan did. With Army and the irrepressible French leading 17-14 at half time, Gipp put on a second half one-man rodeo as the Irish pulled out the game 27-17.

"How'd you like Gipp as a football player?" I asked McEwan after the game.

"Gipp is no football player," retorted McEwan. "He's a runaway son of a bitch!" One of the more volatile English instructors in West Point's long history, Mc-Ewan's descriptives remain as pungent as they are concise.

Self-reliant as a wild mustang, George Gipp came out

100

of the iron-ore country near Calumet, Michigan, on Lake Superior's Keweenaw peninsula. He came up the hard way, but at making his point on a football field, Gipp could open with sevens and keep rolling 'em. He had more than his share of speed, power, daring and deception. At times he even baffled Rock. The following, told to me by a former Notre Dame star and assistant coach, occurred during the intermission of the historic 1920 Army game.

"Being behind by three points, Rock was really laying into the boys," he said. "He had about finished and Gipp, standing nearby, asked me for a drag of my cigarette. Rock looked up and spotted Gipp leaning against the door, his helmet on the back of his head, puffing the cigarette.

"Rock exploded, 'As for you, Gipp,' he crackled, 'I suppose you haven't any interest in this game?'

" 'Listen, Rock,' replied Gipp, 'I've got five hundred dollars bet on this game; I don't aim to blow any five hundred!' "

Rock was younger then. Later, not even Gipp would have got away with it.

One of Rock's greatest gangs was his 1924 team that featured a veteran array of backs functioning behind a powerful, combative line.

In the fall of 1923, Army met Notre Dame at Ebbets Field because the World Series between the Yankees and the Giants was taking place at the Polo Grounds. I preferred the football game. That afternoon I took along "Brink" Thorne, Yale's great 1895 captain. We had only sideline passes so Brink and I watched from the rim of the playing field. In one wild end run, the Irish backfield of Harry Stuhldreher, Jim Crowley, Don Miller and Elmer Layden swept off the field over the sideline. At least two of them jumped over me, down on my knees.

"It's worse than a cavalry charge," I said to Brink. "They're like a wild horse stampede."

That thought occurred to me a year later at the Polo Grounds when that same backfield beat Army 13-7 en route to an undefeated year, and the "Four Horsemen" emerged on my copy paper. I'm afraid it was those four football players, who averaged only 157 pounds, and the glory they won that made the phrase stick.

They were an amazing four men. Fullback Elmer Layden, better than a 10-second sprinter, weighed 164 and was the heaviest of the lot. Quarterback Stuhldreher, at 154 pounds, was the lightest; and the halfbacks Miller and Crowley were in between. Layden could run, block, kick and handle a forward pass. Fast and shifty, the Four Horsemen had a brand of rhythm that was beautiful to watch. They were a hardy lot and were seldom hurt. They could all block and tackle and carry the ball—the memory of them made me scoff a little during the days of platoon football, with offensive and defensive specialists cluttering up the premises each Saturday afternoon.

All were keen and smart. Rockne liked players on his squad like these four—all individualists who did their own thinking.

Jimmy Crowley was one of the wittiest men I ever knew. In practice one day, Rock said to Jimmy after he had muffed some play, "What's dumber than a dumb Irishman?"

"A smart Swede," Jimmy replied. No further conversation.

They were and are a great bunch. I'm proud to list them among my closest friends, and that's been true for a quarter of a century and more.

What circumstance brought The Four Horsemen together under Rock? I asked Don Miller that question one day recently at Toots Shor's. With Miller were Layden and Crowley, three of the original four. It was a nice reunion.

"Actually," said Miller, "I didn't have much choice in the matter. My mother had sons at Notre Dame all the way from 1905 through 1925. My brother Harry made Walter Camp's Third Team as a halfback in 1909. Another brother, Walter, played in the same backfield as George Gipp in '19. I met Elmer, Jimmy and Harry for the first time when we were thrown together during our freshman year. How did you 'happen' at South Bend, Jimmy?"

"Curley Lambeau was my coach back at Green Bay High," said Crowley. "He played with Gipp at Notre Dame in '18. We were State champs and when Curley mentioned Gipp and Notre Dame . . . well, I was on my way."

"I matriculated at the University of Iowa first," smiled Layden. "I'd played football and basketball at Davenport [Iowa] High. But I picked up a knee in basketball. The next fall at the University, they examined the danged knee and decided it wasn't worth the gamble. My high-school coach, Walter Halas, George (Chicago Bears) Halas' older brother, contacted Rockne. Rock was never too sure of that knee . . . but it never bothered me." (I recalled the Yankees took a gamble on a rookie named Joe DiMaggio, knee and all, after he'd been turned down by scouts from several other teams.)

Stuhldreher played high-school ball at Massilon, Ohio, the long-time hotbed of early professional football, and then finished off at Kiski Prep. Harry's older brother, Walter, was a senior at Notre Dame when Harry entered.

And that's how four midwest kids happened to matriculate at Notre Dame. Compared to today's hunt for high-school heroes, it doesn't sound like much, does it?

Crowley currently manages a television station in Scranton, Pennsylvania; Stuhldreher handles public-relations work for United States Steel; Layden is a top salesman for the General American Transportation Company in Chicago; and Miller has his own law firm, Miller and Kennedy, in Cleveland.

Compared to many of the high-speed horses galloping around big college backfields today, the Four Horsemen were pony-sized.

"If we stepped on a scale today, I don't know who'd be more embarrassed—the scale or us," cracked

Crowley. "But in those days our playing weight was legit. Before the Princeton game, at Princeton in '25, Rock invited the press to our dressing room. Then he called us out. 'You've been questioning the program weight of my backfield,' he snapped. 'Here's your chance to find out . . . exactly.' Rock then signaled us on the scales— one by one. Elmer then weighed one hundred and sixty-one. Miller and I were about the same, at one hundred and fifty-seven, and Stuhldreher was a few ounces under one hundred and fifty-two."

"We weren't very big—then," said Miller, "just big enough. After all, Rock's entire attack was based on speed and deception—scientific football. We breathed and lived Rock's rhythm and cadence and then play execution followed. Also, we all had to block on rotating plays. No prima donnas . . . Rock saw to that."

"Another thing," added Layden, "Rock used to load us down with extra-heavy practice gear. On Saturday, when we climbed into game suits we felt like four Lady Godivas. Actually we were four pounds lighter on Saturday than on weekdays."

"That's right," chuckled Crowley. "We might not have been any faster but we sure felt faster. Psychologically, it was great."

It's been years since The Four Horsemen last shone as four satellites in what was perhaps Rock's greatest football constellation. I'd written countless leads before they arrived—I've written thousands more since.

"Granny," said Miller. "Rock put us together in the same backfield but the day you wrote us up as The Four Horsemen, you conferred an immortality on us that gold could never buy. Let's face it. We were good, sure. But we'd have been just as dead two years after graduation as any other backfield if you hadn't painted that tag line on us. It's twenty-nine years since we played. Each year we run faster, block better, score more TD's than ever! The older we are, the younger we become—in legend. Another thing. In business, that tag line has opened more doors . . . has meant more to each of us in associations,

104

warmth, friendship and revenue, than you'll ever know."

That's as nice a compliment as a fellow can receive.

Rock had another remarkable character in his assistant, "Hunk" Anderson, tougher than saddle leather at 170 pounds. A bulwark up front on the '19, '20 and '21 teams, Hunk took over the coaching reins at Notre Dame from 1931 through 1933, immediately following Rock's death.

I never saw Hunk in trouble but once, in '35 or '36. He was then head coach at North Carolina State. He was expecting a big year but his team lost steadily.

"What's your trouble down there?" I asked Hunk.

"I don't read enough American history," he said. "I thought the Civil War was over. I have an all-southern line—good, big and fast. All my backs are from the North. My southern line is cutting down my northern backfield before any of them can start."

Rockne was the star between-halves orator. After one of his exhortations, Notre Dame was likely to rush out and sweep the grandstand away. One of his best was but one line: "So this is Notre Dame," he'd say after a comparatively sloppy first half, and then leave the room. The explosive result carried the day.

Rockne's "Let's win this one for the Gipper," is ancient history. It's the kind of history, however, that American sports thrived on during an age when school spirit, college try, or what-you-will, added up to a great deal more than cynicism—which has no place in collegiate football.

In 1928, the Irish had perhaps the least successful of Rock's teams. Army was loaded with talent, depth, and most of all a red-headed back named Christian Keener (Red) Cagle, who could handle a halfback slot on anybody's all-time eleven. The Army coach, "Biff" Jones, a solid organizer, brought the Cadets down to the Yankee Stadium loaded for Irish.

Friday night before the game, Rock called me at our flat at 1158 Fifth Avenue, where Kit and I still make our New York home.

"Grant," he said, "the boys are tucked in for the night. How about coming down and sitting around with Hunk and me here at the hotel?"

"Better still," I replied. "Hop in a cab and come up here. Kit wants to see you. We can warm our sides by an open fire, have a spot of Tennessee 'milk' and watch the rest of the world go to hell."

That evening, sitting by the fire, Rock said he expected to be up against it—but good—next day.

"You recall Gipp," said Rock. "He died—practically in my arms—eight years ago next month. He's been gone a long time but I may have to use him again tomorrow.

"You saw Gipp on one of his better days—against Army in 1920," continued Rock—not in that staccato voice but in a quiet, hushed tone. "He fell sick later that same season. In our final against Northwestern, at Evanston, he climbed out of bed to make the trip. I used him very little that day. We were away and winging—the final was 33-7. But in the last quarter the stands chanted Gipp's name so loud and long that I finally sent him in for a few plays—on that ice-covered field with the wind off Lake Michigan cutting us all to the bone. I got him out of there, quick; but after returning to school with a raging fever, Gipp went back to his sick bed. He never got up. Pneumonia had him backed to his own goal line. He lived barely two weeks. Shortly before he went, Father Pat Haggerty baptized him into the church. After the little ceremony, I sat with him on his bed. His face seemed thinner than the Communion wafer he'd just taken—and just as white—but his forehead was strangely cool.

"Gipp looked up at me and after a moment, he said, 'Rock, I know I'm going . . . but I'd like one last request. . . . Some day, Rock, some time, when the going isn't so easy, when the odds are against us, ask a Notre Dame team to win a game for me—for the Gipper. I don't know where I'll be then, Rock, but I'll know about it and I'll be happy.'

106

"A moment later Gipp was gone.

"Grant, I've never asked the boys to pull one out for Gipp. Tomorrow I might have to."

The following day that '28 Army-Notre Dame game played, as always, to an overflow sellout. At the half it was 0-0. The rest is history.

A sobbing band of fighting Irish raced out for the third quarter. When Notre Dame lined up for the kickoff, I knew they were playing with a twelfth man— George Gipp.

But Red Cagle didn't see any ghost as he circled deep behind his own line, reversed his field and galloped for great chunks of terrain. Cagle's runs and passes carried Army to Notre Dame's 2. There, I recall, a cadet named Murrell plunged over. Bud Sprague, Army's burly tackle, missed the conversion. Notre Dame fired right back, smashing and clawing 80 yards, and Jack Chevigny rammed into the end zone crying, "Here's one of them, Gipper!" The point after was missed, and after getting the ball the Irish started another march. Rock sent in Johnny O'Brien, a pass-catching, one-play demon. O'Brien, juggling the ball as he fell, held on to Johnny Niemiec's long pass into the end zone to put Notre Dame ahead, 12-6.

Cagle wasn't through. With little more than a minute left, the Army flash gathered in the kickoff on his 10 and, circling to his own goal line, started moving. He covered 65 yards before being thrown out of bounds on Notre Dame's 35. After an incomplete pass, Cagle swept 21 yards to the 14. That was Cagle's last shot. He'd played himself off his feet and had to be helped from the field. His replacement, Johnny Hutchinson, attempted two passes, the second connecting on the 4. Hutchinson smashed to the 1-yard line but before the Cadets could fire again, the game was over.

Notre Dame carried that day, 12-6. Somewhere, George Gipp must have been very happy.

My friend Jack Lavelle, one-time Notre Dame guard, recalls his freshman year at South Bend.

"Under Rockne," said Jack, "there was a saying, 'Freshmen get nothing but abuse . . . but plenty of that.' How true. Some of us waited in line for three days just to get a uniform. Shoes? No matter how beat up they were, they always told you, 'Here you are, freshman. Gipp wore these!' It was a toss-up as to who wore more cleats or slept in the most inns, Gipp or George Washington. The pair I got had nails as big as shark gaffs sticking clear through the insoles. I tried to change 'em. They told me the *South Bend Times* was plenty thick . . . to make my own inner soles."

Notre Dame has long featured agile, keen, faking quarterbacks. That brings up Rock's meeting with Nate Leipsic, in my opinion one of the world's greatest magicians.

It was early in Rockne's career. He was in New York when I suggested we go to an afternoon cocktail party given by Mr. Vincent Bendix, the airplane builder, at his apartment in the Fifties. Never overly keen about parties, Rock wanted to know why we should go.

"Nate Leipsic is going to entertain," I replied. "You'll see him do some great tricks—proving again how much faster the hand is than the eye. This ought to fit into handling a football . . . especially in the quarterback's faking."

We went to the party. Rockne was astonished at Nate's skill. There was one trick where Rockne was given two rubber balls to handle, one in each hand. "Keep your grip tight," said Leipsic. Rock did. Then Nate waved a hand and said, "Open them up." When Rock did, he had two balls in one hand, none in the other. Rock got Leipsic to repeat this trick five or six times.

He also had other mysterious tricks repeated. "I've learned a lot today about deception in handling a ball," Rock said. "One thing I'm going to do is to send my quarterbacks to a magician. This matter of handling and faking with the ball is one of the biggest things in football. I aim to make it bigger." I can't recall a Notre

Dame quarterback who wasn't a good faker. Nate Leipsic himself would have faked an opposing team out of the park.

Rockne was a man of great force, deep charm and an amazing personality. I have never known anyone quite his equal in this respect. Coaches who have been my friends include: Percy Haughton of Harvard, an exceptional coach; "Hurry Up" Fielding Yost of Michigan; Bob Zuppke of Illinois; Fritz Crisler of Michigan; Lou Little of Columbia; Jess Hawley of Dartmouth; Dan McGugin of Vanderbilt; Bernie Bierman of Tulane and Minnesota; Alonzo Stagg of Chicago; Pop Warner of Cornell, Pittsburgh and Stanford; John McEwan and Biff Jones of Army; Tad Jones of Yale; Tad's brother, Howard Jones, of Southern California; John Heisman and Bill Alexander of George Tech; Bob Neyland of Tennessee; Red Blaik of Dartmouth and Army; Tom Hamilton of Navy; Frank Thomas of Alabama; Frank Cavanaugh of Fordham; Jock Sutherland of Pittsburgh; Frank Leahy of Notre Dame; and too many others to mention.

But whenever there was a gathering of coaches in any city, there was usually just one question: "Where's Rock staying?" That's where they all gathered.

There have been so many fine coaches, such great inventors as Pop Warner, Lonnie Stagg and Bob Zuppke, that no one can pick the greatest. But Rockne was the greatest of all in the way of human appeal.

I consider Warner, Stagg and Yost the advance guard of the football inventors. I think that Rockne and Percy Haughton were two of the greatest coaches, with Rockne's personality and rare human touch lifting him to the front. The man had an incisive manner of speech that electrified those around him. His manner of raising the pitch of his voice rather than lowering it at the end of a sentence was an spontaneous as it was effective. You never could misunderstand Rockne.

No, you could never misunderstand Rockne—and

there's a little story behind that, too. Gus Dorais, Rock's college roommate and later his assistant, told me why.

"From the start, Rock's mind traveled quicker than his tongue," said Dorais one night in New York. Rock had been dead some ten years but to Gus, much of Rockne will never die. "Don't forget, Rock was about four years older than the rest of us when we were in school. He was always threatening to quit, but of course he never got around to it. Anyhow, in those days and some years later when he became head coach, he was a stammerer. In 1918, his first year as head coach, Rock attended an alumni dinner at which he was called upon to speak . . . and he stammered pretty badly. He was ashamed of himself and next day he told the Father who was toastmaster that he'd made a mess of himself. Father told Rock he had done nothing of the sort and passed it off.

"One month later Rockne had become a terrific public speaker," continued Dorais. "But there was a reason for that strange, machine-gun staccato of his. His thoughts tumbled out in bursts . . . but he had to give his tongue a breather between those thoughts."

I've sat through a lot of dinners through a lot of years. In my mind Jimmy Walker was the paragon of after dinner entertainers, but Rock was the only man who could follow Jimmy Walker. Rockne had a colossal memory. I've been with him at clambakes in some big towns where clusters of strange faces would congregate around him. He'd pick out a face in the crowd and go over and shake the fellow's hand.

"I saw you . . . last spring . . . in Atlanta. . . . Now don't tell me. . . . It's Smith . . . Bob Smith . . . How are you, Bob?"

And Bob Smith, or whoever, would leave walking on clouds. That's one prime reason why as many as 21 special trains were needed in the Chicago railyards when Notre Dame traveled to Los Angeles to play Southern Cal. Those trains were loaded with Rock's friends.

110

He was the greatest personal salesman I've known. It was small wonder that at the time of his death, Rockne was slated to take over the presidency of the Studebaker Corporation. He would have been the Eddie Rickenbacker of the automotive industry. However, where Rick is the prototype of the accepted picture of dynamic big business brass, Rock was just the opposite. His dress— a gray or blue suit—was neat but seldom pressed. His hats—brim turned up, capping a kewpie-doll skull and a bashed, pixy nose—made him an incongruous picture the first time you saw him.

I recall I was with Westbrook Pegler, who didn't meet him until Rock was famous. Peg was amazed.

"He looks like a beaten up tin can," wrote Peg.

Rockne never forgave him.

The Vanderbilt Hotel was Rock's home in New York. And whenever he was in town, his suite looked like a roadhouse. Because Rock—and Notre Dame—were on the road so much during those years, there was always a lot of baggage about. One of Rock's little tricks was to scatter rocks indiscriminately through everybody's bags. He liked to see them lug rather than carry their suitcases. He'd point to any bag and ask one of his aides to pick it up. If the fellow didn't practically lose his arm, Rock knew the bag wasn't loaded and would then take it himself.

I've been at gatherings, particularly coaches' conventions, when the noise erupting from a main room sounded like a reunion of bellowing steers. Rock, with his flair for the dramatic, usually made it a point to arrive perhaps ten minutes late. When he did enter the room the noise would throttle to a whisper. You could hear a pin drop. They'd just stand there and stare at him. Like Ruth and Dempsey, Rockne was a man of the crowd . . . and whatever the crowd, he was its leader.

"Whenever Rock opened his kisser," commented Harry Grayson, "the throng became silent as a tomb."

The Rockne coaching clinics—at the opening of his

111

spring practice—had to be witnessed to be appreciated. High-school coaches from all over the map would descend on South Bend thirsting for a morsel of the Rockne wisdom. I came through there in '29 and took in the first day of the clinic. Between six and seven hundred coaches were on hand. From twirling the baton to blowing the tuba, Rock was the whole show. Standing on an elevated coaching platform with his hundreds of disciples seated around him—and the Irish varsity on a nearby playing field—Rock would go into his spiel.

"Now we'll run the pass play. . . . Marchmont (Schwartz), run that pass play." He'd point to the team and the coaches would stampede over to the sidelines . . . and Marchmont would run that pass play.

"Now is it perfectly clear . . . perfectly clear?" he would say. "Don't be bashful. . . . This play is for you coaches. . . . You men . . . Marchmont, run that pass play again!" And Schwartz would run it, faking to this man, throwing to that one. Small wonder that practically every high-school coach in the midwest sought the personal accolade of sending a future star to Notre Dame.

The soul of propriety at various alumni gatherings throughout the country, Rock, nevertheless, wasn't against imbibing a bit. During such off-the-cuff evenings—with "practical" and important alumni making a fuss over him —Rock would at times get carried away and sign contracts to coach at Columbia, University of Southern California and I don't know where. Then he'd have to bail himself out, telling them that while his football belonged to America, his soul belonged to Notre Dame.

Saturday evenings during football season, we used to have "open house" at our apartment, with food and drink for any and all coaches who happened to be in the neighborhood. (I remember Yost used to sit there with his ear cocked to the radio trying to catch the scores despite the noise of the crowd.) Those kaffe klatches were great fun, and many times were responsible for some pretty fair columns. Also, whenever he was in town

112

for the Army game, Rock would come up for a late "brunch" on Sunday. In '23 and '24, he brought along his little quarterback, Harry Stuhldreher, for bacon, eggs and coffee. The recollection of Rockne's "brain" Stuhldreher, sitting there all slicked up, his feet not even reaching the floor, is a picture that Kit and I treasure.

During Rock's dozen years as head coach—from 1918 to 1930—years when Notre Dame picked up followers by the millions, the Rockne System became the great vogue, from Yale to St. Mary's. The more the Irish won, the greater became Rockne's vision of not only giving Notre Dame spectacular seasons but of giving his alma mater the Number One place in the football world.

Rockne took his teams far and wide, seeking the intersectional powerhouses of the country. At West Point; Atlanta, Georgia; Princeton; Lincoln, Nebraska; Palo Alto; Chicago—wherever Rockne went he was a Pied Piper picking up followers by droves.

I saw Rockne at New York's Polo Grounds in December, 1930. Phlebitis had claimed his once swift legs. Muffled in a blue blanket, he was wheeled into place beside the bench of the Notre Dame All-Stars, who were playing the New York Giants in Mayor Jimmy Walker's answer to the depression. The game, played for the relief of the unemployed, was a pushover for the Giants. Benny Friedman had a field day with his passes and the Owen brothers, Steve and Bill, had a huge barn party in the line. Several of Rock's old stars, Jack Cannon at guard and Adam Walsh at center, along with graduating Frank Carideo at quarterback, played some great football. However, brought together from the four points of the compass at the last moment, they simply were no match for the Giants.

The following day Rock and I had lunch together at the Park Lane Hotel. Despite the condition of his legs, he moved pretty well and seemed in good spirits. Holly-

113

wood wanted his technical direction for a football picture, and he wanted me to write the script. I agreed.

"We ought to make it next spring or early summer. It'll take only three or four weeks. I'll go out there sometimes this winter to get things in order."

"All right, Rock," I said, ". . . and good luck."

I believe that's where Rock was heading when his plane, carrying a half dozen other passengers, crashed in a Kansas cornfield on March 31, 1931.

On the afternoon of Saturday, April 4, a vast assemblage of people from every walk of life gathered at Notre Dame to pay their last respects. They were all there, from the butcher's boy down on Main Street to the personal representative of the King of Norway.

Rock's last team carried him to his grave, near his beloved university, beneath the great branches of a gigantic oak. Knute Kenneth Rockne, an Olympic personality in American football, had barked his last command.

A SPORTING PHILOSOPHY

Let's keep trying to win;
Let's keep playing the game;
Let's keep trying to spin
The whirligig top called fame.
But isn't there something more—
This life we know isn't long—
Something beyond the score?
So let's keep room for a song.

There is the dawn and the moon;
There is the flaming glow;
But here is the sunset soon—
Sooner than you may know.
What do we get out of life
Picking the right and the wrong?
Weariness, hatred and strife—
So let's keep room for a song.

114

THE YALE-ARMY GAME—1925

(N. Y. *Herald Tribune*, November 11, 1925)

NEW HAVEN, CONN., Oct. 31.—Yale beat the Army, 28 to 7, this afternoon with a rejuvenation of speed and power that astounded 78,000 spectators, including 1,400 cadets who sang their songs and thundered their cheers in vain.

It was a great Yale team that came pounding its way back from the Pennsylvania defeat to reach the heights again where the strength and swiftness of its drive cut through the conquerors of Notre Dame for four touchdowns, with three coming in the final period after the Army had tied the score.

Despite the fact that Cutler was injured and out and that Kline was not at his best, the Blue sent so many stars to battle that the Army was overwhelmed after Harry Wilson's sensational 85-yard dash with an intercepted pass had lifted the Cadets to even terms with only fifteen minutes of play left amid the gathering shadows from a cloudless sky.

For the first three periods Yale and the Army had an even fight, but in the final quarter, with the outcome still in doubt, it was the speed and ferocity of the Blue defense that cut the Army down and drove it in rout from the field. This final quarter must take its place as one of the most unusual of all periods in football lore.

Yale had scored in the second canto through a steady march, interspersed with forward passes, with Larry Noble finally shooting across the line with only three seconds left for just one more thrust as the half was over. Failure to make four yards on that play as Gill boxed in the Army tackle would have cost a touchdown, as time ended the moment Noble whizzed across the line.

115

Up to the third quarter the Army attack had been battered into pulp. Every Cadet drive was hurled back, play after play, forcing a kicking game that seemed endless. The Army hadn't made a first down with more than half the game completed, and then as the third quarter wore on, West Point finally got its chance on Yale's 40-yard line. Here the Cadet attack suddenly came to life as Trapnell ran twenty yards and a series of line plays carried the ball to within five yards of the Blue goal. On the next smash Trapnell cut through, hurdled an Eli tackler and had only a stride left for the touchdown when Wolfe nailed him with such stunning force that the ball bounded away, to be covered by Yale.

A recovered punt far down the field left Yale on her way to another touchdown, when Harry Wilson leaped for a Blue pass, pulled it down on his own 15-yard line and then cut for the sideline. At mid-field, Wilson, close to the line, swerved to the right, eluded the only Eli tackler in his path, and with three interfering runners he raced the remainder of the way across the line. And there was no Yale man close as he passed the goal line.

From a team that had been completely smothered in the first half the revived Cadet attack now looked to have its chance for victory when Yale put on a defense counter charge, led by Joss and Sturhahn, that helped to make new football history.

In the first part of that final quarter Yale turned in the remarkable achievement of making two touchdowns, though her running and passing attack had shown a net loss of three yards. Without making a first down, or anything approaching a first down, in this brief interval, Yale rolled up fourteen additional points through the sheer greatness of her defense. It may seem incredible that a team could fail to gain a yard in ten minutes and yet score fourteen points, but this is precisely what happened.

The first defensive surge came when Yeomans attempted to kick from behind the goal line. There must have been five sets of Blue jerseys leaping for the ball, which was partially blocked, as it finally fluttered down

116

only ten yards away. And as it struck the ground the brilliant Allen was coming at top speed; he flicked it from the air and rushed across the line.

About three minutes later Harding, of the Army, on his 35-yard line, circled back for a forward pass, but as he stopped and turned both Joss and Richards were on the spot. Joss bowled him over, and as the ball flopped from Harding's arms, Richards grabbed it and ran thirty-five yards across the West Point goal for the second touchdown that had found no need of a Yale attack. The Blue defense had become swift and strong enough to outscore any attack that might be needed.

Joss, on this last play, had reached Harding with almost incredible swiftness, only one of many brilliant plays which the Yale captain made all afternoon.

In fact, it was the overwhelming and predominating supremacy of the Blue line which rolled up the score. It was a Yale defensive play which led to the final touchdown, or rather made the last score possible, for Bradley intercepted an Army pass and ran to the 30-yard line before he was thrown. Here two line plays and a Yale pass placed the ball only a yard from the Army goal, whence Foote went sailing across.

Yale, this afternoon, gave one of the finest exhibitions of defensive football ever seen upon a gridiron. The smashing, savage charges of Joss, Sturhahn, Allen, Richards and others kept the West Point attack bottled up and befuddled most of the afternoon. The leading star on the Army team to match a part of Yale was Born, the end who, in two places in succession, drove the Blue back for seventeen yards, a feat that is seldom matched in any big battle of the year. Born played the finest sort of football and the Army line did its share in curbing Yale's advance, but it had nothing to match the final quarter uprising of Yale forwards.

The contest was fought beneath a cloudless blue sky, with a keen, cutting breeze of no great force adding spice to the aftermath of an October snow. The field was fast, and Yale showed a decided reversal of form in handling the ball. Following the fumbling of the Pennsylvania and Brown battles, the Blue this afternoon fumbled only once, and this lone fumble was promptly covered by a Blue jersey.

The two fatal Army fumbles were the result of hard, clean tackling by blue-jerseyed players, when both Trapnell and Harding were struck with enough force to jar bricks from a solid wall. The two tackles made on these two occasions by Wolfe and Joss were almost hard enough to break a normal mortal into several parts, including head, body and legs.

There is no doubting Yale's great strength this afternoon. The Blue team came upon the field to avenge that Pennsylvania defeat, and not even the team that beat Notre Dame 27 to 0 had a chance to roll back this surging blue tide. The Army fought bitterly and stanchly up to the final turn in the final quarter, when Yale put on a defensive campaign that carried the day more effectively than any attack shown this year. Yale was a unit in this big revival, the line and backs working together in flawless fashion after the first slow quarter, when neither team could work up any punch or drive.

Yale's victory, hooked up with Penn's defeat, scrambles the situation to an even greater extent, but it would have taken a sensational outfit to hold Yale in check this afternoon. For this was a football team that had no idea of being licked, no matter what the opposition.

There was a wintry tang in the air, but the sky above was blue as the Yale flag when the cadet corps finished its ceremonious march around the field to the applause of 78,000 spectators. The field was dry and fast, swept clean of the first October snow. Yale won the toss and elected to take the favoring wind.

It was 2:14 P.M. when Captain Joss of Yale kicked off and Wilson, the big Army back, came crashing on his way to his own 30-yard line. Three Army plunges failed to make a yard, so Yeomans kicked to Bunnell on Yale's 10-yard line, where he was thrown heavily. Noble promptly lifted a long spiral to Army's 24-yard line.

118

After a brief kicking duel Yale got the ball on the 40-yard line, and with the aid of a line play by Kline and a penalty made first down at midfield. Noble, attempting to circle the Army right end, was thrown heavily by Born for a four-yard loss. On the next play Noble swung back fifteen yards for a forward pass, but once more Born, the Army's brilliant right end, swooped down on him like a hawk after a chicken and threw the Yale man back with a thud on Yale's 33-yard line for a thirteen-yard loss.

These two brilliant plays by Born caused Yale to lose seventeen yards, so Noble punted into Army territory once more. Yale's line defense smothered three Army plays and Yeomans punted to midfield. Kline and Noble together made eight yards, and Noble's kick was partially blocked, Army recovering on its 35-yard line. Two Army plays made less than a yard through the strong Yale line, so Yeomans kicked to Yale's 2-yard line.

Neither team could make any headway at this point. The running attack on both sides was completely smothered and the war turned into a kicking duel with small advantage either way. Standing on his 20-yard line Yeomans kicked well into Yale's territory where Bunnell, after a fine catch, came rushing back almost to midfield on the best run of the day.

Through all this period the defensive strength of both teams continued to overwhelm and smother every form of passing and running attack and each team was forced to kick repeatedly after failure to gain. The first quarter ended with Yale in possession of the ball on the Army's 40-yard line. The only first down made by either team resulted from a penalty against the Army for offside. The net amount of ground gained was less than ten yards for either team in this period, one or the most remarkable defensive exhibitions of the year.

The Army had the ball on its 20-yard line just after the second period opened. At this point Hewitt and Harding were rushed in and on the first play Buell circled Yale's right end for five yards and was thrown out of bounds. An offside penalty took this gain away, so once more the

119

Army had to kick, Bunnell being hauled down on Yale's 40-yard line. Yale lost three yards in two plunges and Allen had to kick again. There was little variety to either attack, with both sides resorting to old-fashioned plunging football. It was plunge, plunge, plunge for about two yards and then kick, kick, kick, for play after play.

Finally, with the ball on Yale's 40-yard line, Noble fell back and shot a long pass to Kline, who took the ball out of the air on the Army's 30 for a net gain of twenty-eight yards on the first spectacular play of the afternoon. The pass was perfect and Kline took the ball with three Army tacklers around him. They brought Kline down with such force that Foote was sent in to relieve him.

Yale was threatening now for the first time in the game. A double pass made five yards, and while Foote fumbled Yale recovered. Allen then drove his way through the Army line for a first down. Yale speeded up her attack and Allen spurted through Army's left tackle for nine yards. The Yale stands were now in an uproar as Allen made his first down on the Army's 11-yard line. Yale was driving, but the Army defense, fighting in desperation, held the next two plunges to a short gain. It was now third down on Army's 6 and Yale went into a huddle to talk things over.

The next play was a straight thrust at center, which the Army line swept back without a gain of an inch, and on the fourth down Noble attempted to circle Army's left end, but he found the road blocked on Army's 5-yard line and the Cadets took the ball. It was a close call for the Army, but its defense held in fine shape, at a critical moment. Hewitt, from behind his own goal line, punted forty-three yards downfield and Yale had to start all over again. This time Yale could not start, so Allen kicked into the Army end zone for a touchback.

The cadet section was now in unending turmoil, with a wild roar of encouragement for the hard-fighting Army team. After an exchange of punts, Yale got the ball at midfield, and once more Noble, drifting back toward the right at least twelve yards, whirled and sent a long pass down the field to Gill, who took the ball at a dead run on Army's 30 and sprinted sixteen yards more to within twelve yards of the Army's goal before he was finally covered and thrown. So once more Yale, with first down on the Army's 12, had a fighting chance.

The first Blue thrust was halted, but on the next play Noble broke through tackle for five yards, and the goal was now only seven yards away. With a well worked double pass Noble went to the 4-yard line, and on the next play Noble, driving at top speed, split the Army defense, and with a final plunge carried the ball over the line for a touchdown. Something like 50,000 Blue supporters came roaring out of their seats with enough racket to shake down the Bowl.

There were just three seconds left for this last play, and Noble had to make four yards on that lunge to get a touchdown. Allen kicked the goal as the period ended. The Army in this first half failed to make a first down as the cadet attack was cut to pieces and pounded into powder by Yale's great defense.

Yale started slowly, but after the first period her forward passing game opened up the Army defense, with Noble the big star of the day. In his touchdown, however, Gill boxed the Army tackle and left an open hole for the play.

During the intermission the cadet corps refused to be discouraged, and with the support of the band sent forth its melody, "The Army Gray."

This was one of the finest musical melodies of the year. The great crowd of nearly 80,000, after the stirring Army song, then heard Yale counter with its famous "Boola."

The shadows were starting across the field when Yale kicked off to start the third period.

Wilson ran the ball back to Army's 28-yard line. Up to this point the Army had not made a first down, and once more the Bulldog defense was more than the Army attack could meet, so Hewitt kicked to Yale's 35.

On an exchange of punts Harding took the ball on his 35-yard line and, after slipping, recovered his footing and

121

ran twenty-five yards down the side line to Yale's 40 before he was stopped. This was the first time the Army had carried the ball into Yale's territory. Amid a terrific cyclone of noise from the cadets, Trapnell circled Yale's right end for twenty yards and put the ball on the Blue's 20. It was a thrilling run. On the next play Yale was offside, so the Army was now only fifteen yards from Yale's goal. A wide-sweeping run by Trapnell was spilled by Sturhahn without a gain. The Army completed a short pass, but it made no ground. It was now third down on Yale's 15-yard line, with five yards to go.

The Army went into a huddle to figure out the next play. It resulted in a brilliant forward pass from Harding to Wilson, who carried the ball to Yale's 6-yard line. Trapnell then swept outside of Yale's tackle and, after hurdling a tackler in Blue, he was hit so hard on the 1-yard line, just as he was going over, that the ball bounded out of his grip, and Yale's Richards recovered it on the 8. The Army touchdown was less than two feet away when the ball got away from Trapnell and bounded ten yards clear of the mass. It was spinning along the ground in the open when Richards dived for it.

Yale tried two running plays and then kicked to midfield, where Harding took the ball to Yale's 44-yard line. A great one-handed tackle by Sturhahn cut down Trapnell, who was almost away on another run. The Army kicked out of bounds on Yale's 25. Born and Saunders together threw Noble for a loss, so Allen drove a low kick down the field, which struck Harding's hands on the Army 28 and bounded away. Noble dived for the ball just in time to cover it for Yale. Noble and Kline on two powerful rushes made a Yale first down on the Army 17. A double pass was cut down by Trapnell with a flying tackle for a loss of two yards.

The breaks up to this point had all been in favor of Yale. But at this moment one of the most thrilling plays of the season followed. With the ball on the Army's 19, Noble attempted a pass to Yale's right side, well down the field, and Harry Wilson, leaping for the catch, intercepted it on his own 15 and, with perfect interference forming around him, the Army back ran eighty-five yards for a touchdown. Wilson cleared the last Yale man as he passed midfield and from this point on he was protected by a wall of Army blockers. Wilson sprinted this long distance, and the cadet stands were in the wildest possible frenzy. Reeder then fell back and drop-kicked a goal, tying the score.

The Army kicked off and Yale ran it back to the 35. On the second play Noble, attempting to circle end, had his blue sweater ripped from his back by the fierceness of an Army tackler and time was taken out while he got another jersey. Yale then kicked to Army's 10, where Harding was thrown in his tracks. This ended the third period.

On the first play of the fourth period Yeomans was thrown for a seven-yard loss by Bradley. So the Army had to kick. Yeomans, standing behind his own goal line, attempted to punt. But the Yale line charged through and partially blocked the attempt, and Allen, who was coming up like the wind, took the half-blocked ball on a bound on Army's 10-yard line and swept over for a touchdown. Allen then kicked the goal and Yale went into the lead by 14 to 7.

Yale kicked off and Wilson came back to the 30-yard line. Trapnell made six yards on the first play, cutting around Yale's end. Harding attempted a forward pass on his own 35-yard line, but Joss was on him like a flash, the ball popping out of Harding's arms by the force of the tackle. Richards, on the spot, scooped it up and set sail on a 25-yard run for Yale's third touchdown! Allen kicked the goal. Yale 21-Army 7.

Once more Army kicked off. Yale could not gain, so Allen kicked to Army's 36-yard line. At this point Fishwick went in for Bunnell. Army's Wilson made first down on Yale's 45. Yeomans added five more through center. An Army pass failed, so Yeomans punted over Yale's goal line for a touchback. Yale was penalized fifteen yards for holding and the ball was placed on the 5. A running play failed and Allen punted out of danger to Yale's 42.

Yeomans then threw a long pass to Baxter, who was finally nailed by Allen on Yale's 10-yard line for one of the longest gains of the day. It was a brilliant pass, brilliantly handled by Baxter, and only a sensational tackle by Allen saved the touchdown. He had to dive for his man to get him on the 10 Buell tried sweeping Yale's right wing, but was thrown for a two-yard loss. Harding attempted a pass, but was throttled by Wolf for a seven-yard loss. Another forward pass by Yeomans was intercepted by Bradley on Yale's 17. Two Yale plunges lost four yards. Allen kicked to midfield.

An attempted forward pass was intercepted by Bradley on the Army's 20, where he had an open field, but a one-hand tackle around the neck brought him down. Buell was hurt on the play. Two Yale plunges took the ball to Army's 18-yard line. After a no-gain line plunge, Failing shot a pass to Fishwick, who was thrown out of bounds just a yard from the Army goal. Allen's line plunge netted only two feet. But on the next play Foote crashed through for a touchdown and Allen kicked another goal, putting Yale in front by the wide margin of 28 to 7.

Yale now began to make numerous substitutions, relieving most of the first team. It was almost dark when the Army kicked off again. The field was dark in shadows and a cold wind swept down from somewhere out of Iceland.

Yale punted into the Army territory just as time was called, with the final score, 28 to 7, in one of the greatest Yale victories in years.

124

RED GRANGE'S LAST GAME

(N. Y. *Herald Tribune*, November 22, 1925)

COLUMBUS, OHIO, NOV. 21.—The flying feet of Red Grange will cover no more ground on a college gridiron. The most advertised player in football history closed out his career today upon a fast field as Illinois beat Ohio State, 14 to 9, before 85,200 spectators, the greatest crowd that ever saw a sporting event in America inside of any stadium.

This great throng had gathered from one coast to another to hear for the last time the thudding hoof-beats of the redhead's march, and they saw him win the game for the Orange and Blue by two series of advances in the first half, where he either rushed or passed the ball up and down the field for a double attack that led to both Illinois scores.

Playing under a smashing nerve strain, where for over a week he had been the most worried and the most harried athlete in the country, Grange gave the 85,000 spectators all they had come to see. He was not at top of his brilliant peak, but he was the outstanding star of the day. His Orange "77" flashed often enough in the golden sun to lift the crowd more than once to its feet, as he cut his way off tackle or circled an end for eight, twelve or fifteen yards while heading for Ohio's goal.

Grange closed out his college career today with a total gain of 3,637 yards for his three years of play, which amounts to two miles and 117 yards. This afternoon the "Galloping Ghost" carried the ball twenty-one times for 113 yards, an average gain of 5.4 yards for each attempt. He ran back kicks and kick-offs for twenty-eight more, passed for forty-two yards on nine attempts, and just two minutes before the game ended he hauled down a long Ohio pass on his own 20-yard line, and as 85,000 or more came up with a roar he was on his way.

These 85,000 souls understood here, in the gathering shadows, that they were looking upon the last amateur run of a backfield star, whose ballyhoo had driven Dempsey and Wills from the sporting pages. They were looking upon the final sprint of the Galloping Ghost, including all the adjectives you can think of or find in the dictionary.

They were looking on the young collegian who, for three years, had been the most widely discussed athlete any college had ever sent to a competition. All through the afternoon this almost incredibly great crowd had seen him carry the ball on runs ranging from two to twenty-six yards, but now they saw him in the open with no one close as he swung under way, with the flawless rhythm that has helped to make him famous.

There were deep shadows on the field now, but No. 77 still flamed as he crossed one chalk mark after another. For just one moment it looked as if he might get away, but after he had covered forty-two yards on this final return at least six Ohio tacklers swept upon him and forced him out of bounds. And the eighty-five thousand were satisfied at last. They had seen the ghost, the phantom, the specter, or what you will, gallop lightly over fast turf, for nearly half a length of the field, before the smear of many tacklers brought him to a halt.

Grange today was playing the seventh game of the season and the twentieth of his career. It was the first time in seven games that he had dry footing for his dancing feet. It was something to have this chance, and something more to work before the greatest of all football crowds, watching every move he made. It might be stated here that Ohio State was also watching every move, and there were many times when shoals of tacklers threw themselves into the paths forming walls no man could quite break through.

Grange slashed away at tackle with great force, putting all he had into these attacks. There was an added in-

126

spiration in this great crowd. No stadium has ever held as great a gathering before, although California hills may have helped to bring out a greater crowd at Berkeley. They were packed in the straw just off the field. They were perched on the topmost barriers. They were huddled and crowded in the various corners and turns, and they were all admirably handled, where everyone had a chance to see these famous feet eat up November turf.

It was Grange who started the Illinois advance early in the first quarter. On his first play of the afternoon he made only a foot. There was, of course, a thundering echo from Ohio's side, as he was stopped with such abruptness. But on the next play he slashed his way along for twelve yards, and thirty seconds later he ripped on through for twelve yards more. Illinois was now threatening, and while the Buckeye defense was looking for another Grange rush the redhead passed to Earl Britton, on Ohio's 14-yard line—a perfect pass to the proper spot.

In two sudden thrusts Grange then carried the ball to within a stride of the line, where Britton took it across. But it was Grange who carried the ball most of the way. The second quarter was a repetition of the first, with Grange leading the Illinois rush, usually back of strong interference, with Britton helping to clear the way. Kassel, the big Orange and Blue end, was a great help here, as he caught two passes, where the last was handled deftly across the Ohio line. Grange was on the sidelines when the third period opened, and his absence had a depressing effect upon the team.

Ohio came on with a rush and just before the period ended Marek took a pass from Wendler and by the best exhibition of running shown all afternoon the sophomore star in Scarlet and Gray fought his way across the line. Marek had to dodge one man, jump another in the open, and break the grip of a third, before he scrambled across. It was about as fine a play as any game has seen this year. Marek was a star all afternoon, second only to Grange.

127

As the fourth period came on, Grange seemed to be tired and worn down. He was listless, most of this period, with a drooping look. He let punts sail over his head making no attempt to run them back. It was not until he intercepted the pass near the close of the game that he suddenly came back to life. His final exhibition was more workmanlike than brilliant.

It was fine football, but not up to the greatest he has shown. But, considering this last week, where for three days he was forced to seek seclusion, and considering further the fact that eleven men in Scarlet and Gray were watching every lift of his eyebrow and every quiver of his pulse, his final showing was impressive.

There was a thrill every moment Grange was in the game. There was a lack of thrill when he left it for the third period. He was fully as much personality as he was speed and running strength. It was not only what he did, but what he might do, at any moment. On at least six occasions he was almost loose where one lineman might dive for his foot or grab with one hand to slow down his march.

It was all like a tremendous circus, multiplied ten or twenty times. Among the 30,000 or 40,000 visitors who rolled in upon Columbus, there was almost no talk of a football game. Every tongue was spinning but one name —Grange. The game itself was completely overlooked in the performance of one man, where either failure or greater glory meant a dramatic afternoon of sport. Thousands predicted that the terrific nerve strain of the last week and Ohio State's strong defense would leave the famous redhead floundering, an abject figure in his final college stand.

There were just as many thousands confident that on a fast, dry field the Galloping Ghost would return to his own. No one knew—and this suspense and expectancy only added to the thrill.

More than two hours before game time the advance guard of the great crowd started for Ohio Field, and the tremendous stadium. In this tidal wave of people there

128

were travelers from California, Oregon, Maine, Massachusetts, New York, Tennessee, Georgia—a cross section of America—that had come to see Grange in his final game, to read at close range the story of his closing play.

I saw Bob Zuppke, the Illinois coach, a few hours before the game. Mr. Zuppke's famous philosophy was still intact. "This is something I've never run across in coaching before," he said, "but to make certain, I've just told my team they are playing Ohio State this afternoon."

At two o'clock, thirty minutes before game time, the big stadium looked packed. And yet as far away as one could see, there were still marching lines headed for the numerous stadium gates. When the Ohio State band, 128 in number, moved across the field to Frank Crumit's melody, "The Buckeye Battle Cry," over half the stadium rose with a cheer. Bright Scarlet and Gray flags in the yellow sun fluttered all over the place with as brilliant a flare of color as any game has ever known.

It was Grange who started the Illinois rush. The Illinois cheer followed the first appearance of a football player wearing "77" on the back of his blue jersey. No. 77 headed the Orange and Blue rush. After that first rush the harassed Grange was immediately surrounded by motion picture machines and camera men, who followed him back and forth across the field. Here, after all, was the man who had scored thirty-one touchdowns in nineteen games, and many of these had come from runs of sixty, seventy and eighty yards, where no hostile hand had been placed upon him. Both Grange and Cunningham, the two rival captains, each wore the "77" numerals as they went into action, this action being preceded by the firing of a cannon.

Illinois won the toss and took the favoring wind which swept up the field. Before many minutes had passed in this period Illinois had intercepted an Ohio pass on the 31-yard line and a roar went up as the Orange and Blue backfield went to position.

On the first play that followed it seemed that every

129

man on the Ohio team went for the Redhead and he managed to squirm just one foot through the mass. But a moment later he hurtled just outside of tackle for twelve yards and he was running with such force on this dash that when Karow, the star Ohio fullback, brought him down Karow had to leave the field. Two plays later, Grange ripped outside the tackle for another twelve-yard dash and this time it was Hess, the big Ohio guard, who hauled him down.

Grange was apparently putting everything he had into every play and he was a hard man to pull down, even by a brace of tacklers. The Redhead finally varied his dashes by tossing a pass to Britton for an eighteen-yard advance and from Ohio's 14-yard line Grange then slashed through tackle for eight yards to the 6-yard line. He then cut through for four more on the next play after which Britton scored from the two.

On the kick-off Grange brought the ball back nineteen yards, eluding two tacklers on the way. Grange got six yards and then Britton kicked sixty yards down the field. Once more the strong Illinois attack got under way, until Grange finally shot a long incomplete pass to Kassel.

There was no further scoring in this quarter. Ohio got her two points when Reitsch, the Illinois center, passed over the goal line on a missed signal where one seemed to be guessing, and Daughterty fell on the ball for a safety. After a brief series of plays back and forth, Illinois took over the ball on its 40-yard line. On the first play Grange cut his way around right and raced almost to the side lines, and then with a sudden swerve cut back as three tacklers missed him.

The Redhead ran twenty-six yards on this play before he was nailed on Ohio's 34-yard line. A pass from Daughterty to Kassel got twenty-two more on a brilliant catch by the Illinois end. After Grange had passed to Greene he whipped another to Kassel over the goal line for another touchdown.

In this half Grange carried the ball sixteen times, for a net gain of eighty-one yards. He ran two punts back for nineteen yards, ran back a kick-off for thirteen yards, and made eight passes for forty-two yards more. His total activities in this period were responsible for a net Illinois gain of 155 yards and they were also directly responsible for both touchdowns, although the Redhead made neither.

The two teams started the second half with Grange on the side lines, and Illinois was now a different team. For most of the period neither team could make much ground, but finally Ohio got a passing game under way, and a long pass from Wendler to Cunningham put the ball on the Urbana 30-yard line. Another pass followed and then Wendler shot a pass to Marek. The flashy Ohio back caught the ball on the 15-yard line, raced to the side lines, jumped one tackler, broke loose from another and crossed the goal line amid the most outlandish din a football field has known this year.

Ohio kicked the goal and with Illinois leading only 14 to 9 Zuppke promptly rushed Grange back to the war.

From that point on there was no great amount of steady advancing by either team. Grange ran fourteen yards from his own 20 to carry the ball out of danger before Britton again kicked just as the fourth quarter started. It was just after this that Captain Cunningham, of Ohio, in the grip of two tacklers, twisted around for a great pass to Marek on Illinois' 48-yard line. This was one of the great plays of the afternoon. There were two Orange and Blue players gripping Cunningham as he threw the ball.

A moment later Grange intercepted an Ohio pass on his own 20-yard line and raced forty-two yards before he was thrown. Two minutes later Grange intercepted a Buckeye pass as the game ended. This was his final play upon a college gridiron.

THE SPORTLIGHT

(N. Y. *Herald Tribune*, November 23, 1925)

CLEVELAND, NOV. 22.—What about Grange and his place in football history? Now that Urbana's famous Redhead has made his last collegiate run, you will find this query upon more tongues than a thousand horsepower could wag in a month. Grange was a great football player. He was one of the greatest of all ball carriers. On a dry field he would have been as spectacular this season, possibly, as he was last year.

But as an all-around star upon both offense and defense, Grange was not up to the standards set by Jim Thorpe, George Gipp, Willie Heston, Ned Mahan, Swede Oberlander, Eddie Tryon, George Wilson or Ernie Nevers, to mention a few.

He was not their equal on defense, nor yet their equal at all forms of attack. He was not up to Oberlander this season by several notches, and as quarter he was no better than Benny Friedman, of Michigan. But Grange, in addition to his ball-carrying skill, has grace, rhythm and personality. He was a quiet young man upon the gridiron or around the campus, yet he had the vital spark. He was proof that one doesn't have to manufacture the flame by lighting many bonfires. He was proof that one cannot manufacture the flame in this way. He had it within himself.

Grange, more than all, was a threat. He has been something like Jack Dempsey and Berlenbach in the ring. When these two fought there was always the feeling that every hook, punch or swing might be a knockout. When Grange took the ball there was always the feeling that each run might be a touchdown. Oberlander's rare passing needed Lane, Tully and Sage to complete the job. Grange needed the interference of Earl Britton or the work of his line to clear the way.

132

But where Lane, Tully or Sage could be seen completing Oberlander's passing, those who helped Grange were lost in the scrimmage and the mass. At the last appearance of Grange before nearly 86,000 spectators, we sat next to Jess Hawley, Dartmouth's brilliant coach. His eye and his keen brain miss nothing. Each time Grange started Hawley remarked, "Watch that interference." And that same interference was helping prodigiously.

Hawley knows football values better than most since he has coached both East and West. "Grange," he said, "is a great football player. He has class. But he doesn't outclass. He was the best man on the field today. But not the best man on any field. He can do one thing exceptionally well. But he can't do many things exceptionally well. There is a certain grace and beauty to his running which catch the eye. From the standpoint of the crowd he is just what they want. From the standpoint of the team and the football coach he is valuable. But from what I saw today there are others more valuable since they can do many things which the crowd cannot see."

Grange was about the only man who could gain ground for Illinois. But when someone else was taking the ball there was no longer that smashing interference which cleared the way. You hear Grange and Mahan compared. Yet neither could do all the things in modern football which Thorpe, Gipp, Oberlander and Wilson, of Washington could do. Nor yet Ernie Nevers, of Stanford.

They could run the ends and tear at a line. They could pass and kick. They could block. They could back up a line and spill a play or spill a runner. But most of these things, or many of them, are merely taken for granted by the crowd. The crowd knows football in the open, but it doesn't know it man to man. If Grange had been the greatest blocker in college football, he would have been almost unnoticed. His great gift lay where the crowd could see. And the crowd could see not only unusual

133

skill beyond the line of scrimmage but also unusual symmetry and rhythm, judgment and speed.

Against Ohio State he crashed outside of tackle with fine driving force for ten, twelve and fifteen yards. But his greatest skill was in the open where he had obtained his start. From this point on no Thorpe or Mahan could touch him. He was a greater broken field or open field runner than either. He had a better change of pace. He was harder to catch. He wasn't as hard to bring down as Thorpe perhaps, but he was a more rugged runner than Mahan. There was considerable power in those elusive legs. He was, above all, always a touchdown threat. Therein you have the appeal of Grange.

He scored thirty-one touchdowns in twenty games—not so phenomenal. But most of these touchdowns were scored on long runs from fifty to eighty yards. He ran kick-offs back for touchdowns several times. He ran seventy and eighty yards through powerful teams on numerous occasions. He made most of these touchdowns against powerful opposition. He made eight of them in two years against Michigan and Pennsylvania. If he had drawn fair weather and fast fields this season he would have added several more. He made none against Ohio State on Saturday, yet in each instance he was directly responsible for both touchdowns scored. He was an eternal threat for three years and this is bound to have its effect upon the mental stability of the opposing team.

No team ever knew when he would get away. With the opposition watching Grange there was always a chance for some other back. He was tackled harder and oftener than any back in football for three years. He had his share of rough treatment, most of it fair football, but when it was somewhat unfair he never kicked. He had no alibi to offer for anything that happened. He had the complete respect of every team and every man he met upon the field. This is more important than his long runs, but it will not be remembered as long.

Our modern civilization is not so concerned with sportsmanship as it is with results. It is not so concerned with standards as it is with victories. But Grange on the football field met both tests. There can be no complaint with any decision he makes to enter whatsoever field he might choose. Scarcity is what made radium worth more than gold.

OTHER STANDOUTS

Yesterday Michigan proved its greatness in the Middle West with one of the most powerful teams in the game. Michigan sent the greatest line of the year into action where a crashing Minnesota attack with five star backs could make no headway at all. After which Friedman, Oosterbaan and others did the rest. Dartmouth, Michigan and Washington finished their seasons with impressive teams that must rank with the best. And it might be in line to recall also the fine finish which Princeton and Illinois made after starts that were none too cheering. After all it is the finish that counts.

It may be a long time before any one sees a more impressive crowd than the gathering of 85,600 which packed the Ohio State Stadium yesterday. There may be greater crowds. But there will not be another crowd drawn from as many portions of the map—from California to Maine.

Hundreds even slept at the base of the stadium to get their chance in the first rush for unreserved seats. It was something more than a football game. At least 40,000 of these came to see one man. Grange performed ably through the first half until he wrenched his back. But he proved then what he meant to a team when he was right and ready.

He will not be remembered as the greatest of all, but he will have his own place among the gridiron immortals, which the experts and the psychologists will attempt to explain at their leisure through the years. And they will be partly right and partly wrong. That is the exit to which any criticism of genius always leads. For when genius can be explained it is no longer genius.

135

THE 1926 WORLD SERIES

(N. Y. *Herald Tribune*, October 11, 1926)

For just one brief moment in the seventh inning the screeching and the roaring gave way to a sudden hush, gripping in its intensity as the straining eyes of the crowd looked out across left field. Under the heavy blanket of this silence that seemed to be part of the shadows of a dark day the Yankees had the bases full; there were two out and the Cardinals were leading 3 to 2, with Tony Lazzeri waiting at the plate.

And then, as suddenly as it had stopped, the screeching and the roaring broke into a greater wave of sound as an old, familiar figure came shuffling into sight from the hidden bull pen in left field.

He came shuffling on, stride by stride as he loafed along, with the same old badly fitting cap cocked on top of his head as if balanced there by a trick.

He paid no attention whatsoever to the emotional salvo of thousands who had turned from cheering a Yankee rally to pay tribute to an old arm.

So it was that Alexander, sixteen years in the service, last of the grenadiers, came to the mound again to send his "whoosh" ball whizzing through at the vital moment of the seven-game series. Here was the spot where $50,000 rode upon every pitch and every swing, where a base hit meant a Yankee victory and the end of Tony Lazzeri meant the end of Yankee hopes.

Jess Haines had just given way to the old master who now stood looking Lazzeri over before he began to pitch. Without a quiver or a tremor, unhurried and unworried, Old Man Aleck started back to work. Strike—strike—ball—strike—and the oldtimer started for the bench

136

again with the winner's end rolled up in his tobacco soaked glove.

It was upon this last pitched ball that struck Lazzeri out that the young hard-fighting Cardinals rode to the baseball championship of the world.

Needing both games on New York turf to reach the peak of fame and the top of the golden pyramid, they beat the Yankees, 3 to 2, in the seventh and decisive game in spite of the brilliant pitching of Waite Hoyt and Herbert Pennock that with even fair support would have shut the game and hustling Cardinals out.

For it was through an open breach in the left wing of the Yankee defense, through a complete cave-in of the Yankee levee where Mark Koenig and Bob Meusel both crashed together, that Hornsby's galloping Western tribe rushed on to win the most dramatic battle of the year on any field.

A fumble by Koenig, a looping fly that fell between Koenig and Meusel, an outfield muff by Meusel, and then Tommy Thevenow's timely single in the killing fourth turned the fine pitching of Waite Hoyt into a Yankee rout and Haines and Alexander together held the struggling and desperate New York attack at bay by the margin of a single run.

The Cardinals won their championship not only by the big crash in the left wing of their rival's defense but also with a defensive wall that could not be broken. Led on by the daring and dazzling play of Thevenow at short, the Western youngster who also drove home the two $50,000 tallies, they refused to waver or to fade at any stage of the dark, gray afternoon.

These 39,000 fans who had braved the threat of heavy skies and impending rain saw Babe Ruth take his only chance at bat and hammer his fourth home run of the series into the right field stands. They saw the same bounding and irrepressible Babe kill Bob O'Farrell's near triple in the second inning after a wild, thirty-yard spring and a one-handed stab in the foggy ozone as the ball was whistling by. They saw the Babe walked four times out of five trips to the plate as they booed and clamored for his chance to hit. And on the last play of the game they saw the Babe, with two out and Meusel up, dash for second on the closing New York chance as O'Farrell's deadly throw cut him down.

But above all this the crowd found its main melodrama in the ancient right arm of an old-time pitcher marvel who figured in his third triumph and who came on just when the big scene was swaying in the air between tragedy and triumph. Alexander had stood the Yankees on their domes just a week ago. He had crowded them back to the bosky dell only the day before this final game. He was supposed to be out of the carnival for good and all with his double performance on its way to history. Even the events leading up to his sudden return were somewhat hectic.

Babe Ruth, after walking in the first, had started the scoring off Jess Haines in the third with a home run that came near breaking its way through the layer of haunting clouds. It was a home run that cracked all altitude records for a batted ball, for at the crest of its flight the ball resembled a buckshot burst from the sky. But it was hit for enough to drop beyond all human reach into the right field stand.

With Hoyt moving steadily and evenly on his way, Ruth's big blow was an impressive start. But after Hornsby had faded in the fourth Bottomley singled. Bell's sharply driven grounder got away from Koenig, the ill-fated son of destiny who must have killed an albatross in his youth to become an ancient mariner of woe. After many of Koenig's errors, three runs have followed, and three runs were on their way through the gap once more.

Hafey then lifted a short fly which both Koenig and Meusel pursued, and which Meusel might have bagged if Koenig had not been on the same narrow trail. This filled the bases, and then O'Farrell pumped a high fly to left which Combs could have gathered in his teeth. But Meusel, carrying the better throwing arm to battle, decided to shut off the run at the plate. The left fielder ranged far,

138

and then as he settled under the ball the ball in turn struck squarely in his hands and bounded out as Bottomley came across the plate.

Thevenow's timely whack sent two more Cardinals over. Hoyt had given his support four chances to retire the side before a run had reached the plate. It was rough sledding on pitching that was good enough to win.

The Yankees got another run back in the fifth when Dugan singled and Severeid's double sent him home.

They now needed only a tally to tie and the big chance came in the seventh. Combs opened with a hit, starting a hullabaloo in the stands from a crowd that was cheering each team for every worthy play. Koenig sacrificed and Haines walked Ruth for the third time. Meusel forced the Babe, but Gehrig's walk filled the bases. By this time Haines had developed a sore finger from violent use of the knuckle ball and it was at this moment the boding hush fell upon the scene as the crowd peered through the foggy, misty shadows in the direction of the bull pen, waiting for the high, cocked cap of Alexander to show itself for the second time in two big days.

Once more the depressing strains of Alexander's Rag Time Band were to begin the dirge of Yankee dreams.

"There was ease in Aleck's manner as he shuffled
 to his place;
There was pride in Aleck's bearing and a scowl on
 Aleck's face;
And as he cut the first one through with speed that
 ever mocks,
Not a rooter in the stands doubted 'twas Aleck in
 the box."

Tony Lazzeri, the youngster, had no chance against the last of the grenadiers. The arm that had been baffling the flurry of hostile bats for sixteen years had no thought of losing its zip where $50,000 rode upon each curve and fast one. The $50,000 extra meant the winner's end, $2,000 for every member of his tribe, and so Alexander merely decided to put $50,000 worth of stuff on every pitch.

After he had whiffed Lazzeri in the one main inning the Yankees never had a chance. He retired the next five men in order until he faced Babe Ruth, and after getting two strikes and three balls on the scowling Babe the Cardinal veteran seemed to see a baseball disappearing from his sight across the fence, so he passed Ruth on to first, where Bob O'Farrell ran him to death on an attempted steal.

Outside of the rallying rescue of Alexander the main hero in the Cardinal picture was Tommy Thevenow at short. It was Thevenow who drove across the two decisive runs in the rickety fourth. It was Thevenow in the same inning who robbed Severeid of a two-base hit with Gehrig on second, all set to score. Severeid's line drive started for the outfield space when the Cardinal shortstop crouched and sprang with the agility of a kangaroo. As the ball whistled above his head, he stuck up a gloved hand to kill off the rally and save at least a run. And runs in this hand-to-hand battle were going at $50,000 each.

Later on it was the same Thevenow in the seventh, who in the midst of a big Eastern rally scurried far over to break up another hit with a great stop and a greater throw. The infield seemed to be full of Thevenows whenever Yankee bats harried the ball and sent it spinning on its way. And when Thevenow was not on the job, Lester Bell joined in at third to lend an able and a helping hand on hard grounders that were dug up from the soft dirt and hustled along to first, waist high.

The defensive play of these two young infielders in the deciding game of a championship series was a feature no fan present will every forget. If either had skidded for just a step there would have been another ball club holding the top of the world and collecting the winner's end. They supported Haines and Alexander alike where the same support given Hoyt and Pennock would have made Babe Ruth the hero in a Cardinal defeat.

Herb Pennock pitched the last three innings, and the

140

star sidewheeler permitted no runner to cross the plate. He and Hoyt had done their share, but the big gap in the left sector of New York's defense had already done its deadly work and changed the tide from east to west, from the Hudson back to the big river of the Middle West.

The Yankees fought grimly and savagely to break through this unyielding Cardinal wall. But after they had scored their final run in the sixth they could make no opening through which even a scoring eel could slip as the Cardinals stood up before charge after charge without a sign of giving way an inch of the ground they had won.

The one Yankee who might have saved the day once more was only given one chance in five times up to show his stuff. The big Babe had his mighty howitzer trained on the right field stands, but Haines and Alexander kept it spiked with a flock of passes. The impotent Babe pawed the muddy ground with his restless feet and waved his big mace back and forth, but through most of the afternoon he had to look upon wide balls thrown beyond his reach. In his fourth game at St. Louis and his seventh game here his record shows four home runs out of four times up with six free passes, a double record that will last as long as Alexander's arm has defied the passing years.

The big emotional feature of the series came in the seventh, when 39,000 fans who had been cheering their lungs out for the Yankee rally turned in a flash to cheer even louder for the veteran on his way to the box. They were pulling for the home club until the cocked-up cap came bobbing along. And then, without a dissenting vote, they began rooting for a forty-year-old arm, still winging the ball across after sixteen years.

They were all for the pitcher who was still defying the beckoning finger of Time as he moved upon his winning way. The Chicago discard of two months ago had suddenly become the crowning figure in baseball's greatest drama, and he had even the Yankee crowd openly and loudly exulting in his third and final triumph. The victory goes officially to Haines, but it was Alexander who took

141

over the chaplet of wild olive blooms to wear upon his seamy brow.

St. Louis won a deserved victory through a steadier defense. When the high spot of the long series arrived Yankee bats and Yankee pitching arms were up to a winning standard. But where the Cardinal defensive wall remained undented, the Yankee wall split and through this gap the winning runs gave the National League its second series in two years.

The Cardinals are now on their way to another upheaval of noise back home where the Ozark Hills must brace themselves to meet the shock. Hornsby alone will miss most of this welcome, as the Cardinal manager goes to his mother's funeral in Texas. The wonder is that he did as well under the depression that hovered over his work through the longest week of his life.

The young new champions, fighting to the final play, deserve their place at the top of the game.

CASEY'S REVENGE

There were saddened hearts in Mudville for a week or
    even more;
There were muttered oaths and curses—every fan in town
    was sore.
"Just think," said one, "how soft it looked with Casey
    at the bat,
And then to think he'd go and spring a bush league trick
    like that!"

All his past fame was forgotten—he was now a hope-
    less shine.
They called him "Strike-Out Casey," from the mayor on
    down the line;
And as he came to bat each day his bosom heaved a sigh,

While a look of hopeless fury shone in mighty Casey's eye.

He pondered in the days gone by that he had been their
    king,
That when he strolled up to the plate they made the
    welkin ring;
But now his nerve had vanished, for when he heard
    them hoot
He "fanned" or "popped out" daily, like some minor
    league recruit.

He soon began to sulk and loaf, his batting eye went lame;
No home runs on the score card now were chalked against
    his name;
The fans without exception gave the manager no peace,
For one and all kept clamoring for Casey's quick release.

The Mudville squad began to slump, the team was in
    the air;
Their playing went from bad to worse—nobody seemed
    to care.
"Back to the woods with Casey!" was the cry from
    Rooters' Row.
"Get some one who can hit the ball, and let that big
    dub go!"

The lane is long, some one has said, that never turns
    again,
And Fate, though fickle, often gives another chance to
    men;
And Casey smiled; his rugged face no longer wore a
    frown—
The pitcher who had started all the trouble came to town.

All Mudville had assembled—ten thousand fans had come
To see the twirler who had put big Casey on the bum;
And when he stepped into the box, the multitude went
    wild;
He doffed his cap in proud disdain, but Casey only
    smiled.

"Play ball!" the umpire's voice rang out, and then the
    game began.
But in that throng of thousands there was not a single fan
Who thought that Mudville had a chance, and with the
    setting sun
Their hopes sank low—the rival team was leading "four
    to one."

The last half of the ninth came round, with no change
    in the score;
But when the first man up hit safe, the crowd began to
    roar;
The din increased, the echo of ten thousand shouts was
    heard
When the pitcher hit the second and gave "four balls"
    to the third.

Three men on base—nobody out—three runs to tie the
    game!
A triple meant the highest niche in Mudville's hall of
    fame;
But here the rally ended and the gloom was deep as night,
When the fourth one "fouled to catcher" and the fifth
    "flew out to right."

A dismal groan in chorus came; a scowl was on each face
When Casey walked up, bat in hand, and slowly took
    his place;
His bloodshot eyes in fury gleamed, his teeth were
    clenched in hate;
He gave his cap a vicious hook and pounded on the plate.

But fame is fleeting as the wind and glory fades away;
There were no wild and woolly cheers, no glad acclaim
    this day;
They hissed and groaned and hooted as they clamored:
    "Strike him out!"
But Casey gave no outward sign that he had heard this
    shout.

The pitcher smiled and cut one loose—across the plate
it sped;
Another hiss, another groan. "Strike one!" the umpire
said.
Zip! Like a shot the second curve broke just below the
knee.
"Strike two!" the umpire roared aloud; but Casey made
no plea.

No roasting for the umpire now—his was an easy lot;
But here the pitcher whirled again—was that a rifle shot?
A whack, a crack, and out through the space the leather
pellet flew.
A blot against the distant sky, a speck against the blue.

Above the fence in center field in rapid whirling flight
The sphere sailed on—the blot grew dim and then was
lost to sight.
Ten thousand hats were thrown in air, ten thousand threw
a fit,
But no one ever found the ball that mighty Casey hit.

O, somewhere in this favored land dark clouds may hide
the sun,
And somewhere bands no longer play and children have
no fun!
And somewhere over blighted lives there hangs a heavy
pall,
But Mudville hearts are happy now, for Casey hit the ball.

THE NEW YORK UNIVERSITY-CARNEGIE

TECH GAME—1928

(N. Y. *Herald Tribune*, November 25, 1928)

PITTSBURGH, Nov. 24—The Violet tonight is the crowning flower in the football garden of the East. It blooms far above the thistle of Carnegie Tech, the rose of Harvard, the lily of Princeton and the bluebell of Yale. For this afternoon, New York University crushed Carnegie Tech's great team, 27 to 13, with a storming attack that would have smashed down the defense of any team in the country.

This attack was led by a runaway buffalo, using the speed of a deer, and his name was Ken Strong. This man Strong weighs 201 pounds and he runs the 100 in about ten flat. Today, he ran all over a big, powerful team, smashed its line, ran its ends, kicked fifty and fifty-five yards, threw passes and tackled all over the lot. Today he was George Gipp, Red Grange and Chris Cagle rolled into one human form and there was nothing Carnegie had that could stop his march.

While Strong was storming the field a young fellow named Howard Harpster, wearing the plaid and crimson of Carnegie Tech, was throwing a football after the manner of a sniper. Harpster completed more passes against a stout defense than any two passers have completed in a single game all season.

Strong and Harpster were the two outstanding stars of one of the most decisive battles of the year, a battle where New York University rose to supreme heights in the East as one of the great teams of 1928. In the crash of battle Captain Lassman of New York was badly hurt near the close of the game. Rushed to the hospital with

146

a serious concussion, two doctors worked over Lassman in the dressing room before he could be taken away.

Carnegie Tech, conquerors of Pittsburgh, Georgetown, and Notre Dame, had no chance against the big, charging line in Violet and the crushing attack led by Strong and Hill. It was only reasonable to suppose that Carnegie would be on the down-grade after three tough games. However, almost any team would have looked on down grade against the savage assault made by the Violet at Forbes Field in this battle for the Eastern Championship.

Early in the game, when the two teams seemed deadlocked, Harpster, the sniper, crossed the New York defense with a magnificent pass of forty-five yards that settled in the arms of Sweet, an end, who caught the ball in the open and dashed over the line. As the two teams had been unable to make much headway it looked for a brief spell as if this spectacular pass might be decisive.

But in the second period, Chick Meehan's fast and powerful outfit went to work. Once they marched more than sixty yards, with Strong leading a counterattack, ably seconded by Hill and Riordan, only to be halted near the goal line when Strong fired an incomplete pass over the goal line. Then, from eighty yards out, the Violet started another march, including a Hill run of thirty-three yards.

As the march moved along and the ball moved inside Carnegie's twenty-five yard line, Strong crossed the Tartan tribe by throwing a diagonal pass to Barrabee. The pass was true as a rifle bullet. Barbee was covered and had to jump for the ball on a sensational catch for his touchdown.

The two teams entered the second half tied, 7 to 7. In the third period, New York again put on a hammering, sprinting offense. Again Strong outguessed his rivals by throwing another pass to Barrabee for the second Violet touchdown. Once again it was Hill who dashed thirty-four yards to make this play possible and to bring the ball within scoring distance.

This scoring play was something out of the ordinary—

a triple pass from Hill to O'Herin to Strong, and when Carnegie's defense dashed in to smash Strong, he pegged the ball to his waiting end.

Later on this same period, Strong broke away once more. He fought his way through the line, cut back, reversed his direction and then ran forty-one yards to take the ball across. At least five tacklers had a shot at him as he whirled and spun and broke away to reach open country.

Carnegie was trailing badly when the fourth period opened, but Harpster was still sniping any man in sight who could catch a football. From just beyond midfield he finally swung back, ducked to one side and then from more than forty yards out he passed to Shaughnessy on the 2-yard line. Shaughnessy was completely covered but made the catch. Karcis then crashed over for Tech's second touchdown.

Later on this same period Strong again ran forty-three yards deep into Carnegie territory, and a few plays later from the 5-yard line he crashed paydirt with such speed that he came near falling on his neck.

This was a game loaded with movement and fast action. It was the clash of two giant teams that had unusual speed. The New York line, headed by Lassman and Grant, was more than Carnegie's strong line could handle.

New York University could handle Carnegie's running attack, but had no defense against Harpster's uncanny passing. He must have completed twenty passes. Near the close of the game this brilliant Carnegie quarter completed nine out of eleven. Each time the ball was thrown with speed and deception straight into the open hands of some mate.

Harpster would fake to the right as he started to pass and then whirl in the same motion with a pass to the left. It was the finest all-around exhibition of forward passing I have ever seen, not barring the brilliant work of Oberlander and Friedman a few years back.

All through the game this Carnegie rifleman tied up

N. Y. U. with the the speed, deception and accuracy of his passing. In addition, he ran well, kicked exceptionally well, and intercepted two or more long passes that came near upsetting the entire game.

Harpster stood Meehan's team on its head for the first quarter. Both on offense and defense, but as the battle wore along not even he had quite enough to stop the combined drive and power of the New York rush.

Strong had able support from his line and he had able support from Hill and other backfield stars, but one rarely sees a 200-pound back with such speed, brains and courage. When there was no other way to get through Strong rammed his man and usually knocked him cold.

Strong was something more than a big, powerful runner. He picked his openings, cut back at the exact moment, reversed his field and used his head as well as he used his feet. He was the best running back I have seen in years, including Grange, Mahan or Cagle!

Strong wasn't the entire show, however. Lassman and Grant again gave a fine exhibition of tackle play. Hill was a star all afternoon, both at blocking and carrying the ball. Riordan played well and so did Hemeck. The entire New York delegation put on a brand of football that no team in the country today could have stopped short of two touchdowns.

It had everything a great football team needs—except the ability to break up Harpster's passing game; and no armament has yet been found to stop the stuff he was shooting all afternoon. Harpster twice completed three passes in a row. He completed eight out of ten earlier in the battle. He completed nine out of eleven near the close of the game. He completed more passes than I have seen all year from the Army, Harvard, Yale, Georgia Tech., Vanderbilt, Princeton and Ohio State combined.

He handled that football as Willie Hoppe handles a billiard ball. He could knock your eye out at forty yards, and Sweet, Shaughnessy and the two Flanagans knew how to take a pass and hang on to it.

New York's stout defense broke up Carnegie's running game. This defense blocked the road for the powerful 225-pound Karcis who smashed Georgetown and wrecked Notre Dame. Karcis could make no headway this afternoon with Lassman, Grant and others nailing him at the line with a distinct thud. When Karcis hit Grant that meant 450 pounds of football flesh crashing at the line and you could hear the echo in the upper stands.

Rosensweig, the end who starred against Notre Dame, was completely covered. That's why Harpster switched to Sweet and Shaughnessy and Flanagan. Carnegie had a defense that bottled up every attack it faced this year, including Niemic and Chevigny of Notre Dame. But this defense crumpled before the headlong rushes of Strong, Hill and other Violet backs who started at top speed, picked their holes with split second timing and hit hard.

I doubt that any team in the country could have stood off this New York attack as it struck this afternoon. Certainly nothing in the East could have checked it on a dry field. It had manpower, weight, strength, deception and exceptional speed. It also had the plays.

Carnegie's first touchdown was a match that fell in the powder keg. It woke New York up. It exploded Meehan's team into action that had fire all the way. Strong, time and again, ran for fifteen, twenty and forty yards on plays that needed exceptional speed and running strength to take him through.

At 1:40 the New York University band made a big hit as it marched across the field with its brilliant flash of violet. It was like a moving violet bed at the edge of a snowstorm. They came eighty strong, backed up by 5,000 rooters, the largest delegation in football history that ever made a trip of this length. The special train broke all records for an overnight trip.

The field was fairly fast in spite of a recent light

150

snow. The day was perfect for football, cold and gray. N. Y. U. won the toss and Strong kicked off into a wind that swept across the field to Letzelter, who came back to the 20-yard line. Moorehead attempted to swing out around right end, but a fine tackle by Strong stopped him. Grant stopped Bull Karcis on the next plunge and a long pass by Carnegie failed. Harpster then kicked to Strong, who ran deep into Carnegie territory.

Neither team could make any headway against the powerful defense, so a kicking duel resulted between Harpster and Strong. Strong then threw a forward pass which the fleet Harpster intercepted and ran back to his own 35-yard line. Carnegie then made a first down on line plunges and a moment later Harpster's long pass just failed. Two line plunges by Letzelter and Karcis gained two yards. A double pass from Harpster to Rosensweig picked up fifteen yards and put the ball on the N. Y. U. 45. Strong's tackle saved a longer run. Karcis picked up a yard and Harpster's pass hit the ground.

Letzelter got three yards, and it was now fourth down. Harpster dropped back to kick. Follet recovered on his own 2-yard line. He fumbled, but recovered just in time. N. Y. U. was in a bad way. But N. Y. U. was offside as Harpster kicked; the kick was called back, and it was Carnegie's ball on N. Y. U.'s 38.

Lassman and Grant stopped two line plunges for no gain. A long pass by Harpster was knocked down. It was fourth down again and Harpster kicked over the goal line. So it was N. Y. U.'s ball on its own 20.

On the first play Strong ran twenty-two yards through the Carnegie team to the 42-yard line, before the last man pulled him down. On the next play Strong circled the left end for twenty more. Hill made first down on the Carnegie 45. Hill added five more through the line. Strong got only a yard through tackle. Once again Harpster intercepted Strong's pass on his 25-yard line and ran it back thirty yards before Strong brought

151

him down out of bounds with a hard tackle. So Carnegie again was in New York territory. On the first play Harpster, falling back, threw a 45-yard pass over the N. Y. U. safety man to Sweet who scored. It was a brilliant pass and a brilliant catch. Harpster then kicked goal and Carnegie led 7 to 0.

Carnegie kicked off and O'Herin came back to New York's 29-yard line. On the first play Strong threw a 30-yard pass to Nemecek for a 15. On the next play Strong swept out around Carnegie's end for twenty-five yards to Carnegie's 30-yard line. Follet made four yards through tackle, but Strong was thrown for a loss. It was now fourth down on Carnegie's 25, and Strong's long pass over the goal line hit the ground. It was now Carnegie's ball on its own 25-yard line. Karcis was stopped in his tracks. Once again big Karcis was stopped without gain. So Harpster punted to New York's 46-yard line. Follet hit tackle for five yards as the period ended.

N. Y. U. started the second period in possession of the ball on Carnegie's 48-yard line. Strong then got off a brilliant punt to Carnegie's 8-yard line. Harpster, from back of his own goal line, kicked to midfield, where Follet fumbled, but recovered. Strong's pass was too long again. Carnegie's line was cleverly checking New York's ends. Riordan went in for Follet. Strong kicked out of bounds on Carnegie's 22.

Lassman and Nemecek threw Harpster for a 2-yard loss. Karcis made only a yard through the line. Meyers stopped him. Harpster kicked out of bounds on New York's 43.

Hill got two yards through the line. Strong picked up two more at the same spot. A fine pass from Strong to Nemecek got ten yards to Carnegie's 40-yard line. Strong ran nine yards. Riordan then broke through the strong Carnegie line for eleven yards to Carnegie's 20-yard line. Hill fought his way through six more to the 14-yard line. Strong got three through the line. The New York attack was striking with great speed and power as time was taken out by N. Y. U. This march carried the ball forty-five yards through the most powerful defensive line of the country. It was now third down and three to go.

Hill got just a yard and now it was fourth down and two to go. Strong then crashed through for first down on Carnegie's 8-yard line. Hill went out of bounds on the first play. Strong got only a yard through the line. Once again Strong was stopped with only a yard gain. It was now fourth down on Carnegie's 7-yard line. Strong's pass over the goal line was knocked down. So it was Carnegie's ball on its 20.

On the first play Harpster threw a pass to Letzelter for nine yards. Grant broke up the next play, which, however, made first down. Karcis made his first gain, one of seven yards, but Carnegie was offside. Letzelter was stopped by Lassman. Karcis got five yards through the line. Harpster then punted out of bounds on New York's 16-yard line, a very long kick. This punt was beautifully placed.

Strong threw a pass to Barrabee for a ten-yard gain. Time again was taken out. Strong picked up a yard. Riordan came through for thirteen yards to New York's 38. A reverse play, Hill to Riordan, was broken up for a five-yard loss. Hill ran thirty-three yards to Carnegie's 28-yard line. He had a clear field as he dodged through his secondary men, but Letzelter dived and caught him by the jersey, which he nearly tore off him.

Strong, on a wide end run, was thrown for a loss. N. Y. U. was penalized for holding. Strong threw a long pass to Nemecek which was completed on Carnegie's 29-yard line. Riordan was forced out of bounds. Strong threw another pass to Barrabee, who made a first down on Carnegie's 17.

Once again N. Y. U. had put on a long march of more than sixty yards. Hill hit the line for two yards. A double pass from Hill to Strong, the latter throwing over the goal line, was caught by Barrabee in a brilliant play for a touchdown. It was a magnificent pass

153

and an even finer catch. This play started out as a reverse play and turned into a forward pass. N. Y. U. had come over eighty yards for a touchdown with only a short time to the end of the half. It was a game and brilliant rally. Strong kicked the goal, making the score 7 to 7.

Strong kicked off and Harpster was run out of bounds on his own 27-yard line. Roberts went in for Strong. Harpster's long pass was knocked down. Weiner took Lassman's place and Hormel went in for O'Herin.

Harpster threw a pass to Letzelter for a 22-yard gain. Roberts intercepted Harpster's pass on his own 37-yard line. Gaudet went in for Hormel. It was N. Y. U.'s ball on its own 28-yard line. Hill hit the line for three yards. Ashton went in for Hill. Ashton got another yard. N. Y. U. was offside and was penalized for delaying the game. Riordan made eight yards. The next play ended the half with the score 7 to 7.

N. Y. U. started the 3rd quarter with the original line-up. Strong kicked off and Letzelter came back to the 35-yard line. Carnegie couldn't make any ground so Harpster kicked to Strong on N. Y. U.'s 31. Follet made two yards. Strong then fought his way for fifteen yards to N. Y. U.'s 41. Hill cracked the line for five more. Strong picked up a yard at tackle. Hill got another yard through the line. It was fourth and two to go just beyond midfield. Strong's brilliant punt went out of bounds on Carnegie's 7-yard line. This was one of the finest punts of the afternoon.

Karcis got two yards through the line. Karcis hit the line for seven more. Karcis got a foot on the next play. Harpster kicked to midfield.

Strong circled end for five yards. Follet lost two. Hill broke through the line and reversed his field and ran thirty-four yards before Harpster nailed him on Carnegie's 15. Time out for N. Y. U. Strong swept outside of tackle for six yards, planting the ball on the Carnegie 8-yard line. Strong again made three. On a beautiful double pass Hill to O'Herin to Strong, Strong then

154

threw a beautiful pass to Barrabee for a touchdown. The try for goal was good. Score: N. Y. U., 14; Carnegie, 7.

Strong kicked off over Carnegie's goal line. The ball was brought out to the 20-yard line. Carnegie could make no headway, so Harpster kicked to Strong on N. Y. U.'s 35-yard line. On the first play Strong, running like a wild young bull, dashed eighteen yards to Carnegie's 46 before he was stopped. Follet was run out of bounds, losing a yard. Carnegie stopped Hill without a gain. Shaughency went in for Sweet. Strong's pass was fumbled.

It was fourth down. Strong kicked to Harpster who was thrown on his 16. Carnegie was offside on the play and was penalized five yards, making it first down for N. Y. U. on Carnegie's 40. On a brilliant run Strong ran forty-one yards around Carnegie's left end for a touchdown. He eluded two tacklers, reversed the third and then outran Harpster who is also fast. Strong then kicked the goal and N. Y. U. was leading, 21 to 7.

Strong kicked off to Carnegie and Harpster was thrown on his own 20. N. Y. U. was penalized fifteen yards on account of unnecessary roughness. Harpster's long pass was grounded. On a triple pass, Letzelter made nine yards. Harpster kicked to Follet on N. Y. U.'s 18.

Hill picked up a yard through the line. Strong kicked sixty yards to Harpster, who was run out of bounds on his own 41-yard line. Karcis hit the line for six yards. Karcis got two through center. Karcis smashed through for ten yards. Letzelter was stopped for no gain. Karcis was also stopped for no gain. Harpster threw a forward to Shaughency, who picked up twenty yards before he was thrown on N. Y. U.'s 26. Harpster's passing had been brilliant all afternoon. Harpster's next pass was knocked down just as a Carnegie end reached for it. Karcis hit the line for five yards. Eyth lost four. Harpster made a brilliant pass to Shaughency, who was thrown heavily on N. Y. U.'s 2-yard line. Shaughency made a great play which gained twenty-five yards. On the second

155

play Karcis crashed over for a touchdown. He had only a foot to go and he made it by two inches. Letzelter failed at goal. N. Y. U. led 21 to 13.

Carnegie kicked off to Follet and he turned to the 25. Follet crashed the line for three. Strong ran six yards outside of tackle. Time out. Lassman was injured and was carried off the field. Looks like he is badly hurt. Satenstein in for Lassman.

As it was third down and twelve to go, Strong punted to Harpster, who came back to his own 37. Harpster threw a pass to Flanagan for first down on Carnegie's 47-yard line. Harpster tossed again to Flanagan for another first down on N. Y. U.'s 47. He completed his third pass to Flanagan again, planting the ball on N. Y. U.'s 36. Harpster's long pass on a touchdown try missed Flanagan by only a few inches near the goal line. Riordan went in for Follet. N. Y. U. knocked down another long pass just as the receiver was going to take it. This was fourth down. It was N. Y. U.'s ball on their own 40.

On the first play Strong ran forty-three yards through almost the entire Carnegie team. He changed pace after the old Red Grange fashion and was finally cut down on the side with only one man left. This dash carried the ball to Carnegie's 20. Follet hit tackle for two and Strong made three more. Hill made it first down on Carnegie's 9-yard line. Hill hit the line for five more. Strong, on a cutback play, dashed over for another touchdown. Strong failed at goal. N. Y. U. now leading, 27 to 13.

N. Y. U. kicked off to Harpster, who came back to his own 37. On the first play Harpster passed to Letzelter for nine. Karcis fumbled and N. Y. U. recovered on Carnegie's 40-yard line. Strong threw a pass, which was interfered with and N. Y. U. was given the ball on Carnegie's 33. N. Y. U. was penalized five yards for delaying the game. Hill failed to gain. Strong's pass was knocked down.

Strong punted to Cagnegie's 14. Harpster threw a pass to Flanagan for five yards. Harpster threw to

156

Flanagan. Both Flanagan and his tackler were knocked out on the play. Harpster again threw his third consecutive pass for first down, putting the ball on Carnegie's 40. Harpster circled end for five yards. Harpster's long forward barely missed. Once again Harpster threw to Letzelter for a twenty-yard gain. He completed another pass to Flanagan. Harpster has completed eight out of the last nine passes. He completed another forward to Letzelter, planting the ball on N. Y. U.'s 34. He completed another to Shaghency. Harpster's long pass was intercepted as the game ended. N. Y. U. started a wild celebration on Forbes Field. Final score, 27 to 13.

BALLAD OF THE GAMEFISH

"Only the gamefish swims upstream."
—COL. JOHN TROTWOOD MOORE

When the puddle is shallow, the weakfish stay
    To drift along with the current's flow;
To take the tide as it moves each day
    With the idle ripples that come and go;
With a shrinking fear of the gales that blow
    By distant coasts where the Great Ports gleam;
Where the far heights call through the silver glow,
    "Only the gamefish swims upstream."

Where the shore is waiting, the minnows play,
    Borne by the current's undertow;
Drifting, fluttering on their way,
    Bound by a fate that has willed it so;
In the tree-flung shadows they never know
    How far they have come from the old, brave dream;
When the wild gales call from the peaks of snow,
    "Only the gamefish swims upstream."

157

GENE TUNNEY, A STUDY IN CONCENTRATION

The Giants were playing at home and Heywood Broun, covering for the *World*, and I were in the press box at the Polo Grounds when Walter Trumbull, sports editor of the old New York *Post,* appeared in our midst with a young fellow in tow. Trumbull introduced his guest, Gene Tunney, all around, and I recall that Broun made quite a fuss over the handsome youngster.

I had glimpsed Tunney several days earlier when he fought "Soldier" Jones, a tough trial horse in a supporting bout to the Dempsey-Carpentier fight at Jersey City. Tunney scored a knockout in seven rounds. He was known only as a soldier-boxer who had won the light heavyweight title of the AEF in France. However, he had not fought as a bona fide heavyweight and certainly looked no part of one.

"What are your plans?" I asked.

"My plans are all Dempsey," he replied.

"Very interesting," I said. "But why not sharpen your artillery on Harry Greb, Carpentier or Tom Gibbons before you start hollering for Dempsey?"

"I suppose I'll have to beat them on the way up," Tunney said, "but Dempsey is the one I want."

I said no more and turned my attention back to Mc-Graw's Giants, who with George (High Pockets) Kelly at first base, were headed for their first pennant since 1917. I recall Tunney later volunteered that he was 23 years old. I couldn't help thinking that this forthright young fellow would make a fine insurance salesman but certainly had no business having his features and brains scrambled by Dempsey's steel fists.

In January of 1922, Tunney defeated Battling Levinsky for the light heavyweight crown but lost it the following May to Harry Greb in perhaps the bloodiest fight I ever

covered. A great fighter—or brawler—Greb handled
Tunney like a butcher hammering a Swiss steak. How
the Greenwich Village Irishman with the crew haircut
survived 15 rounds I'll never know—except that Tunney
always enjoyed more and better physical conditioning
than anybody he ever fought. By the third round, Gene
was literally wading in his own blood.

I saw Gene a few days later. His face looked as though
he'd taken the wrong end of a razor fight. "You know,"
he said, "I must have lost nearly two quarts of blood in
there."

Abe Attell, the former fighter-gambler and long-time
"character" in the fight game, probably saved Tunney
from bleeding to death.

"Abe was sitting near my corner—a spectator," continued Tunney. "When he saw the shape I was in after
the second round, he ducked out to the nearest druggist
and bought his entire supply of adrenalin chloride.
Hustling back, Attell slipped the bottle to Doc Bagley.
Between rounds Doc's long fingers flew. A superb 'cut'
man, he'd managed to stop the bleeding only to watch
Greb bust my face apart in the following round. It was
discouraging."

To me, that fight was proof that Tunney meant to
stick with prize fighting. I tried to tell Gene that Greb
was too fast for him . . . to go after a softer touch. But
less than a year later they fought again and Tunney
won the decision in 15 rounds. I scored that fight for
Greb, but then Tunney met Greb four times more without defeat.

In the buildup for the Rocky Marciano vs. Roland
La Starza title bout in September, 1953, they were
comparing La Starza to Tunney and Marciano to Dempsey—all tom-tom beating. For two years, prior to this
fight, La Starza should have been "learning" against the
toughest monkeys he could find, fighters with the mauling,
brawling overtones of Marciano. That's exactly what
Tunney did preparing for his first Dempsey fight. Instead,
La Starza remained in comparative cold storage, a fact

that became cruelly apparent as the recent fight wore on. One of the prime truisms of the ring remains—namely, if fighting is your business, fight!

Many people are under the delusion that Tunney fought comparatively little . . . that he rocketed into the championship. Gene fought 65 bouts before meeting Dempsey at Philadelphia—with several professional fights in 1917 and 1918 before he enlisted in the Marines in May, 1918. Tunney was no glamour boy; he came up and learned the hard way.

After knocking out Carpentier in 15 rounds in 1924 and dispatching Tom Gibbons in 12 rounds in 1925— along with a string of other tough babies like Jimmy Delaney, Martin Burke, Chuck Wiggins, Tommy Loughran, and Johnny Risko—Tunney again camped on Dempsey's trail.

The Tunney-Gibbons fight, staged at the Polo Grounds in June, 1925, ended in a knockout by Tunney in 12 rounds. Following his fine stand against Dempsey at Shelby, Gibbons had put together an imposing string of victories along the barnstorming route—mostly by knockouts. But when Gene tagged him at the Polo Grounds, Gibbons, then 36 years old, decided he'd fought his last fight. He retired and subsequently became sheriff of St. Paul.

As for Tunney, he finished out the year with KO's over Jack Herman and Bartley Madden and a decision against rubbery Johnny Risko, the Cleveland baker. Then he spent the next ten months preparing for Dempsey at Philadelphia.

In 1925 Tunney fought another fight that has never been recorded. I was the matchmaker and promoter.

Jim Corbett, the old champion and the world's greatest boxer, had written a book called *The Roar of the Crowd*. I was in the business of making sport pictures for the Sportlight, and I finally sold Corbett the idea of boxing three rounds, for pictures, with Gene Tunney.

My "assistant" promoter was Frank Craven, the actor. At that time Tunney had heard of Will Shakespeare and having met Craven he was quite keen about it all. He also knew of Corbett's reputation as a boxer and what Jim had meant from the viewpoint of science and skill. We arranged a spot in midtown Manhattan, atop the Putnam Building.

Anxious to pick up any possible tip from the old stylist, Tunney arrived at the appointed hour, ready to go and attired in trunks. Corbett took one look at them and said, "I'd like to wear long white trousers. I had a pair of good-looking legs in the old days but they don't look so good now. I'm nearly 60 and they are kinda shriveled."

They boxed three 2-minute rounds. Tunney was on the defensive. Corbett was brilliant. He feinted with his left—then punched with his left. A left feint . . . a left hook; a right feint . . . a left jab; a right feint; a right cross. He still had bewildering speed! He mixed up his punches better than practically any fighter I've seen since—with the possible exception of Ray Robinson.

After the exhibition, Tunney turned to me, "I honestly think he is better than Benny Leonard. It was the greatest thing I've ever seen in the ring. I learned plenty," he said.

At 59 Corbett was still the master.

That winter in Florida I played golf with Tommy Armour and Tunney. Gene would hit his drive, toss aside his club and run down the fairway throwing phantom punches—left and right hooks—and muttering, "Dempsey . . . Dempsey . . . Dempsey."

"He's obsessed," observed Armour. "His brain knows nothing but Dempsey. I believe Jack could hit him with an axe and Gene wouldn't feel it. I don't know if Dempsey has slipped, but I'll have a good chunk down on Tunney when that fight arrives."

I should have gone along much stronger with Tommy's hunch but in those days Dempsey, in my book, remained a killer whose arsenal was simply too much for Gene, a skilled boxer who lacked a real KO punch. It would take a stick of TNT to dislodge Dempsey, the kind of

161

dynamite a crude but willing Firpo had thrown that night in the Polo Grounds three years earlier.

Soon after his Florida vacation, Gene was in Hollywood making a picture called "The Fighting Marine." He didn't allow the greasepaint and glitter to interrupt his training or, more important, his thinking. Each afternoon he'd work at the Hollywood Athletic Club where Harry Grayson, now NEA sports editor, got to know him. An ex-Marine himself, Harry spent a lot of time with Tunney. The more he saw him, the better he liked him. Six months before the fight, Grayson picked Tunney to beat Dempsey. He never recanted. Matter of fact, Grayson was the *only* fight writer in America to go overboard on Tunney. We all thought he was crazy.

With Municipal Stadium, Philadelphia, selected as the site of the fight, Dempsey settled down to heavy work at Baeder Field, Atlantic City. Tunney went first to Saratoga, then to Speculator, New York, and finished off his last three weeks' work at East Stroudsburg, Pennsylvania, down by the Delaware Water Gap and only a pitch shot from Fred Waring's golf course at Shawnee. Billy Gibson, Tunney's manager, had the ring pitched next to the first fairway of the town course and commandeered the clubhouse as Tunney's quarters.

During those roaring twenties, fight camps were colorful, with a heavyweight's camp handling more daily paying customers than the average TV fight of today. The *Tribune* had Bill McGeehan, Fred Hawthorne, Harry Cross and Rice beating out copy, stethoscoping Tunney's scholarly breathing and blueprinting Dempsey's primeval snorting.

Ring Lardner, writing a syndicated column, had two passions, Notre Dame and Dempsey. Both represented the West. Ring hailed from Indiana, as did Rockne's Irish. Dempsey came out of Manassa, Colorado—also "West, by God!" Lardner looked at Tunney, a New Yorker, with cold contempt . . . just as McGeehan, a transplanted New Yorker by way of San Francisco, viewed Dempsey with complete intolerance. Why? He

162

hated Kearns because Jack fed Dempsey "exclusives" to Runyon in the Hearst camp.

Tunney went into heavy training at Speculator, New York, about 40 miles west of Saratoga. His camp was pitched near a small river amid gorgeous scenery. Ring Lardner and I went up for a visit. As we arrived, Gene was coming over the brow of a hill with a fat book under one arm. He could have passed for a young college athlete studying for his Masters in English.

Greeting us enthusiastically, Tunney said he'd been rowing up the river and then reflected on his communing with nature.

Ring pointed to the book, "What's the title?" he asked.

"The Rubaiyat," replied Tunney.

Brimming with enthusiasm for nature, Gene commented that he hadn't been able to take his eyes off the scenery. Fixing Tunney with those solemn, prominent eyes, Lardner cracked, "Then why the book?"

Tunney, at Speculator, was in fine physical shape. Later, at Stroudsburg, Pennsylvania, where he'd gone three weeks prior to the fight, he looked wonderful and was boxing sharply. I told him as much.

As for Dempsey—banging away behind closed doors at Baeder Field—well, he didn't look or move like the Dempsey of the Firpo fight three years earlier. Wealth, opulence, a bride and a revamped nose hadn't exactly brought Jack anything approaching soul comfort. Also, he was fighting his old manager, Kearns. Having moved out of Dempsey's camp bag and baggage, Kearns was slapping him with six kinds of injunctions right up to the eve of the fight.

"Lawyers!" snorted Dempsey one afternoon when we were alone. "Honest, Grant, I'd be better off if I could get rid of the whole mob of 'em for one hundred thousand dollars. It would be cheaper in the long run. They're nothing but a pack of bums . . . every last one of 'em!" Thus was Dempsey's state of mind going into that first Tunney fight.

Concerning sparring partners, Jack never spared the

163

horses. For this fight his main hired hand was Tommy Loughran, a particularly clever light heavyweight. Several days before the fight a well-known fight manager and close friend of Dempsey saw Jack's last workout with Loughran. He saw Loughran outbox Dempsey for three rounds by a city block. He paid little attention to what happened until Dempsey sent for him.

"How did I look today?" Dempsey asked.

"You looked fine . . ." the manager said.

"You are crazy," retorted Dempsey. "I was terrible. Tunney would have murdered me today."

They argued back and forth. Then the fellow left with the horrible realization that he had a $20,000 to $5,000 bet on Dempsey. "Jack don't like his chances," he thought. "I got to do something about this."

I saw him that evening in the lobby of the Ben Franklin Hotel. When I commented he looked extra pale, he told me his predicament. Next morning, however, when I encountered him, he looked positively beamish.

"It's this way," he smiled. "I'm walkin' around the corner last night. I'm treadin' that last mile . . . when I bunk into this character. He asts how I'm doin'. I tell him I couldn't be better.

"I tell him I'm just back from Atlantic City seein' that tiger, Dempsey, work. It's like finding gold in the gutter.

" 'What's like finding gold in the gutter?' he says.

" 'My bet,' I says. 'I'm down at four to one on the Champ. Twenty thousand bucks to make five thousand. It'll be over in two rounds. Good return on my investment, don't you think?'

" 'I'd like a chunk of somethin' like that,' he says.

" 'How strong?' I says.

" 'Strong,' he says.

" 'Doubt I can help but I'll see what I can do,' I says. I walk once around the block and bunk into my friend . . . he's riveted to the spot I left him.

" 'Got you down,' I says. 'It wasn't easy! You're in at four to one at twenty G's.' I'd rolled him my whole bet, thank God!"

164

Two days before the fight, the sports section of the Sunday *Tribune* went ten solid pages. The *Tribune*'s owner-publisher Odgen Reid was amazed. As the paper was going to bed Saturday night, Reid exclaimed, "Grant, you're making the *Tribune* more of a sports paper than anything else! At this rate, we're becoming ALL sports, and damn the rest of the world!"

"You could do worse," I replied, trying to manage a straight face.

Matter of fact, that weekend was one of the greatest in sports. George Von Elm defeated Bobby Jones for the Amateur golf crown at Baltusrol. Rene Lacoste defeated Big Bill Tilden in the National tennis final at Forest Hills. The crush on Philadelphia was under way, with $25 tickets being gobbled up at anywhere from $100 to $175 each—and Rickard threatening to call the fight off, so great were Dempsey's legal complications. Down in Miami a tornado was all but knocking Florida's glittering Gold Coast off the face of the earth—leaving untold death and destruction. I had steered clear of Miami, thank goodness, but I was spinning in all the other directions like a roulette ball on a galloping wheel.

That brings up another matter. I'd been fighting a cold all that week with hard deadlines, no sleep and too much prohibition whiskey. McGeehan and I landed in Philadelphia the evening of September 22nd to make sure we'd get plenty of sleep and be fresh for the big fight on the 23rd.

We'd eaten and were headed back to the hotel when one of us recalled a roulette wheel less than two blocks from City Hall. We decided we'd drop by for just a few innocent whirls of the wheel. Along about 2:00 A.M. I was $1,200 ahead; McGeehan was $800 behind.

"Let's get out of here," I said, "and get some sleep."

"Like hell!" replied McGeehan. "I'm going to get even!"

At 5:00 A.M. we had enough, between us, for taxi fare to the hotel. I was ready to curl up with a pint of whiskey and a revolver.

165

When I awakened about noon, I was still 48 years old—and felt 88. Following a breakfast of bicarb and coffee we managed to struggle into our clothes and head downstairs. On the sidewalk in front of the Bellevue-Stratford stood Rickard and his famed malacca cane. He was conversing with Gibson, Tunney's manager, and a few sports writers. The day was foggy and Rickard was worrying about rain and the possibility of postponement. Suddenly a writer came swinging through the door.

"Heard the latest, Tex?" he said. "We just got word that Tunney's flying into town for the weigh-in."

(Don't forget, this was a year before Lindbergh made the world airplane-conscious.)

"Flying into what?" stammered Rickard, nearly swallowing his cigar.

"He's flying in. Gene's in the air now!"

Rickard turned to a dumbfounded Gibson, who had left everything in readiness back at Stroudsburg for Tunney to travel into town by automobile.

"Goddamn that son of a bitch!" exploded Rickard, whacking his cane on the pavement. "What's that Tunney trying to do to me?"

"What's he trying to do to you?" countered McGeehan. "What about himself?"

I couldn't blame Rickard. This is what happened. Casey Jones, the airplane stunt flier and instructor, had flown his little biplane up to Stroudsburg and landed it on the golf course the morning of the fight—after Gibson had left.

Casey could smell out a promotion stunt quicker than the next man. Gene had never been in a plane. Jones convinced him that it would be far easier and quicker, too, to fly down the Delaware River to Philly, a distance of only 70 or 80 miles, than it would be to drive. To prove his point, Casey would take Gene for a five-minute trial hop. Tunney, in fine mental fettle, agreed, climbed aboard and they were off into the wild blue yonder. Once they were airborne, however, the golf course and all surrounding terrain were immediately socked in. Jones couldn't land. He took a compass heading for Philadelphia and drilled into a fog bank.

"I could have reached over that open cockpit and touched the Delaware Water Gap with either hand," said Tunney later. "It was that close! It took us about an hour and twenty minutes to cover 80 miles. I think we came by way of California."

Tunney had been air sick. After the weigh-in, he hid out in a friend's apartment, ordered a steak and went to sleep. The steak burned up. "We had a spare," said Gene. "I stayed awake till that one was on the platter . . . ate . . . and then dozed off for several hours. I felt OK."

With a crowd of 135,000 contributing to the first two-million-dollar gate, Gene Tunney, a superbly cool and efficient boxer, marched out of his corner at the opening bell and hit Dempsey, the fighter, with a high, hard right hand. That blow sealed Dempsey's doom. It started to rain in the fourth round and by the tenth and final round it was a deluge. At the end, Dempsey's face was a bloody, horribly beaten mask that Tunney had torn up like a ploughed field.

Speed of foot, a sharp jab and a right cross that ripped Dempsey's face like a can opener were going for Tunney that night against a man who, despite a rocky training period, had been installed at 4- and 5-1 favorite. Tunney, at 28, had arrived on his toes. Dempsey, at 31, departed—flat-footed. Dempsey had never been knocked out, but had the fight gone 15 rounds, the referee would have had to stop it. Blind by the final bell, Dempsey grabbed one of his seconds and said, "Take me to him. I want to shake his hand."

It's fine to help build a champion. But when his time comes to step down, as it always will, it's unpleasant to tear him down and bury him. I intended to give Tunney a fitting tribute in my overnight story that historical night. And I intended to go as easy on Dempsey as I could. I did neither.

Due to the rain it was impossible to use a typewriter. I dictated the description of the fight to my wire man. With me that night were Lardner and Benny Leonard, the lightweight champ from 1917-1925. Back at the hotel a raging sore throat and a hangover had me in bad shape.

"Take a slug of bourbon and lie down," said Lardner. "I'll file your overnight." Leonard, a Dempsey man, told Lardner that he suspected the fix had been in for Tunney to win. The story appearing next day under my byline blistered the hide off both Tunney and Dempsey. Neither spoke to me for several months. I couldn't blame either, but I couldn't open my mouth. I had a ghost.

Incidentally, where did the ghost writer in sport first show on the scene? According to George Ade, this type of story was first used in this country at the Fitzsimmons-Maher fight in Texas in the early 1890's.

George was quite fond of John L. Sullivan. He covered the Corbett-Sullivan fight in New Orleans in 1892.

"Did you ever see Sullivan after that fight?" I asked him.

"Oh, yes," George said. "I saw him at the Fitzsimmons-Maher fight, staged just across that muddy creek, the Rio Grande, on Mexican soil opposite the Texas town of Langtry. When I ran into John L., he told me he had been sent down by a Boston paper to cover the fight and added, 'I've a young fella from Harvard with me who is doin' the writin'.'

"The fight lasted two punches worth," continued Ade. "Maher knocked Fitz down with the first punch and Fitz knocked Maher out with the second. Here was John L's lead as written by his Harvard ghost, the first ghost writer I ever heard of: *E'en as the mantle of the dewey eve settled over the silvery Rio Grande tonight* . . . It was signed by John Lawrence Sullivan.

The second Dempsey-Tunney fight, in Chicago, exactly one year later, was pretty much a repetition of the first —except for that long count.

There's an old saying that "champions never come back." They all but had to bury that old truism that

168

night at Soldier's Field before 104,943, who had paid $2,658,660 to see the bomb go off. It was Tunney's first defense of his crown. As for Dempsey, he'd chipped a lot of rust off his plates two months earlier against Jack Sharkey. His seven-round KO of Sharkey had been Jack's hardest victory.

There was never a more popular underdog than ex-champ Dempsey going into the second Tunney fight. With old-timers, whether it be baseball players or fighters, the ability to hit goes last. And Dempsey could still hit—as proved in the Sharkey debacle.

At Chicago, it seemed that everybody and anybody short of President Coolidge was calling the shots, and throwing coal on the fires of intrigue. The fight was made to order for Chicago, a boom city that was busting its breeches with prosperity and the honky tonk that goes with it.

In 1927, the sports world wore seven-league boots as Babe Ruth boomed, "It's great to be alive . . . and a Yankee." And The Babe was spearheading the greatest of all Yankee teams to the American League pennant and a clean sweep over Pittsburgh in the World Series. That year Ruth blasted his Homeric mark of 60 home runs. Tommy Armour, the Silver Scot with the deadly long irons, won the U.S. Open, and Bob Jones reclaimed the Amateur title. Lindbergh took his big hop to Paris and the French won the Davis Cup from us—and the U.S.A. didn't get it back for ten more years.

Tunney did his training at Lake Villa, Illinois, while Dempsey pitched camp at Lincoln Fields race track outside of town. Meanwhile, the whole world started to descend upon Chicago. Even Al Capone seemed lost in the crush.

On the afternoon of September 22nd, George Whiteside, Tunney's lawyer, and Leo Flynn, Dempsey's legal mind, met at the Illinois Boxing Commission offices to clear up the knockdown rule—"once and for all." It was firmly agreed to by both parties "that the fighter scoring a knockdown shall immediately go to the farthest cor-

169

ner and wait there until signaled by the referee to resume hammering his man," or words to that specific effect.

That night, every name sports writer in the United States plus a huge assemblage of foreign newspaper men were at ringside—along with 104,943 other paying guests. Never again will I witness the mass of seething humanity that jammed Soldiers Field. Typewriters snarled their keys endeavoring to outdo the next machine with bombastic descriptives and double superlatives.

As clean shaven as Tunney in that first fight at Philadelphia, Jack reverted to his old custom of entering the ring with three days' growth of black beard. He was tan as a month of hard work under a hot sun could bake him. Tunney, by contrast, was pink and white, with white trunks. Dempsey wore black trunks. The betting was even money.

The first six rounds were a repetition of the Philadelphia fight. Tunney boxed beautifully, his straight left jab and combinations jarring Dempsey but not hurting him particularly. I was thinking of my overnight lead in the seventh, when, lo and behold, Dempsey landed a right cross over Tunney's left lead. It landed like a bomb on the left side of Tunney's jaw. The lights in Tunney's mind flickered as a second right to the jaw knocked him into the ropes. As Tunney came off the ropes, clearly dazed, Jack caught him with a short and crucifying left hook . . . then a right . . . a left and a right. Tunney was down on the canvas, his left hand clutching the middle rope near one corner.

Dempsey landed six or seven punches. Had Tunney enjoyed anything less than 100 per cent physical condition, he would have been "out" even at the count of 20 . . . or 30. In the space of two seconds, Soldiers Field became a braying bedlam. As Tunney hit the deck, Referee Dave Barry signaled Dempsey to "that farthest neutral corner." His mind set on just one thing, the final and utter destruction of Tunney, Jack moved straight ahead to the corner where the battered Tunney lay and stood behind him,

170

his arms on the top rope. Barry charged Jack, grabbed him around the waist and pointed to the opposite corner. Then Jack moved. How many seconds elapsed between the time that Tunney fell and Dempsey reached that far corner I'll never know. I do know that when Barry started his count and reached seven, Tunney was on one knee, listening attentively, and was up at nine. A tiger flew at Tunney. But Gene, already in almost complete command of his faculties, back-pedalled and circled out of range until his head had completely cleared.

That was Dempsey's last chance—the only round of the ten I could score for him.

Tunney never saw that first punch, the right cross that landed over his left lead.

"I had injured my right eye in training about a week before," said Gene in recapping the fight for me. "The retina had become partly detached and there was just a spot of astigmatism in it. I caught that punch 'blind' —from nowhere—but it was dead on the target.

"I had never seen Barry in my life until he called us together at center ring," continued Gene. "I recall he explained the knockdown rule, slowly and clearly to us. After he finished he said, 'Do you understand, Champ?' I had never before been called 'Champ.' It felt good. Then he said, 'Do you understand, Jack?' We both said, 'Yes.' He then said, 'In the event the man scoring the knockdown does not go to the farthest neutral corner, I *will not* start counting until he does reach it. . . . Do you understand that, Champ? . . . Jack?'

"We both answered, 'Yes.' "

Tunney defended his title once more, in New York, against a tough but inept Tom Heeney, whose arms that night didn't seem any longer than a seal's flippers. I felt the natural follow-up would have been Sharkey "The Sailor" against Tunney "The Marine," but that's water over the dam. Directly following the Heeney pushover, Gene retired to the life of a country squire, with a beautiful bride, Polly Lauder, daughter of a steel family.

Tunney today, at 55, is a fine figure of a man enjoying

171

robust middle age. He is a director of several corporations with offices on Vanderbilt Avenue near Grand Central Station, and we frequently have a cocktail and lunch together.

Looking over the Tunney of today as compared with the Tunney of 1926 and 1927, I can read the figure of a man who dedicated himself to a task as no other athlete, with the exception of Ben Hogan, ever dedicated himself. For at least six years the Tunney of Philadelphia fame trained for that first big chance as perfectly as a man can train: no drinking, no smoking, proper food, proper exercise, no deviation from the straight and narrow,—all harnessed to a tremendous power of concentration.

We were discussing those Golden Twenties one day recently over luncheon at the Chatham Hotel.

"Life's been good, awfully good to me, Grant," said Gene. "In my trade at the time—prize fighting—there will never be another period like those Twenties. There were a lot of first-rate competitors . . . also, there were millionaire sportsmen around who had a genuine interest in all sports. If you thought you could make your point, those were the days to prove it."

They sure were.

NEVER ANOTHER JONES

The world of sports was set back on its heels with a shock ten years ago when, in 1930, a stocky young fellow, at the age of twenty-eight, announced his retirement from competition. He had just completed an unprecedented grand slam by winning four major golf championships in less than five months against the greatest amateurs and professionals in the world. Worn by the nervous, mental and physical strain of championship golf, he saw no more worlds to conquer. At best, there could be nothing but anticlimax left—such anticlimax as Gene Tunney's victory over Tom Heeney before Gene retired as world's heavyweight champion. So Bobby Jones wisely retired.

When he did, from Alaska to South Africa you could hear this question in the locker rooms: "When will we ever get another Bobby Jones?" As a rule, questions of this sort begin to die away as the years pass and new stars sparkle in the sports firmament. Especially in a game where records today are falling like autumn leaves. But as the golfing greats and galleries gather for the 1940 National Open at Cleveland, you will still be hearing the question: "When will we ever get another Bobby Jones?"

Since 1930 no fewer than eight crack golfers have won the U. S. Open title. But for eight out of nine previous years, from 1922 through 1930, Bobby Jones finished 1-2 against the best professionals and amateurs of golf.

The eight champions of the 30's were Billy Burke, Johnny Goodman, Gene Sarazen, Olin Dutra, Sammy Parks, Tony Manero, Ralph Guldahl (twice in succession) and Byron Nelson. Of this group, certainly Burke, Sarazen, Dutra, Guldahl and Nelson must be listed as magnificent

173

golfers. But this list included no one star who could keep hammering, year after year, at the main championship gate. Not one could approach Jones' one-two consistency—an incredible performance when one considers the destructive inconsistency of touch and timing in golf.

The point has been made that in the last few years the pace of golf has taken a big jump. This is true of golf as of other games. Jones won most of his championships with scores that ranged from 290 to 296. These scores won't get you a pot of tea today. The long-hitting, finely conditioned, tournament-tough golfers of the last few years know they must shoot between 280 and 285 to have a look-in. They know in advance they must rip Old Man Par into fluttering ribbons. They have to produce scores from eight to ten strokes better than those Bobby planted on the scoreboard.

The scores that gave Jones first or second place for almost ten years would win no big Open today. Few appreciate the tremendous feat Jimmy Demaret, the Houston Hurricane, put over when he won seven big tournaments in eleven starts last winter and this spring. Demaret, with a flawless swing and no nerves, had to cut both feet from under Par at every start.

Today Bobby Jones would have to face a far stronger field. But here are the golfers he had to meet and beat in their prime—Walter Hagen, Gene Sarazen, MacDonald Smith, Horton Smith, Henry Picard, Long Jim Barnes, Billy Burke, Willie MacFarlane, Bobby Cruicshank, Harry Cooper, Olin Dutra, Leo Diegel, Tommy Armour, Wild Bill Melhorn, Joe Turnesa, and such British entries as George Duncan and Abe Mitchell.

Fully to understand just how good Jones had to be, you must understand the competitive brilliancy of Walter Hagen and Gene Sarazen in these years. Hagen, one of the incomparables, won the U. S. Open in 1914 and again in 1919. He won four British Opens. He was a true great. Yet from 1920 through 1930 the amazing Haig was never able to lead Jones in a U. S. Open, or beat him to the wire in a British Open. Gene Sarazen, still a great golfer, beat Bob by a stroke in 1922 at Skokie, but that was his only triumph.

The golfers who beat Jones from 1922 through 1930 included such names as Sarazen, Cyril Walker, Willie Mac-Farlane, Tommy Armour and Johnny Farrell. But they never beat him twice. Right here one of golf's major ironies is worth mentioning in passing. Cyril Walker, who missed out at capitalizing his hard-won championship, was living at the Salvation Army hospice in Miami last winter. When his poor health permitted, he picked up small change as a caddie at Miami Beach municipal course.

Will golf ever produce another Bobby Jones?

Almost certainly not. There is no more chance that golf will give the world another Jones than there is that literature will produce another Shakespeare, sculpture another Phidias, music another Chopin. There is no more probability that the next 500 years will produce another Bobby than there is that two human beings will be born with identical fingerprints.

And why? Because to produce supreme genius in any line of endeavor, whether it be art, sports, or making flapjacks, one skin must enclose such a rare combination of human condiments that mathematical probabilities alone will not permit the admixture to arrive more than once.

Genius combines gifts from the gods with an even rarer quality—the ability to develop and realize on natural endowment. Doubtless, many men are born with the rudiments of genius. But few come into the world with the hardihood, the immense capacity for labor, and the passion for perfection that the fruition of genius demands. The pattern must be complete. Robert Tyre Jones, Second, of Atlanta, Georgia, was the complete human pattern for supreme genius.

Let us inquire first what the gods gave to Bobby Jones at birth. Let us examine the foundation, remembering that it is difficult to explain an amazing natural combination of mental and physical co-ordination. It might seem to be raw sacrilege to compare a golf swing to the rhythm of a

175

Keats or a Shelley. Yet Bobby Jones put into his swing the physical ingredients of beauty in motion that poets put into beauty of thought.

Thirty-one years ago, back in the summer of 1909, a Scotch professional by the name of Stewart Maiden was giving golf lessons at the East Lake Club in Atlanta, Georgia. From time to time, as Maiden glanced around, he saw a seven-year-old kid with a thin body and a large head watching him intently. After thirty or forty minutes of observation, the child would walk quietly away and start swinging a lone iron club. He was trying to swing the club as Maiden did.

"Who is that wee one?" the pro finally asked a club member.

"That's young Bobby Jones," the member said. "Son of Colonel Bob Jones, you know—the colonel's good."

That summer day in Georgia, Maiden never dreamed that twenty-odd years later the Marines would be called out to help troopers hold back the crowd eager to see that boy's swing—as was the case at Merion in Bobby's final 1930 bow.

Not long ago I asked Instructor Maiden just what interested him most in Bobby's starting years.

"Three things," Maiden said. "One was the complete concentration he gave to what I was telling other pupils, possibly for an hour at a time. This was amazing in a seven or eight year old kid. The second was his willingness to practice and play all alone, hour after hour, while other kids were playing other games. He was never lonesome with a golf club in his hands. He must have been born with a deep love for the game. He was certainly born with the soul of a perfectionist looking only for perfection. The third point was the smoothness of his swing at a time when most beginners are awkward-looking. Even then he had an uncanny knack of timing. He had the feel of what his hands were doing with the club head."

So we find here, in a seven-year-old kid, the combination of concentration, willingness to work, and a natural rhythm.

In the spring of 1914 I happened to stop off at the East Lake course with George Adair, who had a definite influence on Bobby's career. I saw this sign posted on the club bulletin board: "Bobby Jones, age 12. Out in 36, back in 34—70, tying the amateur record of the course."

Colonel Bob Jones, a prominent Atlanta lawyer, was a close friend of mine. Congratulations were in order. "He can do better than that," Bobby's father said. "He missed two short putts in that round."

The next time I ran into Bobby Jones happened to be at the U.S. Amateur Championship, held in 1916 at Merion, a suburb of Philadelphia. Bobby was then fourteen—a short, rotund kid, with the face of an angel and the temper of a timber wolf. At a missed shot, his sunny smile could turn into a black storm cloud quicker than the Nazis can grab a country. Even at the age of fourteen Bobby could not understand how anyone ever could miss any kind of golf shot. He discovered the answer later.

In that 1916 Amateur Championship, fourteen-year-old Bobby proved that he could hit more great golf shots than any man in the big field. He also proved beyond any argument that he could throw a putter or a niblick far beyond the range of anyone else.

I'll never forget his match with Eb Byers. Byers, a great competitor and a former amateur champion, was none too keen about meeting a fourteen-year-old. He was no keener about the match when he discovered that the big gallery was rooting for this chubby, pink-cheeked boy. The kid and the veteran both had a double ration of flame in their systems.

Byers finally missed a short putt. He promptly threw his putter into the top of a tall neighboring oak. Bobby missed one even shorter. He just as promptly threw his putter clean over the oak. It was Jones who won the match too. It was only his kid temper that kept him from

177

winning that 1916 championship. As it was, he came to the last eight from a big field. Every pro who saw him was enthralled by his perfect swing—a full body turn, with a smooth movement never hurried at any stage.

From that 1916 start it took Bobby Jones just seven years to reach the top. Through seven suffering years he took an incredible beating. He was still the best golfer— the finest shot maker—in each tournament. But he couldn't win. His fiery temperament was against him. He ran into every form of hard luck. He had conquered golf—but he wasn't able to conquer himself.

"Never mind his club-throwing temper," Long Jim Barnes, a double champion, told me then. "It simply means Bobby is never satisfied with any pretty good shot. It has to be perfect, or it is no good at all. That's the way any great artist must feel. He is only a kid; he will handle himself in time. The beatings Bobby has taken so far, beatings that would break the heart of an average man, will help to make him great. Great competitors only learn from defeat—not from victories."

Jones had a remarkable knack of stepping off into the quicksands, of getting himself into heavy trouble. But then he proved the iron in him by facing the issue with a heart that saved the day. From many of his near disasters I can give you two outstanding examples.

The eighteenth hole at Inwood probably saw him reach the most dramatic moments of his career. This crisis almost broke him. I think it made him. Standing on the last tee he was leading Bobby Cruicshank, great golfer and greater competitor, by four strokes in the U. S. Open of 1923.

This was a killing margin. Imagine anyone giving Bobby Jones four strokes on a single hole. After a good drive, Bobby's long second shot over guarding water pulled up to the left of the green, some twenty-five yards from the pin. Even a six on this hole meant certain victory. But he muffed his short approach into a trap, missed his fourth and finally wound up with a ghastly seven. He

178

had taken five strokes from only a few yards off the green.

To add horror to the nightmare, Cruicshank rapped a brilliant second shot seven feet from the cup. He sank his putt for a three to square the 72 hole score. I thought twenty-one-year-old Jones would be crushed.

"I'm glad Cruicshank tied me," he said later in the locker room.

"Why?" I asked.

"Because," Jones said, "I don't want to win any tournament with a seven on the last hole. They'd only remember my terrible finish and nothing else. I'm glad to have another chance to prove I'm not that yellow."

The big test came in next day's play-off. The two chunky Bobbies stood on the same last tee, still neck and neck. Neither hit an exceptional drive. But Cruicshank was too far back to carry the water hazard against the wind. He had to play for safety. Jones found his ball resting on a close, sandy lie. He had a long carry to face. If he missed the next shot, the water was waiting. If that happened, he might have written with Keats: "Here lies one whose name was writ in water."

This was the same hole that had wrecked him the day before. But instead of refusing the gamble, he picked out his midiron and lashed into the ball. As it struck the green it missed the pin by only a few inches, to stop six feet from the cup.

That was the shot that started Bobby Jones on his nine-year triumphant processional against the greatest golfers in the world. If Bobby had missed that shot, one of the most difficult in golf, no one can say what might have happened to a competitive spirit that had absorbed such a beating for so long.

Some time before this, young Jones had curbed his inclination to throw clubs. He had taken charge of himself. He was now out to play against par—not against Bobby Jones.

Almost any professional will tell you that the most

179

nerve-shattering shot in golf is the vital win-or-lose putt, from eight to ten feet away.

Yet I've seen Bob Jones save at least six championships this way—each time when the nerve-strain was tightest. On each occasion he stroked the ball as smoothly as if there were nothing at stake. The most striking exhibition came at the Winged Foot Club of New York in the Open Championship of 1929.

Jones apparently had the championship won, in spite of two terrible breaks that cost him sevens on four-par holes. He was six strokes in front of Al Espinosa, with only six holes left. Jones lost those six strokes in five holes. On the final hole be needed a par 4 to tie. His second shot hit the green and traveled halfway down the bank of a steep bunker. With 8000 spectators packed around this closing green, his third shot stopped twelve feet from the cup. He needed a twelve-foot curling putt to save himself from the greatest collapse in golf—a collapse that would have meant losing seven strokes in the last six holes.

I have never seen such gallery tension as when Jones calmly studied the line of the putt for a few seconds. Then he stroked the ball as perfectly as he had ever stroked in his career. I can still hear the roar from the crowd.

He proved he had it when the going was toughest, and the next day he won the play-off easily.

"Championship golf," he told me once, "is an entirely different game from friendly golf. From the start there is the tension and the strain. There is also the Thundering Herd storming along the course, many of them almost directly in the line you want to play. I have to think of at least three things before I play any shot— the smoothness of the back swing, taking my full left-side turn and then cocking my wrists at the top. You can't take anything for granted in golf. When I was leading by eighteen strokes at Augusta, with only three holes left, I thought of nothing and I finished those three easy holes six over par—something that would break a duffer's heart. I knew I couldn't lose and I was too tired to concentrate any longer."

One of the great curses of golf is attempting to steer the ball away from the trouble. One of the greatest golfers and one of the best of all instructors once told me this: "Bobby Jones is the only golfer I ever knew who never tried to steer a shot. If a championship depended on one swing, he would always take his full body turn and then let it go. There was no thought in his mind of playing anything safe. He played the shot as it should be played, and then let Fate decide the issue."

"I know exactly what he means," Horton Smith said. "The net of it is this: Bobby has a fine swing—and he trusts that swing. Many of us have fine swings—but we don't trust them in the clutch. Tension licks us. The temptation to steer a swing where there is trouble ahead is irresistible. Bob always whistled that temptation away."

There is a major golf lesson in this one idea. Play the shot. Forget everything else. As Bobby often told me: "Too many golfers think ahead of the stroke. All they should ever think of is the stroke itself—of the correct way of making the stroke. This is 70 per cent of golf."

But there is another answer to the question: "Will there ever be another Bobby Jones?"

Let us go back to St. Andrews, Scotland, in 1936. Here is the true shrine of golf.

Bobby Jones had won one of his last championships there in 1930, six years before. I was with Bobby on that 1936 visit to Scotland. An ordinary friendly golf game was arranged one morning. We left for the famous course around ten o'clock. There had been no publicity connected with Bobby's visit. But when he teed off with two local professionals, over 400 spectators were around the first tee. From mouth to mouth, word had been passed that Bobby Jones was back. "He's the King of Scotland," one excited Scot told me. And Scotsmen don't excite easily.

The gallery grew to 6000—more than many golf championships ever draw. They wanted to see Bobby Jones

181

again. They wanted to see Bobby Jones more than anyone else in the world. For St. Andrews means golf, and Bobby Jones meant golf to St. Andrews. He meant what St. Andrews idolized—form, style, sportsmanship. The return of young Tom Morris, long since dead.

When Bobby sank his last putt for a seventy, with almost no play or practice, the roar that came up from 6000 Scottish throats would have drowned out a naval battle.

I happened to be standing beside a veteran Scot. He was smoking a pipe and the tears were running down his face.

"Isn't it graund?" he said.

"Just what do you mean?" I asked.

"We have Bobby back."

When I heard that St. Andrews crowd roar, when I saw tears on the parchment cheek of that seventy-year-old Scot, when I pondered the full picture, then I knew there would never again be another Jones. Whatever any future giant of the links does to par, nobody ever will replace Robert Tyre Jones in the hearts of those to whom golf is something more than a game.

But to get back strictly to strokes and scores, who are the modern golf royalties who are candidates for Bobby's many-starred crown? Just now the hottest of them all appears to be Jimmy Demaret, who got a slow start in the game, but ran away from his competition last winter and this spring. Some who saw the twenty-nine-year-old Texan take the Masters' Tournament at Augusta with a 280, and saw portly businessman Robert Tyre Jones withdraw from the same tournament with a lame back when he was in the ruck, probably cannot picture the Bobby of ten years ago, a winner over Jimmy. If so, they never saw the Bobby of ten years ago.

In search for another Jones, certainly Ralph Guldahl, the rough and ready Texan who won two Opens in a row, cannot be overlooked. Then there's Byron Nelson, the Open champion, to round out the Texas trio at the top. Those Lone Star campaigners have been coming. Right up with them we must rate Sluggin' Sam Snead, the big money winner of 1938-39; Billy Burke, whose sound swing and great heart are likely to bring him back to the top; Henry Picard, the present P.G.A. champion; Horton Smith and Paul Runyan, a pair of reliables; Craig Wood, the brilliant unlucky one; Ben Hogan, still another Texan; Harry Cooper, the consistent veteran; Clayton Heafner, the comer from Carolina; John Bulla, the Chicago threat; Oliver and Dudley, the powerful Eds; and Dick Metz, another comer.

How would the Bobby Jones of 1930 compare with these? He never had the distance off the tee that Sammy Snead and Ben Hogan have today. They could outhit him, but Jones was straighter, and Jones was long enough. Henry Picard, Jimmy Demaret, Dick Metz, Ralph Guldahl and several others are better long iron players. As good as Jones was on the short game around the greens, he had nothing on Horton Smith, Paul Runyan, Billy Burke and Johnny Revolta.

Some experts will tell you that the Bobby Jones of 1922-30 could never have completed such a record against the par-blasting campaigner of the last few years. Today the winner usually has to peel the everlasting hide off par to pick up the big money. Ben Hogan, for example, had to beat par by something like thirteen strokes to win the last North and South Open.

Could the Bobby Jones of 1930 meet this new challenge? I think he could. For, in addition to his great skill, he was able to concentrate longer and he was better able to take a nerve beating than another golfer I ever knew. He took more than his share for fifteen years—from 1916 through 1930—and that's the real reason he quit. This is where most fine golfers who can play all the shots bog down. Gene Sarazen once said, "You can't take sixes and hope to win." Ordinarily, this is true. Yet Jones' cards showed sevens where he still finished in front.

I'll give you one clinching proof. He had just returned from winning the British Open in 1926 and was playing the U. S. Open at Scioto, Columbus, Ohio. Playing the last hole on his third round he missed every type of shot and took a seven, leaving him well behind the leader. When I went into his room at the club he was shot to pieces, almost a nervous wreck.

"Forget about it," I said. "You can't win everything."

"I was about ready to take it easy," he replied, "and let it all go. But I can't forget that terrible seven. Now I'm going out to win, or break my neck."

Bob was five strokes back of Joe Turnesa, with nine holes to play. On the last nine he had to face a swirling wind storm. But he won. Under all conditions it was the greatest stretch running I ever saw in golf. For here was a weary, nerve-exhausted competitor, a badly beaten man. He refused to admit he was beaten—and went on to win.

There are golfers today who can play every shot as well as Bobby Jones ever could.

But I'll never see another Jones.

This rare photo, on display at the Hall of Fame, shows Ty Cobb as a member of the Augusta, Ga., South-Atlantic League Club in 1905. On it Cobb inscribed the following notation: "This is a photo of myself as an 18-year-old recruit, to my knowledge, the first baseball photo taken of me. I am donating it to the Hall of Fame with fond memories of those days."

Rice's four all-time pitchers were Mathewson, Young, Johnson, and Alexander. "Of these four," wrote Granny, "Alexander was the keenest control artist I ever studied. He won 30 games or more for three years and his earned run average was around 1.65 year after year. Alex could throw a ball into a tin cup." The photo shows Alexander as a member of the St. Louis Cardinals in 1926.

Baseball's Iron Horse, Lou Gehrig, played in 2,130 consecutive games for the New York Yankees before he was forced to the bench on May 2, 1939. Two years later, in June of 1941, Lou died of amyotrophic lateral sclerosis. In Gehrig's death, just as with Babe Ruth's seven years later, baseball and Rice lost two irreplaceables.

WIDE WORLD

Babe Ruth taking one of his famous swings. Fat and wheezy, Ruth had been in retirement for seven years when this photo was taken on August 21, 1942. Ruth once said, "I copied my swing after Joe Jackson. His is the perfectest. Joe aims his right shoulder square at the pitcher with his feet about 20 inches apart. But I close mine to about 8½ inches for a better pivot. However, once my swing starts, I can't change it or pull up. It's all or nothing at all."

Joe DiMaggio, a true champion, achieved the summit despite severe handicaps. He broke into the Yankee lineup with a questionable knee that made him "thumbs down" for scouts from other teams. After that he was dogged by heel spurs and calcium deposits. Nevertheless, Joe was a lifetime .325 hitter and one of the most graceful outfielders of all time.

WIDE WORLD

Jesse Owens, one of Rice's all-time great athletes, is shown as he partici-
pates in the 1936 Olympic games at Berlin. Regarding Owens' performance there, Granny wrote: "In four straight days, he made 14 appearances,
running four heats each in the 100 and 200 meters and jumping six times.
He broke Olympic records a total of nine times and equaled them twice!
Altogether, by his deportment and his actions, he was rather a handy
bloke to have around at Berlin."

Here is Red Grange, famous "77" of Illinois, sweeping right end on the last play of his college career as the Illini defeated Michigan in 1925. Nearly 30 years later, Rice wrote: "Three names leap out at me through the years. Jim Thorpe, Bronko Nagurski and Red Grange. Aside from whatever properties make up football greatness, all three had that indefinable quality known as color."

In 1937, Byron "Whizzer" White of Colorado, was the nation's leading college scorer and an All-America on the Grantland Rice team. Rice commented on White's abilities: "He ran, kicked, and passed. As a blocker and tackler he was better than most. The entire Colorado attack was molded around him."

Today, the Whizzer is Supreme Court Justice White.

*In 1928, NYU beat Carnegie Tech 27-13 to lay claim to the mythical
Eastern Championship. Ken Strong is shown above on a carry through the
Tech line. Strong's performance that day inspired Carnegie's coach to remark: "I've seen Heston and Eckersall, but here's the greatest player I
ever saw. This is the first time I have ever seen one man run over my
team. We beat Notre Dame 27-7 last week to keep us undefeated, but
Strong runs, passes, and kicks us into the ground."*

Knute Rockne's football clinics were special. Every coach in the midwest sought the personal accolade of sending a future star to Notre Dame. Here, gathered around Rockne, are 77 of them from the 1930 team.

Grantland Rice coined an immortal nickname to describe this famous backfield. From left to right, The Four Horsemen of Notre Dame: Don Miller, Elmer Layden, Jim Crowley and Harry Stuhldreher.

A bunch of good sports at Palm Beach. Tex Rickard, Rube Goldberg, Gene Tunney, Rice, and Ring Lardner on the links during the winter of 1926. Several months later Tunney was to beat Jack Dempsey for the heavyweight championship.

Joe Louis and Jim Braddock exchange missed jabs during their title fight on June 22, 1937. Joe went on to win the title with an eighth-round knockout.

"Joe was a clean, fair sportsman. Completely honest in a game where honesty is not a watchword, Joe was a glowing example for all to follow."

Ben Hogan blasts out of a sand trap during the 1953 National Open at Oakmont, Pa. *"Through his complete dedication to his sport, Hogan built in himself that 'more of everything' — particularly brains — it takes to win than any golfer I ever saw."* — Grantland Rice.

Above: Will Rogers and Granny Rice take in a golf tournament in the early 1930's. Right: Bobby Jones and Rice watching the 1932 U.S. Open.

Gallant Fox with Earl Sande up, wins the 56th Kentucky Derby in 1930.
It was Sande's second Derby victory, his first coming in 1925.

*Earl Sande in 1930, the
year he rode Gallant
Fox in the Derby. Hav-
ing already retired
twice, that season
marked his third return
to the saddle. Rice con-
sidered Sande as the
first great jockey he
ever saw.*

Seabiscuit vs. War Admiral. "In one of the greatest match races ever run at 1-3/16 miles, the valiant Seabiscuit not only conquered the great War Admiral, but, beyond this, he ran the beaten son of Man o' War into the dirt and dust of Pimlico." — Grantland Rice.

Eddie Arcaro, displaying top form as he rides Wintervale to victory at Aqueduct in 1961, once told Rice: "When it comes to busting for that opening, it's largely instinct. You've got a split second to decide. You are right or you are wrong. You can't wait."

A SWITCH IN LULLABIES

By GRANTLAND RICE

"Some flew east—some flew west—
Some flew over the cuckoo's nest."
—(Old nursery rhyme)

Somewhere beyond the Southern Cross above the Seven Seas,
Along the bitter far-off roads, their pinions catch the breeze.
Their wings are black against the sky, by desert, surf and dune,
An ancient lullaby is lost against a rougher tune—

Some flew east—some flew west—
And some will fly no more,
Far, far out from the eagle's nest
Their mighty motors roar.
And wing by wing their rule will grow
Above all sea and sod,
Until they strike the final blow
For Country and for God.

Faintly, I hear the old, old song when golden dreams were young.
But louder still I hear the wings where sudden death is flung.
Bravely the eagle rides the air, but in my fading dreams,
The dim, lost lullaby returns—how far away it seems—

Some fly east—and some fly west—
They take an endless track.
Through flame and steel they face the test
Around the world and back.
Their golden youth blots out the sky,
They let the comets plod,
As each one flies to live or die
For country and for God.

PART III

The Old Order Changes

In 1930, Grant Rice was fifty years old. From the twenty-year-old graduate of Vanderbilt—an honor student who played enough infield to rate a call from the Chicago White Sox—the name Grantland Rice carried an authentic ring that had become recognized wherever English is read. Wherever the big game, race, match or prizefight was being staged, chances were that Granny would show. He had no special beat. Whatever the event or the person that whetted his fancy, that was his story. Except for a few weeks rest annually—usually early in January—he swung a seven-day week in behalf of his syndicated column which necessarily had to be written days ahead. Only the writer who has lived with such a deadline, year after year, can appreciate the physical and mental toll involved. He loved to salute victory, but the first World overseas service in World War I had taught him to salute death as even a more constant companion.

Perhaps the most negative personal event that shocked Rice in the early 1930's was Rockne's crashing death by airplane in March of 1931. In September 1933, his dear sidekick Ring Lardner died. After that, it seemed to Granny that his friends were falling like petals in a chill breeze.

If Granny was a fatalist, "sensitive fatalist" better suits him. Perhaps that was why, following Don Marquis' death in 1938, Rice felt impelled to write a bit of verse for the

185

*annual Artists and Writers dinner of that year. He titled
it,* Via Charon, *the Ancient Boatman.*

At any rate, if Rice went right on as an aging but always vibrant Pied Piper of sport, you can bet that, for him, victory or defeat in the arena, more and more symbolized human qualities far deeper than sport per se.

THE SPORTLIGHT

(April 1, 1931)

KNUTE ROCKNE

The sudden, tragic death of Knute Rockne, Notre Dame's great football coach, comes as one of the greatest shocks the world of sport has known. Here was not only a rare genius on the football field, but a personality that for years had caught and held the attention of millions, one of the most attractive personalities this generation has developed along any line.

Knute Rockne could have been an outstanding figure in any career or profession he might have adopted. He had brains, ability, character and the vital qualities of leadership. He stuck to football because that was the game he loved and because it belonged to the type of younger men who were his kind. Football is a game that demands spirit and action, and Knute Rockne had these elements to a rare degree. He knew football and he knew how to teach football, having shown this teaching ability as a chemistry professor at Notre Dame before he took up football coaching. Beyond this he had the knack of appealing to the student in the right way, the knack of holding interest and attention. And more than all, he had the imagination that belongs to genius. And he had the ability to transfer a lot of his imagination to his team.

I spent most of the afternoon and evening with Knute on one of his last trips East. We were discussing then his main fundamentals of attack.

"Any successful attack in this modern game," he said then, "must be based largely upon fine blocking and the element of misdirection. No team can win through sheer

187

power and, after all, that is no way to try for a victory in a game that can find such able use for brains. I have used the shift because it helped along the lines of misdirection—of threatening one spot and then striking at another. But back of it all you must have the blockers who can provide the openings and the interference.

"At Notre Dame we talk little about ball carriers. We talk about the blockers, the men who clear the way. The greatest back in the world couldn't make any ground without good blocking. An ordinary back can get the distance when you open the road. I should say that blocking and misdirection of attack, plus speed, were the three strongest qualities in my offense."

"All that," I suggested, "plus a rare football spirit for which you have been largely responsible."

Knute disclaimed that part of the debate, but it was true. He had an infectious magnetism that went into the hearts and the souls of his men. He carried the brand of inspiration that no young athlete could help but absorb. He was dynamic without being a driver. He was one of the few who could get the complete response from a big squad.

Having the material developed and the plays at hand, Knute understood that the next step was to build up the quarterback who could handle his attack. Few will know how patiently, how hard and how long he worked with such stars as Harry Stuhldreher and Frank Carideo, two of his best leaders.

He made it a point to spend all possible time with his quarterbacks and to so instill them with his ideas that under fire they could meet any situation that might arrive. Those who saw the last Notre Dame-Southern California battle will understand how Carideo's fine generalship struck at such unexpected points that a big, powerful team was completely overwhelmed in the first few plays.

You can get a faint glimpse from all this why Knute Rockne leaves a record that may never be surpassed, certainly on no gridiron of the generation. In handling his men he could be sharp and decisive, but a moment later he would be on hand with a funny line or a funny story that broke the tension of the moment and wiped away any chance for soreness.

I asked him once what he considered the most important details of football success. His answer was this: "To be mentally keyed up but to be physically relaxed." This is a combination that few can find, unless they come under the careful teaching of a Rockne, so much wiser than most to the workings of the younger mind.

Rockne was one of the best of all after-dinner story tellers. He had a great list of anecdotes and incidents, all from actual life, and no one knew better how to put these stories across. They were a part of his method of teaching, for he found them invaluable aids on the field when staleness or weariness set in.

There has been more than one complaint against spring football. The complaint was that it had become a drudgery, and the boys didn't like it. Notre Dame's answer to Rockne's spring call was 350 football players, all raring to go, because there was a Rockne to rally around.

It took the genius of a Rockne to blend the Four Horsemen into one of the most graceful and most colorful backfields that football has known. He was an artist as well as a football coach, and his loss is a vital blow to millions in the years to come. It will be the loss of a great artist who painted his pictures for great crowds upon the background of green turf, a turf full of romance and action and color that will now cover his last sleep. It is impossible to believe that such a vital, flaming, magnetic human is gone.

There are few in this world who can't be replaced. Knute Rockne is one of the few. Here is one wide gap that can't be closed.

THE SPORTLIGHT

(October 3, 1931)

THE RED BIRD TURNS FROM SPARROW TO EAGLE

ST. LOUIS, Oct. 3—No naturalists in this vicinity have yet been able to explain how a red bird can look like a sparrow one day and turn into a soaring eagle twenty-four hours later.

Yet this is the astonishing phenomenon that has taken place in the Cardinal roost with both clubs on their way to Philadelphia in a deadlock at one and one.

In the first battle the Athletics applied raw power and breezed through. In this second test the Cardinals applied raw speed as Bill Hallahan again shut out the famous maulers from the mansion of Mack with only three scattered blows as the battle ended, 2 to 0. The counting factor was the blinding speed from Hallahan's left arm, hooked to the speed in Pepper Martin's flying feet. It will take until next Monday for even the brainy Mr. Mack to untie all the knots in his team that Hallahan employed in defense of the home plate.

And while the left-hander was putting on a great show and a big job, Pepper Martin stole the battle from Mickey Cochrane's right hand by steals of second and third that paved the way for both runs. In each instance Mickey had to hurry the throw to nail the Oklahoma Cyclone, and in both the second and seventh innings Martin's twinkling feet got to the bag in front of the tag.

As a result of Hallahan's great pitching against George Earnshaw and Pepper Martin's aggressive attack the Cardinals are on their way to Philadelphia in a highly pleasant state of mind.

In the first place they have beaten big George

190

Earnshaw for the first time, as George was the fellow who put them on the burning deck a year ago.

The Swarthmore sharpshooter turned the Red Birds into a pie last fall, but while he only yielded six hits and pitched well enough to win most ball games, he was up against a super brand of pitching in this second contest. Hallahan, who had more smoke than a burning oil well, turned on enough speed to limit the slugging Mackmen to three flabby singles from the bats of Mule Haas, Jimmy Foxx and Bing Miller. There were times when the stocky left-hander was wilder than a timber wolf. He gave up seven passes and put himself into more holes than a duffer digging in the sand. But this made no difference. Someone had to hit these free rides around the towpaths, and no one could. His fast and curve balls looked like bird shot as they whistled over the plate. A cove has to have more than a trifle to keep such people as Mickey Cochrane, Al Simmons, Dykes, Bishop and others from getting a hit. He had the stuff that will beat any ball club any time, and there was no let-up. In the first game Paul Derringer turned on too much steam and finally broke. Hallahan turned on just as much steam in the second game by retiring the first eleven men in order who happened to be coming up. They could just about foul him, and that is all.

Bing Miller got the first Athletic hit in the fifth inning, and that shows how smoothly the southpaw was stepping along. And this was the inning that broke Philadelphia's proud heart. The Cardinals were leading, 1 to 0. Foxx opened the fifth with a walk, Miller singled and Dykes moved them up to second and third with only one out. Hallahan then passed Williams to bring up Earnshaw and a better chance for a double play, or a play at any base. It was tidy strategy, for Earnshaw, with the bases filled and only one out, was in a great spot to tie the score and send his team to the front. His response at this critical moment was an infield tap that led to an easy double play, as some 40,000 Missouri fans rose up and told the world all about the good news.

191

When the second battle opened the big crowd lacked the pep and hilarity of the opening day gathering. One Robert Moses Grove plus Cochrane, Simmons and others had left the harpoon in their backs. There was no great display of enthusiasm as Hallahan smothered the enemy for the first two rounds. They had seen Derringer do the same thing. But about the fourth or fifth inning there was a noticeable change in the spirit of the stands. The crowd seemed to be saying about this time, "Maybe this guy Hallahan means business after all. He beat this same club, 5 to 0, a year ago, and so far they can't hit him with a handful of shot at two paces."

As Hallahan went moving along the "St. Louis Blues" gave way to "Hail the Conquering Hero Comes." You could sense the fact that Mr. Hallahan had no idea of blowing up. He kept on bearing down, crowding all he had on every pitch, but he had the left-arm stamina needed to complete the route. He had another slight slinking spell in the seventh, but after that he breezed in.

The bounding antelope who is about to steal this world series from most of the stars is a young fellow named Pepper Martin, better known as the Oklahoma Cyclone. Pepper likes to ride on freight trains in place of Pullmans, where the soft padding irks his hide. He has arms like Jack Dempsey and the heart of a great competitor. In the first he struck back savagely at Grove and got three hits, even in the midst of a losing cause. Pepper came up with one out in the second inning of Friday's battle. The crowd paid its tribute to a game fighter and a sterling athlete. He obliged by socking a double and then stealing third as Cochrane's peg was a trifle off. That made him. This was the stuff the Cardinals needed, not a good defense, but an old-fashioned, headlong attack. This steal put Martin in position to score a moment later. In the seventh inning he opened the pot with a single and then lost no time stealing second. He was well away and traveling at such speed that Cochrane's hurried throw was again off line. An infield out and a squeeze play from Gelbert brought Pepper from third across the plate, where he spilled the redoubtable Mickey Cochrane in three or four directions as Earnshaw tried to shut off this second run.

Martin now has five hits for the two games and more glory than any other star on either club.

The Cardinals looked to be a far different ball club in this second chapter. They were getting better pitching and once in front they dug in and played with much more spirit than they had to show in the opener. They had the keener attack and the better pitching in the battle that tied up the big show to carry the war at even terms into Philadelphia for a Monday start. The fact that Earnshaw was bowled over has helped a lot. You can stand facing one star like Grove, but when two stars begin to gang you it is something else again. Hallahan will have a much longer resting period this time than he had a year ago and his feat of shutting out the Athletics twice in three starts is something to remember anybody by. The early prediction that the series would be the closest of many years may pan out after all. Hallahan's shut out triumph and Pepper Martin's daily thrusts have changed the outlook, which after the first game was bluer than indigo as far as the Red Birds' migration was concerned. Both teams so far have fielded ably and Al Simmons has contributed two backhanded running catches that shut off triples. Watkins also robbed Cochrane of a double or triple by hauling down a long drive as the right fielder collided with the stands.

THE SPORTLIGHT

(June 23, 1936)

Washington Sweeps Hudson

Poughkeepsie, N.Y. June 23, 1936—The Hudson is still stained with a glint of purple and gold imported from Lake Washington in the heart of Seattle.

The old slogan stands—first in war, first in peace and first in all three races on the old river against California and the picked crews of the East. Al Ulbrickson and his Washington crew were shooting for the Olympic carnival, and they figured any crew good enough to win at four miles against this competition would be good enough to win at Lake Carnegie around July 4.

With this idea in mind, a Washington crew that had both stamina and speed proved its place. Trailing California and the Navy by three lengths with a mile and a quarter left, the power blades from the Northwest put on a long sprint, just about the Olympic distance, to beat California three-quarters of a length, as a game, fast Navy eight finished third, but right in the middle of the show.

This was a boat race that 50,000 spectators will remember. The seven crews got away shortly after 8 o'clock last night in perfect weather. It was Rusty Callow's Pennsylvanians that took the jump, with Navy and California alongside for the first time. Washington was far back. Cornell couldn't get started. Syracuse never had a chance. Columbia was in there swinging, holding her own.

As Pennsylvania's Red and Blue fell back Navy took the lead, with California less than a length away. Then California came on with a roar from the Western contingent as the Navy still stuck. It was to be California or

194

Navy. Washington was too far away, three lengths in arrears and gaining no headway.

As the battle between California and the Navy held the attention of the crowd that lined the banks and the boats that kept in pursuit, another shout went up. With a trifle more than a mile to go, Washington was coming up. Yard by yard the Purple and Gold closed in the open space.

With a mile left after a three-mile grind, Washington now had a sprint on its way. It caught and passed Navy. Then it went after California, and 500 yards from the finish the northwestern entry was in the lead.

California's fine crew tried desperately to meet this new challenge. It had first shaken loose Pennsylvania. Then it had shaken off a corking Navy crew that had no thought of buckling. It was the third wave—the third challenge that set a faster pace than the Golden Bears could meet.

For a short distance Washington and California rowed together, but Al Ulbrickson's young giants from the West had too much steam to be throttled. They were rowing with the skill and precision of a crew that knows its job—that had timed its pace perfectly from start to finish—and when the main showdown came, just at the edge of night, Washington had too much left.

Freshmen, junior varsity and varsity races all went the same way, but the main thriller came at dusk when the three leading crews looked like dim wraiths upon the water. California and Navy had rowed themselves out when the new challenger appeared in the last line, coming on with a burst of speed that few believed possible in the last mile of a four-mile race.

Columbia held on well for two miles, and so did Pennsylvania, but what had been touted as a fine Cornell crew was never in the rowing. Cornell was away badly and could never catch its pace.

Veteran oarsmen in the observation cars were especially keen to figure from this race the possibilities of the next Olympic entry from the United States. California had won the last three Poughkeepsie regattas, and so was in sight of Cornell's four-time record from 1909 to 1912. California had won the last two Olympic races.

But the driving power of that Washington crew through the last mile and a quarter, with a big lead to cut away, brought a new name into the picture. The general opinion was that Washington and California would be in charge at Lake Carnegie with the Northwestern contingent having at least a shade.

It was a thrilling race with action all the way—from the spot where Pennsylvania and Navy got the jump to the final spin that told the story. It is difficult to say that a crew beaten by less than a length at four miles is out of it in a much shorter race, but, unless it is Navy, there was no evidence upon the placid sweep of the Hudson that any other Eastern crew would have a look-in against the two Western entries that ran 1-2. The Navy at the shorter span will bear watching. There are three crews that should fight it out at Princeton later on.

But it would surprise no one to see those huskies from Seattle rowing at Berlin against the pick of Europe and Asia in the hardest fight any American crew has ever faced.

It's a long hike from Seattle to Poughkeepsie, but that last mile looked to be even longer with so much open water to close up. Washington had what it took to wipe out these odds, as Al Ulbrickson waved back to the thunder of a crowd that caught its thrill from a game and a thrilling finish.

THE SPORTLIGHT

(August 5, 1936)

OWENS WINS BROAD JUMP; DOMINATES OLYMPIC SHOW

BERLIN, Aug. 5 (by Wireless)—Tuesday was a dark, raw day of rain and wind, but it looked even darker to the fifty other nations participating in the Olympic games as our Ethiopian troops continued their deadly fire.

Glenn Hardin, the Mississippi hurdler, startled the German multitude by proving that the United States had a white man who could win. The tall, wiry Hardin galloped off with the 400-meter hurdle championship, a lone white spot on a sable background, for it was Jesse Owens and John Woodruff, American Negroes, who stole the third-day show.

Owens, in spite of unfavorable weather, has completely dominated the Olympic cast. After winning the 100 meters Monday, he added the broad jump victory by almost jumping out of Germay. It was the day's most spectacular event. Everything was set for a dramatic climax.

Lutz Long, German star, had just tied Owens' best mark near the finish, only a few yards from Chancellor Hitler's box. A hundred and ten thousand spectators paid a thundering tribute, with Hitler as excited as any member of the packed crowd.

The tumult and the shouting was still rolling across Berlin as Owens, without delay, answered the challenge by jumping past 26 feet and finally finishing with 26 feet, 5½ inches, far beyond anyone else. It was an amazing performance under such pressure and through a sweep of voices that was almost rocking the stadium for his rival as he jumped.

Owens has been like a wild Zulu running amock. He

197

has started six times, in the 100-meters, the 200-meters heats and the broad jump, and has broken the Olympic record four times and has equaled the record in his other two starts. He has been deadly poison to Nordic supremacy, not only by his victories but by the best form and smoothest style that coaches from all over the world have ever seen. He makes every event look easier than lighting a match.

The weather has been all against him and the crowds have been unsympathetic, but he has turned out the finest job ever seen in Olympic sport. He will be remembered among the outstanding Olympic artists of all time. He stopped to applaud Don Lash, qualifying in the 5,000-meter run, a few seconds before making his record jump. He apparently was more interested in Lash than in himself.

John Woodruff, Pittsburgh Negro, ran one of the wildest races on record, the 800-meters. Minus all running form, he raced all over the track. He flopped back and forth until the last stretch turn when his flying legs suddenly moved into action as he passed Edwards of Canada and Lanzi of Italy, running both into the ground to win going away. You couldn't tell whether he was going to win or finish last until the final killing outburst of speed and stamina with his kangaroo stride.

Helen Stephens, the Ozark flash from William Woods College, rushed supremacy on the United States palefaces by breaking the world's women's 100-meter record for the third time in two days. She looked like a Missouri hurricane compared with the rest of the field, including the record holder, Stella Walsh. Her long, strong legs tore the track wide open.

Gisela Mauermayer, German girl, broke the Olympic record for the discus throw, giving the German team eight flags to date at the Olympic masthead. It is something to hear a hundred thousand voices singing "Deutschland Ueber Alles" as the Swastika flag catches the wind and a hundred thousand hands extend in the Nazi salute.

198

"We can beat your American white men," one German official said, "but not these astonishing Ethiopians."

Leading German philosophers are trying to explain the situation in this unique Nordic stronghold, but the explanations are largely the bunk. The Negroes are just better runners and jumpers, with more to come later on.

The collapse of the American whites has been terrific. "Spec" Towns, the Georgia hurdler, promises he will come to the white rescue. "I feel like a feather in the breeze," he told me. Apparently the race here is to the swift, and the black and sepia are too strong. The white man's back has been broken as far as America is concerned. The United States would be outclassed except for our black-skinned frontal and flanking fire.

THE GRANTLAND RICE ALL-AMERICA
FOOTBALL TEAM OF 1937

ANDREW BERSHAK
END, UNIVERSITY OF NORTH CAROLINA

JEROME HOLLAND
END, CORNELL UNIVERSITY

EDMUND FRANCO
TACKLE, FORDHAM UNIVERSITY

VIC MARKOV
TACKLE, UNIVERSITY OF WASHINGTON

LEROY MONSKY
GUARD, UNIVERSITY OF ALABAMA

JOSEPH ROUTT
GUARD, TEXAS A. & M.

CARL C. HINKLE, JR.
CENTER, VANDERBILT UNIVERSITY

CLINTON E. FRANK
QUARTERBACK, YALE UNIVERSITY

MARSHALL GOLDBERG
HALFBACK, UNIVERSITY OF PITTSBURGH

BYRON WHITE
HALFBACK, UNIVERSITY OF COLORADO

SAMUEL CHAPMAN
FULLBACK, UNIVERSITY OF CALIFORNIA

The time is two o'clock on a Saturday afternoon, September 25, 1937. The place is Columbus, Ohio. The cast is composed of Texas Christian and Ohio State, two of the country's strongest football teams.

Just thirty seconds before the game begins a torrential downpour, blown in by a lusty gale, beats down upon 70,000 spectators. The two opponents battle back and forth through rain and mud.

The two teams tackle, block, run, pass and kick. Who cared about a deluge, soaked clothing, influenza or pneumonia?

From this opening game the new season was beginning to roll. Over 400 teams and more than 16,000 big-time football players were moving into action. In addition to team results, there were also All-America dreams filling their heads. Many of these dreams were to be spoiled by injuries and by long, hard schedules. In this lamentable list you will find such early probabilities as Daddio of Pittsburgh, Farkas of Detroit, Uram of Minnesota, Hitchcock of Auburn and others who were early leaders. They were all good enough, barring injuries, to make any team.

This campaign was not a medley of upsets. It was rather one of the greatest levelers that football has yet known. It proved again that material and coaching were spread evenly across the country. The supercoach and the superteam were heading toward extinction. In this last season more than a few well-known names fell at the first volley. Powerful Minnesota, pride of the Big Ten, crashed in its second charge—against Nebraska. The Southwestern Conference, largely Texas teams, began an early job of complete extermination and kept it up all fall. This is the cutthroat circuit of football. The Southwest is perhaps the hardest of all the conference championships to win. Its general average is higher than any other one section. Don't forget that schedules such as T. C. U., Auburn, Pittsburgh, Notre Dame, California, Ohio State and a few others face can make a killing difference when compared to the schedules of those who play only four or five hard games.

Along the Pacific Coast they play a round-robin schedule that only a powerful team could hope to face unbeaten. They had few breathers when the knocking down got under way. It remained for one of the strongest California teams in years to take over the prestige of the Pacific Coast. California fought its way through a hard schedule unbeaten, tied only by Washington.

Through the South and the Southeast most of the leading teams were well matched in playing strength—such teams as Vanderbilt, Alabama, L. S. U., Georgia Tech, Auburn, Duke, North Carolina, Tulane, Tennessee— where Auburn carried by all odds the heaviest burden.

The playing strength of the Big Six and the Rocky Mountain Conference was also well above average. For example, Nebraska's strong team, coached by Biff Jones, was tied by Kansas State and barely able to beat Missouri, but whipped Minnesota and Indiana, two of the strongest teams from the Big Ten, and lead a brilliant Pittsburgh outfit into the fourth quarter.

The Big Ten from the Midwest had an off year, as Minnesota, Indiana, Ohio State, Iowa and Michigan were beaten by outside opponents. Notre Dame had no chance to plow through its schedule unbeaten. Who could hope to throw back Minnesota and Pittsburgh on successive Saturdays, even with the strong Notre Dame squad?

As the Midwest fell back, the East, including the Ivy circuit and such teams as Pittsburgh, Fordham, Villanova, Holy Cross, Temple, etc., took over leadership for the second successive year. In the Ivy set-up, Yale, Dartmouth, Cornell and Harvard were all strong. Harvard, in spite of a season crammed with injuries and hard luck, won the old Big Three championship. Dartmouth finished in front of the Ivy circuit, with an unbeaten campaign, although tied by Yale and Cornell.

Pittsburgh and Fordham were outstanding. So was Clipper Smith's Villanova team. Pop Warner, in his 44th coaching year, rounded out his 300th victory at Temple.

The East, after a long lapse in other years, had the majority of outstanding stars—Frank of Yale, MacLeod of Dartmouth, Luckman of Columbia, Goldberg, Matisi and Souchak of Pittsburgh, Wysocki and Mellus of Villanova, Holland, Peck and Hooper of Cornell, Franco and Wojciechowicz of Fordham, Struck and Green of Harvard, Osmanski of Holy Cross—a long parade who have found football again.

We now come to the All-America of 1937. In lining up the 1937 All-America the play of each man, including opposing strength, was thoroughly checked from the first game to the last. There was no prejudice, no partisanship, no angle of race, creed or color. Those who had shown three good years were given some advantage over others, practically as good, who had turned in only one or two years of high-class work.

Here is the list of candidates from which the team was selected:

Centers—Hinkle, Vanderbilt; Brock, Nebraska; Wojciechowicz, Fordham; Herwig, California.

Guards—Routt, Texas A. and M.; Monsky, Alabama; Stockton, California.

Tackles—Franco, Fordham; Markov, Washington; Matisi, Pittsburgh; Kinard, Mississippi; Mellus, Villanova; Shirey, Nebraska; Babartsky, Fordham; Russell, Auburn; Lane, T. C. U.; Beinor, Notre Dame.

Ends—Holland, Cornell; Bershak, North Carolina; Wysocki, Villanova; Jordan, Georgia Tech; Schwartz, California; Benton, Arkansas; Smith, Oklahoma; Souchak, Pittsburgh; Sweeney, Notre Dame.

Backs—Frank, Yale; White, Colorado; Chapman, Meek and Bottari, California; Goldberg, Pittsburgh; Luckman, Columbia; MacLeod, Dartmouth.

There were many other fine football players. But these were the survivors of more than 300,000 words of letters and telegrams, opinions and vital statistics, from Collier's Board, other football writers and coaches from every section of the country.

The men who rated the highest average this season

203

from all opposing coaches were Frank of Yale, Hinkle of Vanderbilt, Chapman of California, White of Colorado and Franco of Fordham. Routt of Texas A. and M. and Monsky of Alabama were not far behind.

The most difficult positions to fill were center, the ends and the backs. At center the leaders were Hinkle of Vanderbilt, the irrepressible Wojciechowicz of Fordham, Herwig of California and Brock of Nebraska.

Pittsburgh players picked Brock over Wojciechowicz. Jock Sutherland rated them about even. The Southwest rated Aldrich of T. C. U. on even terms with Wojjy, but named Hinkle of Vanderbilt superior to both. The West Coast was divided when it came to Herwig, a fine center, with strong support for Ericksen of Washington and Dougherty of Santa Clara. The three-year rating of Hinkle was outstanding. He played eleven 60-minute games in his last two years.

The ends, as usual, left a headache. They included Holland of Cornell, Wysocki of Villanova, Bershak of North Carolina, Schwartz of California, Jordan of Georgia Tech, Smith of Oklahoma, Benton of Arkansas, Souchak of Pittsburgh and Sweeney of Notre Dame.

"The hard luck," as Jock Sutherland of Pittsburgh said, "was that Daddio was hurt. There was no one even close to him, offensively and defensively." Which happens to be true. Bershak of North Carolina had known three seasons of high-class play. Opponents facing Holland named him as one of the best all-around ends of several seasons. His quick reflexes and his catlike speed were leading features. Wysocki came with a rush this season, his first year as a regular, and he was given his chance to roam by Mellus, the Villanova tackle. Benton, Smith and Schwartz were exceptionally good.

The tackle assignments found a hard battle among Franco of Fordham, Markov of Washington and Matisi of Pittsburgh, all well above average.

The problem of the backfield had just as many knots and tangles. There were Frank of Yale, White of Colorado, Goldberg of Pittsburgh, MacLeod of Dartmouth,

Meek of California, Luckman of Columbia, Chapman of California, Vic Bottari of California, Dave O'Brien of T. C. U., Sloan of Arkansas. Who could pick from this list?

In the final selections from Collier's Board and over fifty coaches, Frank, Chapman and White were unanimous choices. Chapman, especially, was just as outstanding as Frank and Francis were a year ago without even a dissenting murmur. MacLeod, Goldberg and Meek were close. Goldberg remained the spearhead of Pittsburgh's attack through an extremely hard schedule. MacLeod was close in all-around value, while Meek was an all-season sensation. There was little to choose from among these three, but Goldberg's value to Pittsburgh was a trifle more pronounced.

BERSHAK—*End, North Carolina*

Andrew Bershak has been a star end at North Carolina for three years, an important factor in the selection. Bershak is one of the best pass receivers in football. He has been a fast, hustling end on both offense and defense, and also one of the iron men of the team.

HOLLAND—*End, Cornell*

Jerome Holland has been a sixty-minute player for two years and his work this year put Cornell up among the leaders of the East. In the Colgate game, he scored three of his team's six touchdowns, two of them on end-around plays. He also played a great game on the defense, breaking down Colgate's sometimes bewildering attack time and again. In the Yale game he broke through on two consecutive plays to throw the ball carriers for a total loss of twenty yards.

FRANCO—*Tackle, Fordham*

Edmund Franco, short, squat and almost unbelievably

205

powerful, frequently has been called a one-man line. No opposing team ever mouse-trapped him unless he wanted to go lunging through—and no team, having done it once, was likely to try it again, for when he got in there he bowled over blockers and piled up the attack. This was Franco's third year of smashing and effective play on one of the nation's ranking teams.

MARKOV—*Tackle, Washington*

Vic Markov of Washington received a unanimous vote as being the best lineman on the Pacific Coast. "His tremendously effective smashing tactics," writes Dink Templeton, "pulled Washington together. He is fast, smart and a hard worker who never loafs for a second." Markov was the outstanding player on a strong Washington team, strong enough to hold even California's fine team scoreless.

MONSKY—*Guard, Alabama*

Leroy Monsky, amazingly fast for his size and power, was outstanding on both offense and defense and was a key man in the Alabama attack, which specializes in the use of the guards. Monsky, captain of his team, led many a charge that put Alabama in front after a strenuous tussle. His fighting courage was the decisive factor in most of these games. In a year that did not produce too many outstanding guards, Monsky not only proved his right to top rating but was acclaimed by many coaches to be among the first three players in the South, regardless of position.

ROUTT—*Guard, Texas A. & M.*

Joe Routt was a star guard of 1936. His play this season showed the improvement that experience brings. A glutton for hard, all-afternoon play, he was at his best when the going was toughest. Routt used a system of stacking up a whole side of the opposing line, thereby breaking up a play and letting someone else make the tackle.

HINKLE—*Center, Vanderbilt*

There was considerable argument about the centers this year—but very little about Carl Hinkle. He was the first man down the field under punts, was magnificent at backing up the line and made more tackles than any other man on his team. He blocked well and was unerring in his knack of calling enemy forward passes and defending against them. As captain, he was brilliant, courageous and tireless.

FRANK—*Quarterback, Yale*

Clinton Frank unquestionably was one of Yale's greatest all-time players. He captained the team, carried the ball, passed, blocked and tackled. Every team that played Yale concentrated on stopping Frank but none succeeded. Dartmouth, with its rugged eight-man line, stopped him on the ground. But it couldn't keep him from pitching passes.

GOLDBERG—*Halfback, Pittsburgh*

Marshall Goldberg leaped into prominence one gray afternoon in Pittsburgh in the 1936 season by running right through the Notre Dame team, not once but several times—and went on from there. He passes and kicks and blocks in the approved Pitt fashion, which is intended not merely to take opponents out but to stretch them out.

WHITE—*Halfback, Colorado*

This year Byron "Whizzer" White, a student leader for three years, hit such a dazzling pace that the Rocky Mountain region regards him as superior even to the practically immortal Dutch Clark, when Dutch was in

207

college. He was the nation's leading scorer. He ran, kicked and passed. As a blocker and tackler he was better than most. The entire Colorado attack was molded around him.

CHAPMAN—*Fullback, California*

Sam Chapman was voted the best football player on the West Coast. He was California's star blocker, best kicker and one of its leading ball carriers. He was a work horse on both offense and defense. He received unanimous support as leading star on one of the nation's strongest teams.

THE SPORTLIGHT

(November 3, 1938)

The Gamest Thoroughbred

Pimlico Racetrack, Md., Nov. 2, 1938—A little horse with the heart of a lion and the flying feet of a gazelle, today proved his place as the gamest thoroughbred that ever raced over an American track. In one of the greatest match races ever run in the ancient history of the turf at 1 3/16 miles, the valiant Seabiscuit not only conquered the great War Admiral, but, beyond this, he ran the beaten son of Man o' War into the dirt and dust of Pimlico.

Head and head around the last far turn, Seabiscuit, ably ridden by George Woolf, beat War Admiral by a full four lengths down the last furlong, with a dazzling burst of speed that not only cracked the heart of the Admiral, but, in addition, broke the track record, which he now holds at 1.56 3/5.

The drama and the melodrama of this match race, held before a record crowd keyed to the highest tension I have ever seen in the sport, set an all-time mark.

You must get the picture from the start to absorb the thrill of this perfect autumn day over a perfect track. As the two thoroughbreds paraded to the post, there was no emotional outburst. The big crowd was too full of tension, the type that locks the human throat.

You looked at the odds flashed upon the mutuel board —War Admiral 1 to 4—Seabiscuit 2 to 1. Even those backing War Admiral, the great majority of the crowd, felt their pity for the son of Hard Tack and Swing On, who had come along the hard way and had churned up the dust of almost every track from the Great Lakes to the Gulf, from the Atlantic to Pacific.

209

After two false walking starts, they were off. But it wasn't the fast flying War Admiral who took the lead. It was Seabiscuit, taking the whip from Woolf, who got the jump. It was Seabiscuit who had a full length lead as they passed the first furlong. The Admiral's supporters were dazed as the Biscuit not only held this lead, but increased the gap to two lengths before they passed the first quarter.

The Biscuit was moving along as smoothly as a Southern breeze. Then the first roar of the big crowd swept over Maryland. The Admiral was moving up. Stride by stride, Man o' War's favorite offspring was closing up the open gap.

The Admiral was under full steam. He cut away a length. He cut away another length, as they came to the half-mile post—and now they were running head and head. The Admiral looked Seabiscuit in the eye at the three-quarters—but Seabiscuit never got the look. He was too busy running, with his shorter, faster stride.

For almost a half mile they ran as one horse, painted against the green, red and orange foliage of a Maryland countryside. They were neck and neck—head and head—nose and nose.

The great Admiral had thrown his challenge. You could see that he expected Seabiscuit to quit and fold up. But Seabiscuit has never been that brand of horse. I had seen him before in two $100,000 races at Santa Anita, boxed out, knocked to his knees, taking the worst of all racing luck—almost everything except facing a firing squad or a machine gun nest—and yet, through all this barrage of trouble, Seabiscuit was always there, challenging at the wire.

So, when War Admiral moved up on even terms, and 40,000 throats poured out their tribute to the Admiral, I still knew that the Biscuit would be alongside at the finish. The Biscuit had come up the hard way. That happens to be the only way worth while. The Admiral had only known the softer years—the softer type of competition.

He had never met before a combination of a grizzly bear and a running fool.

Head and head they came to the mile. There wasn't a short conceded putt between them. It was a question now of the horse that had the heart. Seabiscuit had lost his two-length margin. His velvet had been shot away. He was on his own where all races are won—down the stretch.

He had come to the great kingdom of all sport—the kingdom of heart.

The Admiral had shown his reserve speed. From two lengths away he was now on even terms. But as they passed the mile post with three-sixteenths left—the vital test—the stretch that always tells the story—where 40,-000 looked for the fleet War Admiral to move away—there was another story. Seabiscuit was still hanging on. Seabiscuit hadn't quit. With barely more than a final furlong left, the hard-way son of Hard Tack must have said to the Admiral—"Now let's start running. Let's see who is the better horse."

Foot by foot and yard by yard, Woolf and Seabiscuit started moving away. Charley Kurtsinger gave the Admiral the whip. But you could see from the stands that the Admiral suddenly knew that he had nothing left in heart or feet to match this wild, crazy five-year-old which all his life had known only the uphill, knockdown, devil-take-the-loser route, any track—any distance—any weight —any time.

War Admiral had no answer. Down the final furlong the great-hearted Biscuit put on extra speed. He moved on by. Then he opened a small gap. Forty thousand expected the Admiral to move up. Close the gap again. But the Admiral was through. He had run against too many plow horses and platers in his soft and easy life. He had never tackled a Seabiscuit before.

211

THE SPORTLIGHT

(October 9, 1939)

FOUR IN A ROW

CINCINNATI, Oct. 8,—Cincinnati is now the city of blasted dreams, "where shadows shut the stars out and the dead leaves tumble down." Rushing down the stretch through a gap in the Red defense as wide as the seven seas, the Yankees for the fifth time made it four in a row as they whipped the Reds, 7 to 4, to write another remarkable chapter in world series history.

But this time they had the fourth and final game handed to them on a platter of gold with a platinum crest and a filigree of diamonds. The Red gift to the Yankees, costlier than the gift of the magi, came in the ninth inning, with Cincinnati leading, 4 to 2.

Facing the two-run deficit in the ninth, Charlie Keller, the young series hero, signaled. So did DiMaggio, driving Keller on to third.

It was here that the unkempt fates planted the crown of thorns upon the unlucky brow of Bill Myers, the Red shortstop. Bill Dickey rapped one to Lonnie Frey at second for the easiest, the simplest and surest double play in world series history.

It was the type of double play that could have been handled by an infield combination from an orphan asylum with cramp colic. Frey should have nailed DiMaggio by ten feet at second and Myers should have thrown out Dickey by twenty feet at first. A double play here would have given the Reds their first victory and brought in about $150,000 to Red and Yankee owners for a fifth game.

But Frey hesitated and finally his throw to Myers

212

arrived just ahead of the flying DiMaggio. The ball popped out of Myers's hands for a $150,000 muff as DiMaggio bumped him. Through this raw and mangled gap in the Red defense, the Yankees tied the score at 4 and 4.

The tenth inning was a Red nightmare—an episode that belonged in a roadhouse, or in a tail-end battle for the Fried Chicken League. It was in this inning that the Yankees scored three runs on one lone single as the Reds blew up with a crash that is still rocking Cincinnati's seven hills.

You won't believe what I am telling you—and I don't blame you. But it happened this way—the greatest world series anti-climax I've ever seen in thirty-five years of close inspection.

Frank Crosetti had scored, Keller kept traveling when Goodman fumbled DiMaggio's hit. They whipped the ball to Ernie Lombardi at the plate as big Keller crashed across. Senor Lombardi fell squarely on his broad back. The ball bounded out of his hands and lay at rest two feet from either hand. At this point, DiMaggio was just rounding third. Joe kept on traveling over the intervening ninety feet as Lombardi still lay at rest, a stricken being.

The afternoon was insufferably hot and big Ernie was tired. He could have nailed Keller at the plate by holding the ball. He had no idea that the roving DiMaggio was on his way to the plate. I have an idea Lombardi was muttering to himself a few lines from "The Soldier of the Legion"—"We fought the battle bravely, but, when the game was done, full many a corpse lay ghastly pale beneath the setting sun."

That's about the way it happened.

DiMaggio had turned a single into a round trip without checking his loping stride.

This gives you a faint idea of the greatest world series collapse that I ever saw.

The simplest of all simple double plays—two easy tosses—would have earned the Reds another chance. The Reds had come to the ninth inning without an error.

213

Whereupon they suddenly turned and pumped four rank errors into two innings that gave the Yankees four unearned runs. It was a real catastrophe for Myers and Lombardi, the Reds and more than 32,000 fanatical followers, who had their hearts torn out by the roots. It was a situation loaded with farce and comedy, but it had its full share of heartaches.

THE SPORTLIGHT

(March 1941)

LOS ANGELES, CAL.—The Cubs had a great guy leading them by the name of Gabby Hartnett. A great guy and a great ball player, one of the great catchers of all time.

They have another great guy at the helm in Jimmy Wilson, the odds-on star of the last World Series.

I came to know Jimmy Wilson well in Bradenton, Florida, around 1934.

Early that spring I had a golf and fishing date with a young fellow by the name of Dizzy Dean. We all met that night above the purling Manatee, and Jimmy was there. Someone suggested a rubber of bridge. "Sure, I play bridge," Dizzy said.

"I'll tell you a funny thing about this bum," Wilson told me. "He never played a game of bridge in his life, but still he'd play against Sims and Culbertson for three cents a point, and expect to win."

Ole Diz just sat by and grinned. "I ain't never played before," he said, "but you ain't no Sims or Culbertson either. You're just a catcher. I can make any catcher look good."

The important point is that after Diz had learned what spades, hearts, diamonds and clubs meant, he was about as good as anybody else. Which is no boost for Jimmy and myself.

214

"Yes," Wilson said, "maybe you can make me look good as a catcher, Diz. But at least I made you look good as a human being."

"How's that?" Dean asked.

"I'll tell you, if you've forgotten," Wilson said. "After you had been with the Cardinals a week as a rookie, I kept missing my silk shirts. You landed here a year ago with a fast ball and one shirt. And it wasn't even good cotton. And then suddenly I caught you one day with one of my silk shirts on.

"You know what he said to me?" Wilson said. " 'Listen, Jimmy, you wouldn't want the greatest pitcher that ever lived going around in one shirt all season, would you? I know you're too swell a guy to do a thing like that to a young pitcher who is better than Walter Johnson, Christy Mathewson or Alexander. You know I'm better than those fellows. I jes' knew it would make you feel bad, having to catch me, to have that happen. So I just borrowed one of those silk shirts. It felt good. The only shirts I'd ever worn were made out of alfalfa or maybe no shirts at all.' "

"How many of my shirts did you steal?" Wilson asked.

"Only two," Dizzy said. "They ought to last me for a lifetime, the way I wear 'em, until they fall off."

This is where Jimmy Wilson rose to the true heights of greatness. "I don't think two silk shirts are good enough," he said to Diz, "for a pitcher who is greater than Johnson, Mathewson or Alexander. I've got only one silk shirt left. I think you'd better call around and pick it up, before you grab it anyway. After all, I'm only a catcher handling the great Dean."

"That's the way I feel about it," Dizzy said. "I'll be around tomorrow and pick it up." Which Old Diz did. And then lost the cost of four silk shirts to Wilson playing golf the next day.

It never occurred to Dizzy that anyone could beat him at any game.

He would have played Shakespeare ten dollars Nassau on sonnets, or Shelley twenty dollars Nassau on odes.

215

There was a ball player you won't see again in this lifetime. He may have been a game bird who flew funny —but he always flew.

I saw Jimmy Wilson again, off and on, until we met the day before the last world series in Cincinnati.

"So you'll have to catch most of this series," I said, knowing that big Ernie Lombardi had an ankle bigger than an elephant's instep.

"I couldn't stand up over three innings," Wilson answered. "I've been out of active baseball for two years. I'm over 40 years old and I've been around a long time. I might have gotten in better shape if I'd known five weeks ago I was to be needed. And I wouldn't have been so hot, even then. I'd hate to have to catch a full nine innings now. They'd have to carry me off the field to a hospital. Catching is the toughest job in baseball. I mean both physically and mentally. And I was slipping over three years ago."

Jimmy Wilson had to catch more than three innings. He had to catch more than three games. In one of the hardest of all world series, one that went to the limit of seven games, he had to be a vital factor in six of the seven games played.

He finished each contest completely worn out, too tired and too sore to even move around. His back ached. He could just about lift his right arm. He had incipient charley horses in both legs. He was too tired to sleep at night.

But knowing that the show must go on—that he was the only one even remotely available—he saved the Red cause by one of the gamest exhibitions under heavy pressure I have ever seen in sport.

Jimmy Wilson didn't give Dizzy Dean the shirt off his back. He gave him three shirts off his back.

And he gave the Cincinnati Reds and the National league the hide off his heart.

Which is just a trifle finer fabric than any silk ever manufactured.

216

TARAWA

("The Marines took Tarawa because they were willing to die."—MAJOR-GEN. HOLLAND SMITH)

How could they get to the beachhead, which only the
    dead men knew?
How could they carry the banner, under a flame-swept
    sky?
How could they stand to the beating, before the brigade
    broke through?
They were willing to die.

Facing a point-blank salvo, hearing the final bell,
Storming a surf, white-swirling, meeting death eye to eye,
How could they drive their heartbeats into the maw of
    hell?
They were willing to die.

Never a hope for tomorrow, never the wraith of a chance,
Never a dawn to wait for except where the ghosts drift
    by,
Knowing that night would find them lost to all dreams
    and romance,
They were willing to die.

Here's to the men of Tarawa, who lived through the
    steel and the foam,
Here's to the dead of Tarawa, who wait for our final
    reply.
Here's to the ghosts of Tarawa, who send us this message
    back home:
"We were willing to die."

THE SPORTLIGHT

(August 1944)

THE PRICE ABOVE THE BILLIONS

"They launched an assault from their fox-holes—
We broke it—but paid in good men."—(NEWS ITEM)

We talk about billions we're spending—
Of billions in gold-minted streams.
Of billions to bring the war's ending
And lead us to peace and to dreams.
But here is the story I'm telling
Above all the billions that are—
"We broke through again—but we paid in good men"—
And that is the price of a war.

We talk about money that's flowing
To handle the ten different maps.
We talk of the cash we are blowing
To roll back the Germans and Japs.
But here is the point I am making,
Beyond the last bugle's dim call—
"We broke through again—but we paid in good men"—
And nothing else matters at all.

ANOTHER "THEN AND NOW" YARN

Two or three years ago—time has a habit of passing in a hurry—I saw a football game between Alabama and Georgia in Atlanta. It was a fairly sure touch that the winner would go to the Rose Bowl and bring back $100,000.

As I recall the details, Alabama was leading, 10 to 3, down the stretch. It looked to be Alabama all the way.

218

Then, on Alabama's 38-yard line, with fourth down and twelve yards to go, Frank Sinkwich of Georgia, a Youngstown, Ohio, product, cut loose with a desperation pass.

Alabama knew the pass was coming. At least three Alabama men swept to the goal line to knock down the ball. But a Georgia end made an almost impossible catch with the Crimson Tide all around him. This catch was the vital factor in sending Georgia to the Rose Bowl game.

George Poschner, also from Youngstown, who caught that pass, was a great end. He was the pal Sinkwich brought to Georgia with him. Poschner wasn't supposed to be much as a football player. But it was Poschner who made Sinkwich the star of that game. For, in addition to catching passes, he was tackling all over the field. He was one of the best all-around ends, in that one game, I've seen in a long time.

And then, a day or two ago, I read: "George Poschner in Germany—both legs amputated because of wounds." That's why I figure the billions or the trillions are unimportant compared to what is happening to the greatest bunch of kids this world has ever known. Yes, the older men, the gray beards, the so-called statesmen make wars—

> But, oh, how very young they are,
> Where all the dead men lie.

THE COUNTRY OF YOUTH

This is a young country, and it should be the country of youth. They are the ones who should take charge— not the older men who rarely hear a shot fired in anger. How simple it is for them.

What we need is a sporting program for these 10,000,000 or 12,000,000 service men, which Army and Navy are now arranging, to take up the physical and mental slack. But it happens to be a country run by too

219

many old men who have no idea of the new generation coming on.

Most of these men were smart, in their day and time, and most of them are honest. They simply don't know what it is all about. They know little about the psychology of those between the ages of 18 and 24. And it is those who are taking the big beating. These men more than deserve the major sporting program which Army and Navy are preparing for them, no matter when the war ends.

Three Fathers and Three Sons

Meeting up with Major Christy Mathewson, Jr., heading overseas despite the fact that he has but one leg, recalled again the sharp divergence of three sons from the games that brought their fathers' fame.

The three fathers were Matty, Ty Cobb and Bobby Jones.

"I had only an average fan's interest in baseball," the younger Christy told me, "and my father made no effort of any sort to have me take up baseball. I played basketball, golf and tennis, at none of which I was particularly good. My main interest was always flying and that interest remained as keen as ever even after I cracked up in China and lost a leg.

"I still play some golf, when I get the chance, which isn't often. But under the conditions nine holes are about all I can handle."

In the same way Ty Cobb made no effort to turn young Ty's inclination along baseball lines. Young Ty's interest was all in tennis, where, Bill Tilden once told me, the son of baseball's star had the chance to be one of the best in the game. The older Ty didn't object to tennis as a sport, but he objected violently to the younger Ty traveling around the country, playing in one tournament after another through the summer.

"I am dead against this sort of thing," Ty said.

When the argument developed, the older Ty won out.

In much the same way Bobby Jones made no attempt to interest young Bobby in golf.

"This is something for the kid to decide," Bob said. "Even when young Bob began playing some golf I never tried to give him a lesson or any form of instruction. If a young fellow is keen enough about a game he will find his own way to learn how to play it. I have seen what has happened to too many young golfers under their fathers' ardent instruction. The best way to learn golf is the way younger caddies learn it—by watching the stars play shots, getting the right picture or pattern, and then working at it—the way Hagen, Sarazen, Farrell, Nelson, Hogan and most of the other top players began."

That recalls the fact that, when Bobby was around 7 or 8 years old, he used to follow Stewart Maiden, the East Lake professional, around the course day after day and then slip away to practice for an hour or so. As a result Bobby could break 80 at the age of 10.

"In my opinion golf will be a great game and a great help for the returning wounded," Major Mathewson said. "It is one of the few games you can play with one leg and one arm. A soldier could lose both a leg and an arm and still learn to play pretty fair golf. There have been one-armed players who could shoot in the low 70s, and one-legged players who could do as well."

This is true. For example, there is the case of Ernest Jones, one of the most famous of golf teachers. One of Jones's legs was shot off in the other world war. He returned to his home near St. Andrews, Scotland, and soon went back to golf.

"I had to play on crutches," Ernest said, "as I had no wooden leg at that time. I'd lay my crutches down and try to balance myself on one leg through the swing. My greatest thrill came the day I shot a 73 at St. Andrews. It was in this way that I became impressed with the fact that golf is a swinging game and not a hitting game. If you swing the clubhead your balance remains, even standing on one leg."

"Golf can bring many of these wounded men the exer-

221

cise they need," Mathewson continued. "But above that it will give them something else to think about. It will help to take their minds off their troubles. When you hole a ten-foot putt or when your iron shot stops fairly close to the pin, nothing else matters. I remember dad, who loved golf, used to say that it was tougher to keep on concentrating in golf than in baseball."

The most remarkable golfer I recall is Tommy Mc-Auliffe of Buffalo, both of whose arms were cut off at the shoulders in childhood. He swung the club head with the shaft of his club held between the chin and neck, and often went around under 100.

There have also been cases of men totally blind playing at least fairly well with caddies to show them the right line and estimate the distance for the next shot. One blind Canadian soldier broke 100.

It is good news for many of the wounded to know that limited golf courses are now being built around many hospital centers. There will be a big increase in these helpful layouts later on.

A game that can be played with one arm, one leg, even with no eyes or no arms, that also provides exercise and mental relief, is the ideal rehabilitating sport.

The U.S.G.A. and the P.G.A. have the chance to do a big job.

PART IV

The Typewriter Grows Heavier

In some ways World War II was a rougher go for Granny than the War he'd personally fought in France in 1918. For one thing, a fearful number of the boys he'd covered in various sports—from Tommy Hitchcock on down the age-line—were killed or maimed. At times, writing about the heroes of Sport at home had begun to pall on him.

Then, following the war, he began to notice a new and different trend in sports.

"Sport today," he wrote in 1953, "is much more commercial and much more stereotyped than in my heyday. I doubt if we will ever again have the devil-may-care attitude and spirit of the Golden Twenties, a period of boom, screwballs, and screwball antics. The almighty dollar, or what's left of it, hangs high. A ball player who, when asked to race Mickey Mantle against time before a recent Yankee-Senators night game, replied, 'I'll do it . . . for five hundred dollars,' is testimony to the times."

However, concerning the athlete's ability to excel, right to the end he remained young and enthusiastic when he wrote that the best does not belong to the past; it is with us now. "And even better athletes will be with us on ahead. When we arrive at the top athlete, the Jim Thorpe of the Year 2,000, we should really have something. But by that year I will have slight interest in what the field has to show."

223

THE SPORTLIGHT

(Christmas Eve, 1944)

WHY THE HARD BLOW LANDED ON RACING

It is now easy to understand why the heavy blow of war fell on racing and why it will doubtless fall upon all other big-time sport.

After more than three years of war the discovery was suddenly made that while Germany and Japan were fighting a 100 per cent war, the United States was fighting a 60 per cent war. Entirely too much man power, time, energy, money, gasoline and other needed ingredients have been used up for pleasure and entertainment in place of a 100 per cent concentrated effort by the home front to win the war at the earliest possible date.

Many paid little attention to this problem last summer when it looked as if our winning armies would be in Berlin at an early date. But if anyone thinks the jolt to racing, baseball and football will be heavy, he should think of the incomparable insignificance of such a jolt in connection with the crash that struck two American armies in Germany, Belgium and France.

It took the sudden, unexpected and additional loss of life to wake up our home front—to let it know that 60 per cent was not nearly enough in the way of a winning effort!

After our earlier success in France crowds at the various race tracks began to increase and betting began to take on a growing pace, crowds at baseball games and, later, at football games began setting new records. All of this in the middle of what should have been—and will be—an all-out war.

I have never been able to guess just what part of big-time sport is a morale builder and what part is a morale wrecker. We simply overdid it, a fault that belongs to those at the top as well as those down the line, including the Government, the Army, the Navy and the civilian list.

There was, and is, a place for sport, but not that large a space in the midst of the hardest and most destructive war the world has known.

Until the last few months I found returning service men from many battle fronts, including the wounded, were all out for sport, even on a large scale. But after three years of war's killing pressure—the swiftly growing list of the dead and the wounded, the weary and the battered—I have sensed a strong switch in the other direction.

More and more of the men returning from the various fronts have been asking why such fine athletic speci-mens as so-and-so and his team mates were allowed to play professional baseball or professional football. If clerks and filling station workers could fly planes, carry guns or storm pillboxes, why couldn't noted athletes from 22 to 35 years old at least match the efforts of the non-athletes?

Lately, such questions as these have been increasing in both volume and intensity.

People tried to tell them it was not the fault of the athletes but was due to rulings by medical or draft boards. In the main this was and is, true. The Army and the Navy have been given the right and the power to take and keep any citizen they need between the ages of 18 and 38.

In a big majority of cases the fault has belonged to those in power. It might also surprise thousands if they were told how many 4-F's tried in every way to get into some form of service, only to be rejected by medical boards.

Against this you can also see how a man with one arm or one leg, or families which have lost husbands and brothers, often begin to look with doubt upon fine-looking young athletes dashing from goal to goal or cir-cling the bases in a pennant race. They don't get the angle that while their non-athletic sons and husbands are able to fight in a war these others are not.

There have been, of course, cases of raw chiseling on the part of the athlete. Human nature is still human nature. These chiselers have hurt their own profession. And the fact that thousands of the athletic flock, the pick of the country, have done their full share in fighting and dying is also overlooked.

"Never mind those," they will tell you. "What about these who are not fighting or dying or helping to build guns and planes and ships?"

It isn't always so easy to answer when you see only one arm or one leg. It isn't always possible to give a sane answer to some mother or father whose son is forever sleeping at Leyte or Aachen.

The only answer is a change from a 60 per cent war to a 100 per cent war. There is no better time to start than now in making the new year a winning year.

THE SPORTLIGHT

(March 6, 1946)

THE TRUE DEMOCRACY OF SPORT

ST. PETERSBURG, FLA., March 6—It may be that I am prejudiced. One way or another, everyone is prejudiced. So, completing my forty-fifth year as a sporting writer, it is only natural that I should have a slight leaning in the direction of sport. My recent experience in St. Petersburg has convinced me again that the true democracy in the United States is not to be found among our politicians, our so-called statesmen, our labor union leaders or our capitalists. It is only to be found in sport.

I already have given you the stories of Babe Ruth, Walter Hagen, Billy Burke, Gene Sarazen, Jack Dempsey and others, orphans, caddies or roustabouts, who rose to fame and wealth through their own ability and skill. There is no class distinction, no union or capital protection in sport. Here you are measured by what you are and what you can do. Nothing else counts.

Here is just another example. In the recent open golf tournament at St. Petersburg, with War Bonds as prizes, I was especially interested in two leading amateur contenders. One was Frank Stranahan of Toledo, son of Bob Stranahan, a noted manufacturer and a leading factor in many big financial enterprises.

Here was the representative of wealth, one of the nicest young fellows you'll ever meet. Just out of the Army. A great kid and a fine golfer.

The other amateur was a waiter and bus boy at the hotel where I happen to live. He also was just out of the Army. He is a tall, redheaded kid from Merchantsville, N. J. His name is Al Besselink. He confessed his

227

right wrist was a trifle sore and stiff from carrying break-fast and lunch trays, a new job for him.

Socially and financially, these two were as far apart as the outposts of a Siberian frontier. But they were dead level on the golf course, where both starred. And Besse-link drew even more comment from the gallery than did Stranahan.

Here were two fine young Americans, former serv-ice men, clean and decent and perfectly conditioned, who were to be judged only by their scores. Here was the true democracy, the democracy of ability.

In considering the cases of these two men, Besselink, the waiter, and Stranahan, a rich man's son, hasn't sport something to offer that the labor unions, the capitalists and the politicians have never been able to meet—who is the better man, no matter from what rank of life he may come?

You don't think the labor unions, the capitalists or the politicians ever consider this, do you?

Why shouldn't the fittest, the smartest, the ablest and the gamest lead the parade?

There is nothing revolutionary about this doctrine. It is built upon the soundest of all foundations—the race is to the swift and the battle to the strong, when the race is truly run.

It is only in sport that you get the true records of the recorded deed. How good were you? What did you have to offer? I happen to know that President Truman feels this way about it and others now known as leaders in our national life. At least this is what they have told me. But they all remain reluctant to lead the way.

In sports the record is there for you to see or read. Few of the labor union leaders, the capitalists or the politicians will ever look at the actual facts.

You couldn't get them to understand that in sports Stranahan, son of a millionaire, was on equal terms with Besselink, the waiter and bus boy; that Ruth, the former orphan asylum kid; that Dempsey, the one-time rousta-bout; that Hagen and Sarazen, the former caddies, at 35

228

cents a round, could move into the $50,000 or $100,000 class—just by their own ability.

Among our labor unions our capitalists and our politicians I have discovered that sports offer the only answer. Look to the record—how good are you? Nothing else is important.

Some day the people of the United States will get the same idea. I only hope it isn't too late, for their own good. The day of the fourflusher should be about over. Just look to the record as sport does.

THE SPORTLIGHT

(April 1946)

WHAT MAKES A COMPETITOR?

ST. PETERSBURG, FLA.—Someone had remarked that what made the Cardinals dangerous was their competitive spirit. This was looking back as far as 1926—back to the days of Rogers Hornsby—and includes players like Pepper Martin, Lon Warneke, Ducky Medwick, Terry Moore, Country Slaughter, Dizzy Dean, Frank Frisch and many, many more.

"That's true" Eddie Dyer said. "They give all they have to give, as a rule, and keep hustling to the finish."

That started a bull session as to what makes a great competitor. The discussion soon led up to the name of the late P. Hal Sims.

"Hal Sims," Al Ciuci, the golf professional, said, "has always been my ideal of a great competitor. In the case of Hal, I'd say he had an 85 swing and a 75 game."

"What made him this way? Well, first of all, he had complete confidence in himself. He refused to play any game badly. This included golf, tennis, bridge, pool and billiards—even pistol and rifle shooting.

"He was a man of fine concentration and strong determination. Concentration and determination are two big

229

words in any game. Without them skill looks ordinary.

"I've seen a lot of golfers, including professionals, watch Hal swing and then give him eight or ten strokes. They were looking at an 85 hacker. They wound up against a 75 shooter. They overlooked the fact that from fifty yards away, Sims expected to get down with a chip and a putt—which usually happened."

Some time ago, in a match with Sims, we came to the last green all square. Sims had a putt of at least thirty feet.

"Yesterday," he said, "I holed a putt of this length for $1,500. I'll just imagine this one is for $1,500 instead of $5." He holed the putt.

In another match during a thunderstorm, a stroke of lightning hit the ground with a terrific crash. The lightning struck just when Hal was at the top of his swing. Most of us jumped about two feet. Hal pitched to within three feet of the pin from 120 yards away.

"Didn't you hear that lightning?" someone asked. "What lightning?" Sims replied. His concentration on the shot was so intense that not even a nearby lightning crash could alter the smoothness of his swing.

The answer is that Hal Sims trained his mental attitude not only for playing games, but winning games.

"I can understand that Sims lightning story," Bill Dickey cut in. "When I was at bat, 70,000 people might have been roaring, but I never heard a sound. I was only concentrating on getting a hit."

MUSIAL AND THE CARDINALS

"It was largely competitive spirit that kept us in the race last year," Stan Musial of the St. Louis Cards said. "You see we are not a young club. Kurowski, Pollet, Marion, Brecheen and others came aboard in 1940 or 1943. I landed in 1941. That's quite a while back.

"As a result, several of our men were either sick or hurt. And these injuries came at tough times. For example, last year we had one bad spell with Kurowski out, Marion suffering from a bad back and a few others were laid up as we stepped into a set of three consecutive double headers, four of these games against Brooklyn.

"But things look different now. Kurowski is in fine condition, ready to go. Marion's back is much better. Schoendienst is right again. Our pitchers are much better. I mean in better physical shape.

"I might be crazy, but I honestly believe we can win this pennant by five or six games. Why? Because we have the best ball club in the league. All we'll need is normal luck. In addition to being the best ball club in the league, I'll bank our competitive spirit against that of any other club. We have more experienced players who are not through by any means.

"We literally fought our way to second place last season where another club, with our bad luck, might have eased up and finished fifth. But this Cardinal bunch is a fighting set of ballplayers. I mean on the field. They'll all hustle.

"I know a lot of smart people are picking Boston and Brooklyn," Musial continued. "I still think St. Louis is the team to beat. We'll get much better pitching this season from Munger, Hearn and others. Sure, Eddie Dyer has his problems. What manager hasn't? Maybe at first base and back of the bat? Maybe an outfield job? Don't let anybody tell you that the Braves, Dodgers, Pirates and Giants haven't got even more serious problems.

"I'm banking pretty largely on that argument you started about great competitors. I think we've got our share. We've had 'em for over twenty years.

"Did you know that outside of the Giants in 1933, and the Reds in 1940, with Walters and Derringer, no other club except the Cardinals has won a world series for the National League since 1939? And we've won plenty. How? Competitive spirit, concentration, determination and hustle."

P.S. St. Louis won the pennant in '46 and defeated Boston in the Series.—Ed.

231

THE SPORTLIGHT

(August 21, 1946)

THE PASSING OF HURRY UP YOST

I first knew Fielding (Hurry Up) Yost, Michigan's great football coach, around 1903. This takes quite a nip out of time. Yost was not only one of the greatest coaches football has seen, but one of the most distinctive characters sport has ever known. He was a human volcano, with a tidal wave touch. Hurry Up had a combination of ability and personality that has yet to be surpassed in any field. I mean on the overpowering side.

He started with West Virginia against Lafayette around 1896, stayed over to play with Lafayette, made phenomenal coaching records with Kansas and Nebraska, moved on to Stanford, and then went on to Michigan in 1901, with Willie Heston in tow. Heston was the atom bomb of 1901–1904. From 1901 through 1905, at Michigan, Yost ran up the greatest record in football history.

It is my belief that, in those five years, he had the greatest football machine the game has ever known, and I'm barring no rival. Here was the first of all point-a-minute avalanches that wrecked everything in sight except one 2 to 0 defeat, in five years. And for four years his spark plug was Heston, rated by Yost as the greatest back that ever lived. Yost may have been right. There certainly hasn't been any greater ball carrier.

Heston, weighing 190 pounds, could outsprint Archie Hahn, world sprint champion in those days, for fifty yards. Willie was a human thunderbolt. Against Chicago on a snow-covered field, he jumped two feet over Walter Eckersall, the defending back.

232

With Heston, Boss Weeks, Sweeley, Nell Snow, Gregory, the Hammonds, Curtis, Rheinchilds, Octy Graham, Redden, on and on, Yost had the greatest collegiate material ever assembled on any one field—and Yost got 100 per cent from what they had.

In 1901 Yost took his Michigan team to play Stanford in the first Rose Bowl game.

"I used eleven men in that game," Yost said proudly. "We won, 19 to 0." Even in those days Yost depended largely on speed. He had bulk, but it was speed that counted. His slogan was—"Hurry up, hurry up, hurry up."

Yost was a relentless driver and a killing taskmaster. Football was his religion. But he was the smartest football coach of his time, one of the smartest ever.

Football has known only one Yost, just as it has known only one Rockne.

Right after I met Yost over forty years ago, someone started a football argument. I disagreed with Yost. Before I knew what had happened, a powerful hand was at my throat and it was Dan McGugin, Yost's brother-in-law and Vanderbilt's coach, who came to my rescue. Dan later gave me the soundest advice I've ever known.

"Don't argue or disagree with Fielding," he said. "You can't win."

He might also have added—"And you won't live."

No one ever won a football argument from Yost. Bob Zuppke once got a tie after an Illinois-Michigan game. The two were found together on the field that night at 11 P.M., six hours after the game was over.

Foster Sanford almost got a tie after a Harvard-Yale game that broke up at 9 o'clock the next morning.

Yes, they were vocal giants in those days. And not too bad physically. Yost was six feet two, 210 pounds, raw-boned and almost as gentle as a West Virginia wildcat. He never took a drink, and in place of smoking he chewed up countless stogies, without ever using a match.

Lacking ball carriers, it was Yost who invented his most famous attack—"A punt, a pass and a prayer."

233

Michigan would make four first downs, the other team would make ten first downs, but Michigan would keep winning.

Yost was a master of kicking instruction and kicking strategy. He was one of the first coaches to realize the possibilities of the forward pass, looking back to 1906. He was, at least, one of the first coaches to teach and use the spiral pass. Yost believed in playing out any game to the limit of what you had.

There was the day his trainer called him to the field and pointing to a prostrate player, stretched half unconscious along the turf, said, "This man must come out. He's nearly dead."

"Come out," Yost said. "He's breathing, isn't he?"

If you could still breathe you belonged in a Michigan game.

Next to Heston, Germany Schulz was Yost's leading favorite. Schulz, six feet five, weighing 245 pounds, was the greatest center I ever saw. And I'm barring no modern entry, Mel Hein or Bulldog Turner. Schultz today would be a $25,000 man in the pro ranks. He was faster than most backs you'll see this fall. He was another Cal Hubbard, not as big, but faster.

Fielding H. (Hurry Up) Yost was an amazing contribution to sports. He was, without any debate, the most dynamic personality I ever met. He was a human tidal wave of words and emotional uprisings.

In addition to being a great football coach, you can also add—"He was a great guy."

THE WAY OF THE MOB
THE SPORTLIGHT
(November 10, 1946)

(To Ted Williams, Joe DiMaggio and Eddie Arcaro.)

All you who get the cheering and the plaudits from the
    mob,
Who shrink because they bawl you out upon some off-
    day job,
Who scowl because they call you names that no one
    likes to hear,
Who keep the welkin ringing from the hoarse hoot to the
    cheer,
Who build you up and knock you down, from here to
    kingdom come,
Remember as the game goes on—they never boo a bum.

I've heard them hiss Hans Wagner and I've heard them
    snarl at Cobb,
I've heard them holler "Take him out," with Matty on the
    job.
I've heard them curse when Ruth struck out—or Speaker
    missed a play.
For forty years I've heard them ride the heroes of their
    day.
I've heard their roaring welcome switch to something
    worse than hum,
But Eddie, Ted and Joe, get this—they never boo a bum.

STILL AFTER ARMY

Week after week they are all after Army. Villanova,
Oklahoma, Cornell and then Michigan. Then Columbia.
Now it will be the veteran team that Wallace Wade brings
up from Duke.

Most of the others run two, three and four deep. Army

235

runs less than two deep. Notre Dame runs deeper than all the others, three and four.

But they still can play only eleven men at a time. This is something of a fallacy in this modern game, where they wear out quicker than they ever did in the old days. Maybe the pace is faster. Maybe they are not as rugged as they used to be.

Red Blaik, a fine coach and an old friend, never thought he could go through this 1946 schedule unbeaten. He knew he had the jump in 1944 and 1945. But after 1946 he also knows Army and Navy haven't a chance against the inducements offered all over the map which Army and Navy can't meet.

By inducements I mean something more than scholarships. I mean direct pay which may range from $5,000 to $10,000 a season. This is important to the poorer kids who seem to make the better football players.

It is my belief that after 1946 Army and Navy will fade out of the football picture, as far as winners are concerned.

Sure, they had all the best of it in 1944 and 1945. But 1946 will be different, as Navy already has found out, and Army will find out later on.

It must be admitted that Army and Navy had the breaks in the two war years of 1944 and 1945. But when the war ended, it was a new story. Star football players no longer talked about going to schools where there was strict discipline and no financial help. They became an integral part of the United States—the cash comes first.

This applies to both coaches and players. Unfortunately, the world-wrecking war also tore a heavy gash into sportsmanship, the old idea of a "fair field and no favor, may the best man win."

Sportsmanship is now a word you find in the dictionary.

TO THE LAST OF ALL

"Cowards die many times before their deaths;
The valiant never taste of death but once."
                                        —Shakespeare

Whether it's Heaven—or whether it's Hell—
Or whether it's merely sleep;
Or whether it's Something in Between
Where ghosts of the half-gods creep—

Since it comes but once—and it comes to all—
On the one fixed, certain date—
Why drink of the dregs till the Cup arrives
On the gray date set by Fate?

Is life so dear—are dreams so sure?
Are love and strife so strong,
That one should shrink from the fated step
To a road that is new and long?

The soul—the grave—and the after-trail—
The Mystic River's flow—
How have the living earned their guess
Where only the dead may know?

THE SPORTLIGHT

THE CALL OF THE FAITHFUL

(February 6, 1947)

(Concerning Johnny Mize's drive at Babe Ruth's mark of sixty homers.)

John Mize, spare that mark—do not attain it now.
It shines against the dark, like laurel on the brow.
From long and long ago, we hear the welkin ring
Above the mighty blow that knew Bambino's swing.

John Mize, rap 'em out—but stop at 59.
Keep piling clout on clout—but never cross the line.
Once more from vanished years I hear the sudden roar,
The still remembered cheers, as Babe jogged in to score.

How long ago it seems since Babe lashed at the ball.
The music of lost dreams that lingers over all.
The crash, the smash, the shout, that churned the
    summer air
Keep piling clout on clout—but, Johnny Mize—beware.

THE MYSTIC MARK OF THE BABE'S SIXTY

Twenty years ago Babe Ruth turned in his sixtieth home run in a single season.

Here is a mark that thousands of ballplayers have been swinging at ever since, but only three have seriously challenged. These were Hank Greenberg of the Tigers and Jimmy Foxx of the Athletics, with fifty-eight each, and Hack Wilson of the Cubs with fifty-six.

What the three don't know is that they were halted

238

by the jinx plastered on their robust frames by several million kids, to whom that number sixty has been a shining star in baseball's sky because the Babe put it there.

Just when it began to look as if both Greenberg and Foxx were certain to beat it, star dust, thrown mysteriously by all these kids, got in their batting eyes and they were forced to halt abruptly.

Now big John Mize of the Giants is the latest Ruth challenger for a record season. Big John of the moon-face and the mighty swing will be facing the same jinx. Many thousands of kids would like to see the mauling Mize reach fifty-nine. But not sixty. Especially not sixty-one.

This mysterious kid jinx won't begin to affect Jolting John until he passes the fifty or perhaps the fifty-five point. Then he will feel mysterious forces at work that will turn the baseball into the size of a golf ball. He will find star dust in his batting eye, just as Greenberg and Foxx did. Big John won't quite understand what has happened, but some ten million kids will, as "the prayers of the faithful go up to heaven unceasingly."

Those sixty Babe Ruth home runs, delivered twenty years ago as part of a total cargo of 714—which is beyond anybody's reach unless they use rubber balls and crowd the fences towards the infield—is now a classic number in American sport. It belongs to the greatest power hitter of all time, who was halted only by the 100 to 170 bases on balls handed him each year.

The Babe copied his stance from Joe Jackson. This position is known in golf as the closed stance which, in Babe's left-handed batting posture, meant that his right foot was well in advance of his left. However, Babe's stance was not as pronounced as Shoeless Joe's was, and his feet were planted closer together to give his tremendous body a better chance to work with his hands and arms.

Added to his power was almost perfect co-ordination between mind and muscle, including amazing reflexes. If Ruth had started as an outfielder in 1914 or 1915, when he was a winning pitcher, his home run mark today would have been around 1,000.

No one can question the fact that the ball Babe swung at was far livelier than the pellet Home Run Baker, Ty Cobb, Joe Jackson, Tris Speaker and other hitters had to face before the first war. On the other hand, taking nothing from Johnny Mize, the 1947 National League ball looks to be the liveliest ammunition yet thrown at swinging bats.

In certain places the fences have also been moved in to decrease the home run range.

But this isn't Johnny Mize's fault. He is swinging at the ball that is approved by the National League. He has always been a great power hitter.

The war came along just when Big John was at his prime and after his injury last season few thought he would ever be the same old walloper.

I can't recall a ball club that had such power hitters as Mize, Marshall, W. Cooper and Thomson at this stage of the race—not even Ruth, Gehrig and Meusel. The Giants are now after the old Yankee mark and are quite likely to break it.

Is the home-run business being overdone? Many games have from four to six four-baggers, and many of these are nothing but ordinary outfield flies that happen to catch the shorter ranges.

Club owners have decided that the home run is something the crowd wants, and apparently the 1947 attendance is backing up their judgment. Any number of teams will pass the million mark this season, including Pittsburgh, which has been just above the cellar line. The baseball fan is a rabid animal, and if he thought too many home runs were being hit he would stay away from the parks.

So many puny home runs have cut in heavily on outfielding skill, as the disconsolate athlete stands and watches an easy outfield fly fade over the walls. But if they keep on shortening the fence range, home run records will soon mean nothing at all.

THE SPORTLIGHT

(April 15, 1947)

THE CHANDLER VERDICT

Happy Chandler's verdict in the now famous Durocher-Rickey-MacPhail-Dressen-Parrott case has more than doubled the April oratory of many millions of fans, especially in Brooklyn.

Here is a case in which everybody was wrong, including the Commissioner, who should have stepped into the sorry business long before he was forced to act. Of those involved, Chuck Dressen was the lightest offender. As able a manager as Leo Durocher was, the accumulation of his many offside acts or mistakes finally brought about his downfall.

In our opinion the worst of these mistakes was the lack of active field interest he showed in handling his Dodger squad this spring, when his frequent absences from play and practice were something no manager should have been guilty of with a team like the Cardinals to overtake. These young Brooklyn ballplayers, many of them trying desperately to make the team, needed much more care and attention than Durocher gave them.

It was generally understood, before the Dodgers headed north, that Branch Rickey was looking for another manager, whatever he might happen to say about it. Rickey gave you the idea of handing Durocher more rope, with a noose attached. This was the worst spring training trip any good ball club ever experienced.

Just as Chandler should have acted long before he did, so should Rickey, in place of starting the trouble with his Havana interview concerning MacPhail and gamblers.

There are many who believe that Chandler was entirely

241

too rough on Durocher, compared to the light fines assessed against the Dodger and Yankee ball clubs. A year's suspension for Durocher should have been coupled with drastic punishment for the two who started all the recent trouble, forcing Chandler into some form of action.

Baseball is too big a game, too much a part of our national life, to be treated as Durocher, Rickey and MacPhail have treated it.

The odd turn about this whole bad business is that MacPhail was not shooting at Durocher. I happen to know he was aiming both barrels at Rickey, in the belief that Rickey was trying to frame him on the gambler incident. But, when the charge of buckshot exploded, only a stray pellet grazed Rickey's ear while Durocher caught the full blast.

As a bystander in this case—not an innocent bystander —but still a bystander so far as the MacPhail-Rickey feud was concerned, Durocher's system absorbed most of the ammunition fired.

Durocher, undoubtedly, has been leading with his chin for some time. At this Belshazzerian jamboree, he should have been able to read the writing on the wall some time ago—"Mene, mene, tekel Durocher." But this doesn't alter the fact that if Rickey and MacPhail hadn't collided in March, Durocher would still be the Dodger manager.

Chandler was very unhappy when MacPhail forced the issue. From that point on, it takes no master mind to figure out his philosophy.

Practically everyone was saying or writing that Chandler would mull over the case for a few weeks, and then either forget about it or impose some warning; that the only salvo he would fire would come from a popgun.

"A popgun?" Happy says to himself. "I'll show 'em." So he reaches for a cannon. His system was as full of darts as a bull goaded by a dozen picadors.

In spite of what Dorocher says about Chuck Dressen, Chuck had never been given fair financial treatment by Rickey. He was badly underpaid. If anyone had

242

an excuse, in this weird tangle, it was Dressen. Just why he was socked for a thirty-day suspension, which means more on the money side comparatively than the Dodgers and Yankees have to pay, will remain a mystery.

After the trouble that professional and college football had faced, including gambling and college professionalism, after basketball's scandal, boxing's scandal and racing's troubles, it was to be hoped that baseball, at least, would show a clean page.

This is something that Durocher, Rickey and MacPhail overlooked. They put themselves, their own interests and squabbles, above the good of the game.

This is also something that Happy Chandler should have seen or sensed months ago. The time to put out a fire is when it starts, not to wait until the building is in flames. Durocher should have been called to account some time ago. Rickey and MacPhail should have been squelched weeks ago.

A $2,000 fine means nothing to the Dodger and Yankee bank rolls. But $60,000 and the possible wrecking of a career, under the circumstances involved, is a judgment far out of line. It also imposes a heavy penalty on the new leader chosen and all the Dodger ballplayers who have already received shoddy treatment on the field. This happens to be a queer case, in which everyone involved, including the judge, will be pronounced guilty by the jury of fans—a jury that runs into many millions.

As the late Mr. Gray almost said—

The boast of heraldry, the pomp of power,
  The rush for fame and money to the wire,
Await alike the inevitable hour—
  The paths of glory lead into the mire.

THE SPORTLIGHT

(March 24, 1948)

TRAIL'S END OF GLORY

ST. PETERSBURG, FLA., March 24.—There is a story marching the rounds of Florida today that is beyond all telling. Its setting is deep in tragedy, but its outline is as brilliant as any rim of stars.

It is the story of Babe Ruth, suffering beyond all comprehension, yet valiantly retracing his path of nearly thirty years ago for the good of baseball, for the good of all kids, and for the good of suffering humanity in general—whatever the cause may be.

It is the story of a man who is much greater nearing the trail's end of glory than he ever was hitting his 714 home runs, and giving a vast nation more thrills than any sport has known.

Babe Ruth has been my friend for over thirty years . . . a great guy, set in mammoth proportions of build, heart and appetite, especially when he was starring from 1914 through 1935 in the box, in the field and above all, at bat.

Broken, but not beaten, a relic of the king that was, he is an even greater man today. His head may be bloody—but it remains unbowed.

I have watched his drawn face, wherein anyone could see his inward suffering, as he autographed baseballs and score cards.

Here, in the way of gold and glory, here in the way of continued thrills, is the greatest man sport has ever known. Jack Dempsey? One of the tops. Bobby Jones, Ty Cobb, Tommy Hitchcock, Red Grange, Earl Sande? All great. But the Babe stood alone. He held the throne room and he wore the purple toga because he appealed to more millions, especially to more kids, than all the others put together.

He was Babe Ruth. Recently I've sat and watched him suffer through ball games. His face is drawn. His old bold voice is gone. Physically you wouldn't know him. But the old spirit of sport's all-time top man still carries him along, almost jauntily at times.

The sheer courage of this man is appalling. It more than matches the power and the skill of his home-run days. For here was something I had never seen before —the story of a great star remarching his old paths in agony, with his aching head still held high.

As I recall the shifts and drifts of time, it was back in 1919, just twenty-nine years ago, that I traveled north from Florida with the Giants and the Red Sox.

The Babe had just been launched as a home-run hitter. He had been one of the greatest left-handed pitchers of all time, with an average that still keeps its place around the top. But this was the year that Ed Barrow had picked for Babe's debut among the sluggers.

Back in 1919, the Babe was about as robust as two atomic bombs. He was a young man of mighty appetites and unrestrained desires that were beyond all curbing. He was something the world of sport had never seen or known before. He was something the millions took to their hearts.

Big, rough, gentle, tough, powerful, kindly, generous, natural, profane, he caught the fancy of a world. The United States, Japan, India, England, France, Germany— Oriental and Occidental all knew about Babe Ruth.

Now once again, through Florida's heat, the Babe makes his way . . . St. Petersburg, Tampa, Miami, Clearwater, Sarasota, Bradenton, West Palm Beach, Orlando. I don't believe anyone knows the suffering he has beaten off as he holds his head in two weary hands and bravely waits for the next ordeal.

It would have been so easy—so simple for the Babe to say, "I'm sick and need a rest." For the Babe is sick and he needs a rest. But Ruth won't take a rest. No one today can keep him from visiting a sick kid or a broken or a blind human being. He seems to feel they belong to him—and he belongs to them.

He is taking an incredible physical beating for what the Babe believes to be the general good of the human race. This is true. How many have we like that today in public life, in public office? Just give me one name. Just one.

The Babe knows the "paths of glory lead but to the grave." He has no worry about a grave. His only thought has been that he will travel the few remaining miles for the betterment of the kids, the cripples, the heart-weary and the underprivileged, those who might need help and inspiration, as he once needed such help so badly.

It might be discovered some day that big, rowdy, rough Babe is a much bigger man than a great pitcher or the game's greatest home-run hitter.

If you had only followed him in the gray twilight of his career through Florida, you might have agreed with me that possibly the Babe has done more actual good in this country today than any dozen men you might mention. Or you might make that ten dozen, starting from the top.

There can never be another Babe Ruth. He sits in the twilight of the gods . . . a human being far above anyone we have in public life today.

IT TAKES PLENTY TO WIN
THE TRIPLE CROWN

This is the time of year when we move into that pleasant, thrill-packed month devoted to the Triple Crown. It's the time when racing enthusiasts all over the United States focus their attention on turfdom's most colorful show—the three classic tests for three-year-old thoroughbreds.

The Triple Crown is the term used to describe the Kentucky Derby, the Preakness, and the Belmont Stakes. It's the goal of every breeder to see one of his horses take all three races. But so fierce is the competition that only seven horses have ever been able to do it.

And what horses they were! Sir Barton in 1919, Gallant Fox in 1930, Omaha in 1935, War Admiral in 1937, Whirlaway in 1941, Count Fleet in 1943, and Assault in 1946. That's a roster to stir the memories of any racing fan.

The battle for the Triple Crown opens on May 3 with the running of the Kentucky Derby at Churchill Downs in Kentucky. It shifts to Pimlico, Maryland, on May 10 for the Preakness, and closes with the historic Belmont Stakes on May 31 at Belmont Park, New York.

It's a tough struggle these courageous thoroughbreds are called upon to make. In each of these races the cream of the three-year-old crop is assembled for an all-out effort. Each race is, of course, run over a different track. And, to make it harder, each is at a different distance. The Kentucky Derby is at a mile and a quarter, the Preakness at a mile and three-sixteenths, and the Belmont at a mile and a half. No wonder the list of Triple Crown champions is so small.

Of course, a horse can be the best three-year-old of

any given year and still not wear the Triple Crown. Two of America's greatest thoroughbreds, Man o' War and Exterminator, are examples. Neither was nominated for all three events. Seabiscuit, Stymie, and Armed are other top-flight horses which didn't make the Triple Crown clean-up. The odds against any yearling going on to win these three races are steep, if not prohibitive.

It's always interesting, at this stage of the game, to look at the Triple Crown races from both angles—forward and backward. There are big questions to be answered this month, and there are rich memories of the past to go over and appraise. Right now we're all wondering if 1947 will produce No. 8 in the parade of Triple Crown champions. Meanwhile let's look back over the great races of bygone days.

Colonel Matt Winn's Kentucky Derby is packed with unforgettable moments, going as far back as the victory of Aristides in the first Derby more than seventy years ago. For example, people are always asking me, "Which are the fastest horses that ever ran in the Derby?"

Well, I'd say Johnstown and Count Fleet, both of which had blinding speed. Johnstown, on a fast track, was the swiftest horse I ever saw. He was no good in the mud, but when conditions were favorable he could really move. In 1939 Johnstown won the Derby by ten lengths, running away from the whole field. A week later, on a muddy Pimlico track, this great horse went down to a crushing defeat in the Preakness.

That race is still vivid in my mind. Through the rain and mud, Johnstown broke into a three-length lead, with Challedon in pursuit. Johnstown was racing smoothly until he hit the turn. There his legs seemed to skid apart, and he was through. As Challedon poured it on down the stretch, Johnstown was a badly beaten horse. That's a good example of the part track and weather conditions play in these big races.

For another instance of luck and weather, look back to last year's Kentucky Derby. I'm thinking of the night before the Run for the Roses, when the Main Chance entry headed by Lord Boswell was the hot favorite. King Ranch's Assault, trained by Max Hirsch, had won the Experimental and the Wood Memorial, but was rated an outsider in the Derby.

Assault, on Tuesday, had demonstrated that he had no love for a sloppy, muddy track. He could run over a fast track, and even do well when the turf was slow, but on mud he was not a serious threat. On this Derby eve the rain was beating down over Louisville when I ran into Max Hirsch.

"This will kill us," he told me. "If it keeps on raining we haven't got a chance. If it clears later, and the track is fast, I think we can win it." The rain kept up. Then, toward daybreak, it stopped. The wind came up strong in the morning, and workmen began raking the track. By three o'clock the water was off the track and you could call it fair. I met Hirsch again.

"This isn't perfect for Assault," said Max carefully, "but it gives him a chance."

A little later, as the track continued to dry out, Hirsch told me, "We've got a chance now. A good chance." But the odds on Assault remained 8 to 1, with the popular vote going to the Maine Chance entry. The folks thought Lord Boswell would do it.

When the horses trotted to the post, to the tune of "My Old Kentucky Home," the track was quite dry. Assault, the little horse from Texas, ran away with the race.

All kinds of unpredictables come into the figuring for the big races. Hoop, Jr., six-length winner of the Kentucky Derby in 1945, should have been a shoo-in for the Triple Crown. But Hoop, Jr. was crowded in the Preakness a week later, injured, and forced out of competition.

So many factors must be considered—the horse, the jockey, the track, the distance involved, the weather, and plain ordinary racing luck. You can see what the odds are against any of the 150 horses nominated for the Derby actually whipping home first at Churchill Downs.

Week after week, as the race approaches, the nominated horses begin to drop out. I remember a conver-

249

sation I had a few years ago with the late Colonel E. R. Bradley. We were talking about playing the Winter Book, where attractive odds are given, but where you lose if the horse you select is withdrawn.

"You can name any horse on the list of nominations," the Colonel said, "and I will lay 5-1 that he doesn't even start."

From 150 or more Derby nominees in late February or early March, the parade begins to fall away. By Derby Day usually only 12 or 15 starters are left.

In checking over the possibilities of this year's candidates for the Triple Crown, handicappers had to look over the best two-year-olds of 1946, then survey the early records of these horses in '47. It's a difficult proposition.

Listed among the early favorites were C. V. Whitney's Phalanx; Fervent and Faultless of the Calumet Farm; Maine Chance's Jet Pilot; and Jay Paley's I Will. Also two ex-Bradley horses, Blue Border and Better Value, now owned by Greentree and King Ranch, respectively.

There were lots of other hopefuls. Mrs. John Hertz relied on Owner's Choice, packed with speed but in its early races uncertain over the longer routes. There were U Time and Hubble Bubble from the West, Brabancon, Grand Admiral, Cosmic Bomb, Stepfather, Shim Malone, and on and on. Whitney's First Flight, a brilliant filly, was saved out for later racing.

But from this list—and from the names of others nominated for the Triple Crown events—no one could be sure just which horses would be in shape by Derby Day, when the first leg of racing's three-jeweled diadem is run. I remember how Stagehand, later to win the Santa Anita Derby and the Santa Anita Handicap, broke down a few days before the Derby. Ocean Wave, a Calumet favorite, was removed by trainer Ben Jones only a few hours before the barrier swung open at Churchill Downs.

You have to battle with Fate to get a three-year-old ready to run a mile and a quarter the first week in May. A great two-year-old prospect may easily turn out to be

250

a dud as a three-year-old. And, of course, a strictly average two-year-old such as Assault was in 1945 may turn out to be an equine motorcycle a year later.

Maybe that's why the Triple Crown races have captured the public imagination so firmly. They're unpredictable, exciting, and fiercely contested. No horse runs for exercise in one of these races. Every horse on the track—and every jockey—is giving all he's got every second.

Derby Day in Louisville starts it off. Rich in tradition and sentiment, the Kentucky Derby provides a fitting beginning to the classic series of three races. You have to be there to know the feeling that grips the gigantic crowd when the band plays "My Old Kentucky Home."

As soon as the Derby winner flashes under the wire and his name is telegraphed around the world, racing fans everywhere begin to speculate on his chances of copping the next two legs of the Triple Crown. Part of the answer is supplied the following Saturday, when most of the same horses race around the Pimlico track in Maryland in quest of the Preakness glory. If the Derby winner repeats, excitement reaches a fever pitch in racing circles.

Can he make it three in a row?

The Belmont Stakes supplies the final answer. Rested for three weeks, the three-year-old aces face the barrier in the beautiful New York track. It's a rugged distance for a three-year-old, this mile and a half gallop. It takes a good horse to win the Belmont. Man o' War won it, and so did Sir Barton and Whirlaway and Gray Lag. So did Twenty Grand, Zev, Omaha, Gallant Fox. The list is long, and few flashes-in-the-pan are on it.

What qualities does a horse need to take the Triple Crown, or even one-third of it? First of all the horse must have speed and stamina.

A horse may have the early starting speed to roar into the front and stay there, after the manner of Johnstown and Count Fleet. Or he may be the type to uncork one long, killing run down the stretch in the style of

251

Whirlaway and Assault. Such a final thrust against tiring leaders is always spectacular. The fans love it.

In order to win, a three-year-old must be able to carry 126 pounds, which is hard work when the horse is running more than a mile. And, along with speed and endurance, no matter how well he is trained or how ably he is ridden, the thoroughbred must be dead game. He's got to be the kind of horse of which a jockey will say after the race, "I knew he wanted to run. I just let him go."

It's still too early, as I write this, to tell which horses will put the excitement in the Triple Crown races this year. Maybe some speed horses, like Owner's Choice, will suddenly find the necessary stamina. Maybe some sturdy distance-runners will come up with the speed they have hitherto lacked.

The old adage claims that difference of opinion is what makes horse-races. I don't disagree. To my mind, horse-racing is the greatest guessing-game in sport. And who would want to change it?

THE SPORTLIGHT

(March 24, 1949)

Song of the Everglades

Fang and fin and feather, with the deadly claw around,
Beauty born of jungle and the baying of a hound,
Rattlesnake and ibis, coral snake and crane,
A spot of savage beauty plus a growth of thrills and pain.

Flower land and swamp land—far beyond all words,
Venom from the rattlesnake and songs from countless
    birds—
The egret and the moccasin all share the evening star,
To prove that in the jungle there is never thought of war.

Here is every blend of life that man can ever know,
Poison plus the flaming where the jungle flowers grow,
Fang and claw and orchids where the stately herons sail,
To prove that death and beauty ride together on the
    trail.

Sport's Last Frontier

The Everglades, Fla., March 24.—So far as natural
wildness goes—water and land—swamp and river—jungle
and almost every variety of fish and animal life—the
Everglades' 10,000 square miles remains as sport's last
frontier in this country. In addition to an incredible
spread of bird life, almost every form of fish, and both
bear and deer, are abundant.

The black bear here adds up to 400 pounds or more.
In addition to this there is another wild animal you can
see now and then. You can label him panther or puma—
the Florida form of the cougar or mountain lion. He is a

253

tawny entry, weighing around 170 pounds and close to nine feet from nose to tail tip.

There are sections packed with wildcat, forty pounds of fury in fight.

In one day's fishing I have seen a single boat bring in from twelve to fifteen varieties of fish—tarpon, trout, grouper, red snapper, amberjack, mackerel, pompano, on and on.

In the mangrove district one who doesn't know the Everglades can get lost in five minutes in the winding twisting inland bay, where every mangrove swamp looks exactly the same. And here, of course, is the alligator, who can range up to ten or twleve feet and possibly boast a living heritage that goes back to the days of Columbus.

Here also you find the four varieties of the country's only real poisonous snakes—rattlesnake, coral, moccasin and copperhead.

The rattlesnake belongs to the viper or blood poisoning family, while the coral belongs to the cobra or nerve-attacking breed. The rattlesnake limit in length is around seven feet. The seven-footers are almost as thick as a man's thigh and they carry a punch that Joe Louis might envy, with more than an inch of fang dropping venom. Coral snake poison is more deadly than rattlesnake poison, only there isn't so much of it, as the coral, with bands of gold, black and red, rarely grows beyond three feet.

The rattlesnake is at least sportsman enough to sound a warning at man's approach with a whirr of rattles that indicate hostile territory. These big ones can drive through a cavalry boot.

Major Louie Beard, general manager of Greentree and the Whitney interests, once made this test, not wearing the boot, however.

"This rattler not only pierced the thick leather of the boot," the major said, "but he also knocked it out of my hand."

This desolate but also beautiful jungle is the home of

the fin, fang, feather and claw. With its egrets, herons, cranes, ibises—enough to tax even the memory of Johnny Kieran—it is a birdland paradise.

I forgot to mention the sawfish, twenty feet long, with a sawbone attachment of some six feet. Also the giant ray, which can look bigger than two boats. Also 400-pound turtles, which come in from the sea.

But the gamest animal I've seen in this corral of beautiful desolation is the Florida hound dog.

They'll tell you a pit bulldog is the last word in gameness—or perhaps a wolverine. That may be true. But I doubt that even a pit bulldog or a wolverine would deliberately charge a 400-pound bear or a brown panther, at least the size of a great dane.

The Florida hound dog is a true fighter, caring nothing for the odds against him. He can be outmatched by more than 380 pounds and yet move into action. He can be hurt and crippled and yet limp back into battle.

The hound is a dead game fellow, so when you call anyone a hound, at least from the Florida species, you are handing him a healthy compliment. He may not be too smart in some ways, since I have even seen him attack a coiled rattler. This is never smart business. But the Florida hound dog doesn't seem to care—as long as there is something in front of him he doesn't like.

The human species in the Everglades are the unconquered Seminole Indians, the one tribe that never surrendered to the power and might of our Uncle Sam. You may remember the old lines—sung by the Seminoles:

"Blaze with your serried columns—we will not bend the
    knee—
The shackle ne'er again shall bind the arm that now is
    free."

The Seminoles haven't any particular affection or admiration or respect for either the white or the black race. It may be they know something. Any Seminole girl caught talking to a white man is ostracized by the tribe.

255

THE SPORTLIGHT
(May 7, 1949)

THE RABBIT BALL—AND CONTROL

It has remained for a young rookie pitcher to call a check on your reporter and also enter what is perhaps a well-deserved rebuke. This rookie pitcher is smart—and what is more important—he also can pitch. Up to $100,000 was offered for his services in the box.

"You write," he said, "that Johnson, Walsh, Alexander, Matty and others pitched around 400 innings. Or more. That's right. You also write that no modern pitcher can work 300 innings. Most of the good ones are 250-inning pitchers. That's right, too. But don't forget those old pitchers were throwing a half-dead ball—a spit ball—a fuzzed-up ball—a logy ball that Samson couldn't hit out of a bandbox park.

"Check back with me. Home-run Baker hit twelve home runs in one year, and was promptly labeled Home-run Baker. Here is the king of all home-run hitters. He smashes twelve four-baggers in one season and he is the king. Why, today some of these bums I'm throwing at might pile up twelve home runs in two weeks.

"I'm telling you," he continued, "that today we are throwing bombs to the plate. Every ball we throw is loaded with dynamite. You can take a broom and hit one for three bases.

"You remember those old Yankees headed by Ruth and Gehrig? They set a home-run record that would never be broken, and they were swinging at a rabbit ball. Last year the Giants came along and made those Ruth-Gehrig Yankees look like duffers. They were hammering at a rubber ball, even faster than the one Babe and Gehrig swung at.

256

"To show the difference, if Ruth were playing in the day of Home-run Baker, his top would have been twenty home runs a season."

Which reminds me that I ran into Larry Lajoie a few years after he had quit, and the lively ball had come into us. Larry played in an old-timers game.

"I'm glad," he said, "we didn't have this modern ball when I played."

"Why?" I asked.

"Because," Larry said, "I'd have killed fifty infielders and over sixty people outside the park."

But not even the lashing Larry Lajoie could hit for distance with Babe Ruth. No one could hit with the Babe—not for distance.

Babe once told me a story concerning the shot he called over the centerfield fence in the famous Cub world-series of '32. "A fellow brought it to me after the game," Babe said. "How was it?" I asked him. "A little lopsided," Babe said. "It was knocked out of shape."

The modern ball undoubtedly has put heavy pressure on all the pitchers. The 1948 ball will travel 100 feet farther than the 1910 or 1912 baseball. At least thirty yards or more.

As my young pitcher correspondent puts it: "You don't dare give just a fair hitter one right over the middle. They say we can't hit the plate. We are not shooting at the plate. We are trying to cut a corner—outside or inside by an inch or two. Usually a ball just above the knee. We can't afford to let anybody get a solid sock at the ball.

"I'll say again that no pitcher from the old days, pitching this 1948 model ball, could have won thirty games. Well, Johnson might have blazed them by the bats, and Alexander might have tied them up with his control, but no one else. If Feller and Blackwell and Newhouser can't win thirty games, neither could the others."

It is easy enough to be wrong, but those old-time pitchers, in our opinion, were facing more real hitters. You don't find many hitters like Ted Williams and Joe DiMaggio today. But the old-timers had to face Cobb,

Crawford, Veach, Jackson, Speaker, Wagner, Hornsby, Terry, Lajoie, Collins, Heilmann, Ruth and others.

If I had been a pitcher around 1912 I would not have enjoyed throwing a ball at those fellows—especially Shoeless Joe. As a poet wrote: "O, the brave song his black bat sang."

In spite of all this, I'd rather see these young modern pitchers take a chance on the home-run ball than the bases-on-balls effort. Nothing is as deadly dull—nothing is more costly—than to see a pitcher dishing up one free pass after another, filling the bases, forcing in runs or leaving his team where a single hit can practically wreck the game.

THE SPORTLIGHT

(January 9, 1950)

JACK DEMPSEY'S GREATEST THRILL

BEVERLY HILLS, CALIF., Jan. 9—"No, my greatest thrill," Jack Dempsey said, "was not climbing back into the ring with Firpo. I was too dizzy at that time, anyway. I could see about four Firpos when I got back inside the ropes.

"My big thrill came in my fight with Jess Willard. The morning of the fight Jack Kearns came to me and asked, 'Can you stop this bum in a round?' 'No,' I said, 'I can't stop him in a round. I'm weighing 183 and he's weighing around 260. But I'll knock him out.'

" 'You'd better knock him out in the first round,' Kearns said.

" 'Why the first round?' I asked him.

" 'Because,' Doc said, 'I just bet $10,000 against $100,000 that you'd stop him in the first round.'

" 'You must be crazy,' I said. 'We're only getting $17,500 for the fight. That means we'll only get $7500.'

" 'No, it doesn't,' Kearns said. 'It means we'll collect $117,500. You can punch off his head in a round.'

"That was the spot I was in," Dempsey continued, "when I stepped into the ring that day in Toledo, 31 years ago. I looked at Willard and he looked like two mountains. I knew I couldn't afford to rush in and start punching. He had a right hand cocked for a right-hand uppercut and he could punch. I figured the best way was to take my time, circle him, and wait for an opening. That took about 45 seconds. When I nailed him with my first good punch and he dropped, I could taste my share of the bet. I must have knocked him down seven or eight times. I never saw any fighter take a worse

259

beating. But he kept getting up. I finally caught him right and he fell again and was counted out. The referee lifted my hand. I was champion. More important, I had just won myself $50,000 in three minutes.

"I left the ring. I'll never know again a thrill like the one I felt when I started away. Well, the thrill didn't last long. They claimed the bell had ended the round seven seconds too soon and Ollie Pecord, the referee, had not heard it. They forgot that I had won my bet when Pecord counted out Willard and had lifted my hand. In addition, Willard had taken such a terrific beating that the fight should have been stopped in the first round. He was reeling all over the ring, unable to defend himself."

What Dempsey says is true. He actually knocked out Jess Willard in the first round at Toledo where an incompetent set of officials cost him and Kearns $100,000. They drew down $7500 in place of $117,500 for the fight.

"Only the few who knew what I had been up against in earlier days knew what that $50,00 jolt meant," Dempsey continued. "My earlier days had been tough ones. For example, I had been Carl Morris' sparring partner. I was getting $1 a day for mixing with this 240-pound giant who could get pretty rough.

"I remember once when we had lunch together I had 30 cents left. The lunch was 15 cents. So I said to Carl I'll pay for us both, figuring he'd have to buy the dinner, which cost more. Maybe 40 cents. But Morris said no, he liked to pay for his own food. I had to eat a 15-cent dinner that night. Later his fight was called off and I never got paid. So I left for Los Angeles. Morris shipped me my grip with the few things I had. But he sent it collect. It cost 75 cents and I didn't have a dime. It took me a day to borrow the 75 cents. We were matched later and I bawled him out.

" 'You knew I didn't have a quarter,' I told him. 'Just for that I'm going to knock you out.' We fought four rounds only. But a short time later I caught him in Buffalo. I stopped him."

260

It might be mentioned at that time that Jack weighed 168 and Carl Morris weighed 238. So spotting an opponent 60 or 70 pounds was nothing new to Jack.

"It was tough getting matches then," Jack said. "I had been a sparring partner for Bill Brennan, a good fighter and a fine fellow. I tried to get Bill to give me a match. Bill laughed. He couldn't see his small sparring mate drawing a crowd. But finally we were matched.

" 'I know you'll understand,' Brennan said. 'I've got to knock you out because I'm on my way to fight for the championship. I hate to do this to you, but that's the way it has to be.'

"That crack made me sore. 'It's the other way around, Bill,' I said. 'I'm going to knock you out.' Bill thought that was a fine joke. I only weighed 170 pounds then. But I finally nailed him in the seventh and down he went with a broken ankle, out cold. That fight gave me my first big lift—that and the Morris fight together. I guess the thing that clinched it was the Fred Fulton scrap that lasted 17 seconds."

THE SPORTLIGHT

(January 10, 1950)

THE GAMECOCK CARRIES ON

RIVIERA COUNTRY CLUB, LOS ANGELES, Jan. 10—Ben Hogan today continued his great battle with destiny in the third round of the Los Angeles Open as, on wobbly legs, he made a desperate assault on Jerry Barber's five-stroke lead.

Drenched to the skin and completely worn out the day before when play was called off, Hogan went out in 32 —three under par—yesterday to cut Barber's lead to one lonely stroke.

Texas Ben, followed by an enormous gallery that literally prayed for every putt he hit, was only one stroke back of Barber through the 13th hole. But here the same old handicap rose up as an extra hazard. His battered legs began to give way, just as they had done on opening day. They took on an extra wobble when he bogeyed on both the 14th and 15th holes, to drop three strokes behind.

But, to show the dead gameness of this little Texan, in place of weakening at the 16th, Hogan dropped his putt for a birdie to stick only two strokes off the pace.

It was a magnificent exhibition of raw courage and golfing skill. Hogan's drives again were long and straight and his magnificent irons were covering the pin all through his first-round 32. But even when in trouble on the second round, Ben remained cool and unworried.

From the crowd of 10,000 at least 6,000 were pounding the soggy fairways after Hogan, the walking ghost. His sudden dash back into action with bandaged legs and various broken bones that have only recently mended will be one of the star sport stories of 1950, no matter what takes place later on.

Meanwhile, young Jack Burke from White Plains, N.Y., charged into a tie for third place at 212—just three strokes back of Barber.

Barber, Hogan and Burke are the three leaders as little Ben shoots for one of sports' all-time miracles this afternoon. Hogan is in second place at 211—two under par for 54 holes.

If Hogan wins, this rugged Riviera Club will be taken apart by the wrought-up camp followers of the finest product Texas has ever given to sport.

As Johnny Farrell smartly remarked one day—"We drive for pleasure—but we putt for money." The former Open golf champion called the turn.

I have been in close pursuit of various golfers in the 1950 L.A. Open for the last four days, all after at least a part of the $15,000 that will go to some 15 competitors. Most of these have good long games. But they absorb most of the suffering around the greens, from the tricky chip shot and the long 40- or 50-foot approach putt up to the two-footers that bring in their share of chills.

The greens out here slope to the sea and they have slippery, unseen breaks that just carry the ball across the lip of the cup into the tin itself. A two-foot putt can be quite troublesome at Riviera, as Sammy Snead has often discovered.

Ben Hogan has always been a fine short-game player. You hear of his long straight drives and his fine long irons, but don't forget he can also chip and putt.

Whether putting is an art or a science is still a highly debated matter. I have seen in the last few years no putters who compared to Walter J. Travis, Jerry Travers, Bobby Jones, Walter Hagen and Horton Smith.

Each had a different putting method. With Travis, a great putter, the right hand was in control. With Jones the left hand predominated. Horton Smith kept his feet well apart on the longer putts and then gradually brought them together as the length of the putt lessened.

263

I like Hogan's method. Ben knows that any number of shorter putts are missed by knee and body action. It was Jones' opinion and it is Hogan's belief that the body should be quite still. This isn't true on the longer approach putts, where greater looseness can be used.

But if you used to watch Bobby or you still watch Ben, you will see that Ben locks his legs and body before starting his stroke on any putt from two to ten feet. The test here is merely a matter of hand and wrist action. Hand and wrist are easier to control than hands, wrists, legs and body.

There is always extra tension in the short game. In driving and the long irons you have yards in the matter of leeway. But in the chip shot and the long putt you have only a foot or two and in the shorter putt you have less than an inch. So the tendency is to tighten up and to hurry the stroke. This results in shortening the backstroke.

Jones and Hogan have both been great believers in finishing the backstroke smoothly and without any hurry. They let it float back. And there is no hurried jab in the forward stroke.

"Smoothness is the main factor," Hogan tells you. "Smoothness and ease. You just can't afford to tighten up on the short game where a delicate touch is all that is needed. You need full control of your hands and wrists —and also full control of your nerves. I suppose nerve control starts with the brain. I wouldn't know. But they are mixed together. The main idea is to keep calm, cool and relaxed."

THE SPORTLIGHT
(January 24, 1950)

THEY KEEP ARCARO BUSY

ARCADIA, CALIF., Jan. 24—"They certainly keep me on the hot spot out here." The speaker was a slender, well-built fellow with dark hair and keen eyes. His name is Eddie Arcaro, one of the great jockeys of all time.

"Last year," he said, "I came out here to battle Johnny Longden. Johnny holds all the American riding records for winners. Before I knew it a 17-year-old kid named Gordon Glisson came tearing at me to lead all the jockeys in 1949. Longden and I had a great duel, but neither of us could keep up with Glisson. This kid could ride. For that matter he can still ride with anybody I've seen. What makes him so good? Coolness in tight spots— using his eyes and head all the time—sound judgment, a fine pair of hands, big and strong with the right touch.

"I came back here to Santa Anita again to tackle Longden and Glisson and what happens? Both are still on hand, riding as well as ever. And then I bump into two more of these apprentice wonders. A fellow by the name of Shoemaker bumps into the picture and another one by the name of Glen Lasswell. They are as tough as Glisson. Both are fine young riders who are likely to beat you any time. They know how to get a horse to the wire, which is the main part of a jockey's job.

"I feel fine," Arcaro continued, "and I've got a hunch this will be one of the most interesting racing seasons in years. We've got a good bunch of two-year-olds and three-year-olds coming along and the Derby, Preakness and Belmont races in the spring should be sharply fought. For that matter we've got enough big stuff here— the $100,000 Maturity on Jan. 28; the $50,000 San

265

Antonio Handicap in which Citation goes Feb. 11; the $100,000 Santa Anita Derby on Feb. 18 and the Santa Anita Handicap Feb. 25. There's a bundle of $350,000 to shoot at in less than a month.

"There are a lot of fine horses out here but it will be quite a battle to handle that Calumet charge—Citation, Ponder, Two Lea, Sunlit and six or eight more. This is a tough Calumet section Jimmy Jones has, but I guess they can all be beaten."

Arcaro got a big jump on the field but Shoemaker, Glisson, Longden and Lasswell soon moved up and they are now in one of the wildest jockey tangles of many winters.

THE CASE OF BLACKWELL

Out in the neck of the eucalyptus woods, one of baseball's leading tragedies took place. There is some hope this season that the tragedy might be turned into melodrama, similar to the stories of Ben Hogan and Citation.

The party of the first part is a tall, lean beanpole pitcher by the name of Ewell Blackwell. Three years ago, Blackwell was the best pitcher in baseball, barring nobody at all. He pitched a no-hitter with the Reds and two or three days later pitched eight innings of another no-hitter.

Standing 6 feet 6, as thin as a drink of water, Blackwell not only had rare stuff in the way of speed, curves and control, but he also had the best delivery in baseball.

"He is the only pitcher I know," Hal Newhouser said, "who hides the ball four times and shows you the ball four times. That is, you see it, the ball disappears, then you see it again. No wonder the batter gets cockeyed trying to follow that ball. Then suddenly Blackwell turns the ball loose and it's on you before you can move a bat."

Hal Newhouser is one of those pitchers always trying to improve himself. There isn't a ballplayer in either league who studies the game and the playing of the game with deeper concentration. Ewell Blackwell was a marvel to Newhouser.

Another National League hitter described Blackwell as a tall tree falling on you just before you swing. Anyway, the Red sapling was a great pitcher and his illness practically wrecked the Reds. He had a kidney infection last winter and suffered a serious operation, which left him helpless most of last year.

But now the tall Red is making a strong comeback. He is up above 190 pounds again and is sure his arm will be in shape to reach the 20 winning class. The Reds have a pretty fair ball club—or they would have with Blackwell back. They still need pitchers more than any club in their league and the return of the Human Eucalyptus Tree would be a big help in the 1950 battle to emerge from the cellar. With the Yankees, Dodgers, Red Sox and others all looking for another starting pitcher, you can figure what Blackwell will mean to the Reds of 1950.

THE SPORTLIGHT

(January 25, 1950)

The Double Battle

BEVERLY HILLS, CALIF., Jan. 25—Mickey Walker, the Toy Bull Dog of other years, had just laid aside his brush, canvas, easel and whatever else goes with painting a picture.

For Mickey, the embattled welterweight who fought such heavyweights as Jack Sharkey and Max Schmeling, has been an artist for some time. Mickey even paints "moods" and "illusions" as well as landscapes and seascapes. But a big part of his heart still belongs to the rosin.

It has been just eleven years since Mickey absorbed anything resembling alcohol, which is a good, solid seat on the Good Old Cart.

"My biggest thrill," he said, "well, I guess it was an evening I spent with a fellow by the name of Harry Greb. It was a long evening, starting in the ring around 10 o'clock and winding up around daybreak.

"I'd heard Greb hadn't been training right. In fact he staged a visit to a restaurant I was in, staggering a little. It was an act. I was sure I could beat him. He was just as sure he could beat me. I knew after the first minute of the first round that I was in for a stormy night. Greb was in perfect condition. His act had been phony. I was never in better shape. He almost knocked me out in the second round. I almost stopped him in the third. But he was a dead game guy and he could take it. Ask Gene Tunney. Neither one of us wasted two seconds. We threw all the punches we carried and I knew Greb carried a lot. He was fast and strong and rough. He was only a dangerous puncher when he got tired and quit

268

moving around. Then he could hurt you. I was in at 148 and Greb was around 160. He had too much for me. I knew by the twelfth round that I had little chance to win. But we kept on punching to the final bell.

"It was a great fight," Mickey said. "But I liked our next fight better, that same night. I lost the first one and I think I won the second. I'll tell you about that one."

"After the fight Doc Kearns and I dropped into Duffey's Old Tavern. I heard someone call my name. It was Greb. So I went over and sat with his gang. Later on they all left us, leaving only Harry and myself. By that time my right eye was closed tight and badly swollen. We became friends and the ale we drank didn't hurt us any.

"Finally about 3 A.M. we decided to look up another tavern. As we got to the door I said to Greb—'Say, if you hadn't closed my right eye I could have licked you.'

"Greb turned on me with a snarl. I thought he was going to bite me. 'Say,' he said, 'you couldn't lick me if I cut off both arms.'

"Now," Mickey said, "we had just fought before a packed house at Yankee Stadium at plenty dollars a seat. We had just been paid very big money. And here we were heading for another fight with just three spectators who were paying nothing.

" 'Come on,' Greb said, 'let's fight it out here.' He started taking off his coat. As he got the coat about halfway off, which locked up or tied up both arms, I nailed him on the chin with everything I had. It was a nectarine, full of juice. Greb spun and crashed into the side of a car so hard he dented the running board. I never threw a harder punch and he was wide open.

"I guess I was lucky. You couldn't kill Greb with an axe. He bounded back from the car and started for me, when a pair of cops arrived. Our three no-pay spectators were still there. They shoved me in one cab and Harry in another.

"Greb was a great fellow. I never liked anyone better. The next day Tex Rickard sent for us. He offered us

$100,000 each for a return match. Now $100,000 isn't goulash. But Greb turned to me and said—'Mickey, there are too many guys around I can beat easier than I can beat you. I like the easy dough. I can make just as much fighting them. Besides, I happen to like you. I wouldn't get any fun punching you. Besides, the little guys bother me. You and Tiger Flowers. I like the heavyweights.'

" 'I feel the same way,' I said to Greb. 'One hundred grand is a lot of cash, but there must be easier ways to make it. And I don't get any fun swinging at you.' So we turned down Tex Rickard's $200,000 offer and Tex could never understand why.

"I'll tell you about Greb. He was a great guy. He was a great fighter and one of the gamest men I ever met. And don't believe all those stories about his being out of condition. He fought himself into shape. No man could travel 15 rounds at top speed and be out of shape. He had superb skill and the heart of two lions. I've seen Greb go faster and harder in the 15th round than he did in the first. He liked to upset Broadway gamblers by faking a drunk now and then. But when you went out to meet him you got a shock. You knew you were in the ring with a trained athlete, ready to go the route."

OPEN LETTER TO A COLLEGE PRESIDENT

*The troubling subject of football recruiting is the reason behind this impassioned plea from the Dean of U.S. sportswriters to the men who run our universities. Stripping aside all the phony phrases that blanket the problem, he says the mixed-up situation shrieks for action if the game is to be saved from extinction.—*ED FITZGERALD

*   *   *

College football, as you must know, Mr. College President, is now trying desperately hard to return to a saner path than it has known for many, many years.

It is trying to break away from the deep, tangled wildwood of professionalism and deception and hypocrisy into cleaner country through the aid of an NCAA committee headed by the able Prof. Hugh Willett of Southern California. It is my opinion, and the opinion of many others, that no such effort would be needed today if you and your fellow college presidents had met the issue years ago and handled it sanely and firmly instead of turning football over to your coaches, graduate managers, and alumni.

You must have sensed that football's fanatical fervor, its demand for victory, was something far different from baseball, crew, basketball, track and field, or any other college sport. Just why football should have been nominated by the student bodies, alumni, and public at large as the one game to establish a national college ranking is anybody's guess, since football requires neither more skill nor courage than several other sports.

271

However, it must have been easy to see years ago just what the trend was and to understand that under such terrific competition, things must continue to grow worse. Yet, with one or two exceptions (like Dr. John Hannah, president of Michigan State) you were largely responsible for letting the situation get out of hand.

In the beginning, the coaches and the alumni created the semi-professionalism, the proselyting, and the recruiting. But when the demand for victory became so insistent that coaches had to act as athletic salesmen and recruiters or facing a flaming blast if they failed to win, they looked to you in vain for help. The alumni, older men living in the past, groping for their lost youth, practically took over college football.

Great stadia, seating from 50,000 to 105,000, began to spring up in front of your eyes. $1 tickets turned into $5 and $6 tickets. Single games began to draw $400,000 or $500,000—this for an amateur sport supposed to be a minor part of college life!

Since only 50 players out of 10,000 or 15,000 students, less than half of one per cent, had any chance to make the team, the physical development part was numerically unimportant. Certainly no game could look to be strictly amateur to a college player when he began to count up the immense sums realized largely through his ability to crash a line, throw a pass, run around end, or make a tackle. Being normal human beings, many of these young men naturally wanted their share of the swag. And more than a few got paid—up to $10,000 a year.

Prove it? The deals were made too secretly and too craftily to become public. But I can assure you that more than a few grid stars have told me later just what they were paid, and it was just about the same amount they would have received from the Chicago Bears or the New York Giants.

Alumni groups began collecting funds for their football teams. Some of these were advertised in the newspapers. Just recently, one leading coach told me this: "How can I compete with so-and-so? They have $150,000 to spend. I only have $80,000." Since then, his fund reached $150,000, and he had a winning team last fall. You, Mr. College President, should have known about these conditions. You should have known that under the lashing of angry alumni, your coach had to be part of the winning-team plan.

I believe that you, in your official capacity as head of your college, should have looked over your football roster to ask: "Why is it that nearly half or more than half of our squad has come to us from locations 1,000 or 2,000 miles away? Why did so many good football players seek us out to get their education? What new courses have we that they need and want so badly that they can't find at larger universities nearer home?" How many of you can honestly say that you have carefully investigated this part of football's buildup?

This practice isn't universal, of course. I know that such places as the University of Missouri, the University of Nebraska, and many Texas colleges have players largely from their own home state, and rarely go outside. But I know of others who get 60 or 70 per cent of their star players from far-off locations, indicating a marvelous recruiting system with plenty of financial inducements.

I have been reading lately statements by many college presidents that, as far as they know, their alumni have given their players no financial aid. In too many cases, "as far as they know" is about as far as a midget can throw an elephant. I think only a few college presidents helped to develop this football tidal wave. I know of only two or three who were out to have only winning teams, where scholastic quality was ignored. In many places, as a matter of fact, the professors have gone out of their way to drive out football players, to end what they considered the ignominy of being called "a football school."

But you must have seen, Mr. President, that the demand for football winners has become so great that losing coaches and their families, their wives and children, were insulted and persecuted by furious and almost insane student bodies, alumni hatchet men, and downtown quarterbacks. I know, because I have talked to their wives and children. I have heard what I know to be true stories that begin to make you wonder whether football, as great a game as it is, should be allowed to survive in its present form.

It should be stated here that the Ivy League presidents got together back in 1947 to formulate a code that each was to follow. Although these presidents waited quite a while to act, they arranged a first-class working agreement that seems to have settled most of the old disputes. Part of this code dealt with matters of proselyting, post-season games, alumni help, and any form of direct pay. It was impossible to work out any scholarship arrangement, since each university in the Ivy group might have a different standard. Some have softer courses and easier admission approaches that others won't tolerate.

It will, of course, be impossible to have any set standard of scholarship to cover the entire map of the U.S.A. If the Ivy League can't handle this part of the situation, how can 300 widely scattered colleges do anything about it?

During the football season, sports writers begin to get vile, insulting letters that no one but morons or imbeciles could write. Yet many of these same writers become respectable as soon as the football season ends.

The football writers can take it. They don't care one way or another what an infuriated and partially insane college student or college alumnus thinks about them. They know that this breed is so deeply prejudiced that his opinion is completely unimportant. But just how so many students and alumni can stand to see platoons of imported semi-pros representing their college colors is beyond me.

In baseball, the Yankees, Red Sox, or Dodgers can win only two-thirds of their games and still come up with the pennant. They can lose 50 games a year. But in football, the team or coach that loses more than two games has had a disastrous season. Actually, an even break is all that any sane, normal college should ask. Now the entire debris is thrown at the doorstep of the NCAA, but if you presidents had all followed the example of Dr. Hannah of Michigan State, there would be no such mess.

As president, Dr. Hannah has taken football under his care and that of his faculty. Football is their full responsibility. The football coach is a member of the faculty. Dr. Hannah realizes that football today is a big part of student life, but not a dominating factor. It's just one of many things that must be looked after. Dr. Hannah realizes there must be a defeat for every victory. To the average alumnus, this creed is poisonous.

Years ago, I recall one famous college president who made an appointment to talk certain things over. "I've been running football at my college," he said. "I have recently taken a certain stand that my alumni don't like. I have argued with them, but have gotten nowhere. So I am going to abolish football. I would rather have 500 real students than 2,000 football players."

He didn't abolish football, but at least he won his point—even though it cost his team an overwhelming defeat.

As the case stands today, with spring practice about over, you should be thankful that football is in such able hands. I mean the fate of football. Dr. Willett, chairman of the NCAA committee, has all the virtues needed to handle the job. He is patient, where unlimited patience is needed. He is unprejudiced, where any prejudice would be fatal. He knows the magnitude of his job and I believe he has assistants who are just as capable.

"A ruling that would suit one place," he told me, "might not suit another. Football players can be given helpful jobs at many places close to centers of population. At other places, there are no jobs available. You can't make a set rule that will cover this entire country. Certain colleges have much higher standards for admission and for later scholastic requirements. But there are others who must take a lower level. The problems of state universities and privately endowed universities are entirely different. Our object is to meet the problems of all colleges and universities who want to see football preserved, but not made a matter where only victory counts. We are going to stop direct pay to football players. There is a difference between financial graft and financial help to get an education. We want discrimination against no one. We would like to have the help or the assistance of all coaches, graduate managers, college students, and especially presidents." Considering your failure in the past as far as governing and controlling football's tidal wave is concerned, it is essential that you, Mr. College President, respond now to the latest movement to bring the great game of football back to its true place in college life—on a par with baseball, crew, track, basketball, etc.

It is enough to be a good football player so long as the player doesn't develop a swelled head or consider this mark his main objective in college. It may be, Mr. President, that you are deeply interested in what the NCAA committee is fighting for.

To get closer to the situation, I have asked for some advice from an old friend who knows most of the answers. He is a famous football coach who has operated with success in three big conferences. Here is his reply— one that is worth close inspection not only by the NCAA but also by every college and university president in the country:

Dear Grant:

You asked me to pass on to you some of the ideas which have occurred to me regarding the NCAA code and related subjects. My comments will probably not suggest anything new to your thinking, but I am glad to submit them for what they might be worth.

The whole problem of subsidization of athletes is a

complex one for many reasons. Member institutions of the NCAA vary greatly as to the size of enrollments, educational standards, opportunities for jobs and other available means of student aid, cost of living, etc. All of these factors and other circumstances should be considered before enacting legislation and setting up codes.

There is no perfect solution or panacea for everything that might be wrong with football, but the best and most workable plan I have seen is the one that the Southeastern Conference abandoned two years ago in order to come under the NCAA Code. As simple proof of this, I understand that the Southeastern Conference today is in worse shape than it ever was under its own rules and regulations. In this regard I cannot help but admire the stand taken by the University of Virginia's Board of Governors and its president when they resigned from the NCAA with the statement that they could not honestly subscribe to the letter of the NCAA code and still carry on their intercollegiate athletic program. I predict that some day the NCAA will adopt a code similar to the one that was shelved by the Southeastern Conference schools.

There was one rule in particular which I felt to be a very good one. It provided "that from no source whatever may an athlete receive more than the grant-in-aid provided, except from sources upon whom the boy would naturally depend for support." This rule, if enforced—and I think it can be—obviously would eliminate the high-powered alumnus who is so active today in buying up football players.

The idea of a college football player working his way through school during his spare time sounds good, is thoroughly meritorious, but I do not feel that it will work in the average case. Football as it is played today, plus the spring practice period, is a terrific drain on a player physically, mentally, and emotionally. Accordingly, the football player in an A-grade college who is carrying successfully a normal academic load will not have enough spare time to hold a job which will completely defray his actual and necessary school expenses. It is almost a practical problem then of substituting something in place of the phony work jobs assigned in most schools that play football.

Money and big-time football are so closely related today that the two can hardly be separated. Show me a place today where they are playing big-time football and I think I can show you a place where there is a lot of money associated in some way with the football program—by gate receipts, slush funds, alumni aid, or whatnot. Much of this money is gravitating in some way to the players, and not always in conformity with the NCAA code. I feel that a set of sensible, workable rules should be set up, and if necessary, enforced by some militant individual—say of the character of Judge Landis. Violations should carry punishments other than fines. I do not think that any rule will ever have teeth unless the boy can be declared ineligible if he has entered into a shady agreement. I am probably in the minority at this point, but I believe I am right. I have found that the average prospective athlete knows the code and rules about as well as anybody else. This would also cause an alumnus and coach to think a little longer before getting some boy into a jam whereby he might be declared ineligible.

The majority of coaches want to do the right thing and are seeking a solution to the problem. The pressure created by big post-season bowl games has caused a lot of coaches to follow a pathway which is foreign to their convictions about recruiting.

I am an alleged football coach and not a hypocrite nor a reformer, but these are some of my thoughts on the subject.

We submit this as a major answer to the problems the NCAA committee must face and we submit this as part of football's new plan for the future that you, as a college president, must consider. Football is too great a game to face destruction. But something must be done about the present situation, which has gotten far beyond control when it comes to the basic principle of sport—"A fair field and no favor."

Football today needs every friend it can call upon if it is to keep its important place in any college schedule. And I firmly believe the full support of all college and university presidents is needed in the new setup that must take place if football is to survive.

WRITERS AND PALS

I believe that I came along in gayer, happier times for both newspaper readers and writers. Somewhere in the late 1920's, there was a sudden change. In those earlier days columnists wrote verse and paragraphs. There was Franklin P. Adams of the *Mail* and *Herald Tribune,* whose two columns—"Always in Good Humor" and "The Conning Tower"—were magnificent. Bert Leston Taylor (B.L.T.), who conducted "The Line-A-Type-or-Two," in the Chicago *Tribune,* was equally wonderful. These were the two stars, but there were many others who were excellent.

Frank L. Stanton, the serious poet in the Atlanta *Constitution,* was in front of them all. Others were: Judd Mortimer Lewis in the Houston *Post;* John D. Wells in the Buffalo *News;* Don Marquis of the old *Sun,* whose "Archie, the cockroach" and other superb verse held high attention; Eddie Guest; and Henry Sydnor Harrison from Virginia.

These and some others ruled those days of column readers. They suddenly gave way to Westbrook Pegler, Heywood Broun, Alexander Woollcott, Ralph McGill, Walter Lippmann, Frank Kent, E. V. Durling, John O'Donnell, Bob Considine, and many more. Certainly Frank Adams, Bert Taylor and Don Marquis had an appeal that could equal that of any columnist of the present era with, perhaps, the exception of Westbrook Pegler. Pegler's fiery diatribes which keep you wondering what he will say or whose scalp he will lift.

Nevertheless, I got a far greater thrill in reading Adams, Taylor or Marquis in other years than I have got since. Maybe it was because I was a graduate of the verse and paragraph school from the days of the Nashville *Tennessean.*

Frank Adams was the best light-verse writer I ever read, in this country or Europe. He translated the Odes of Horace into modern verse. Here's just one sample of his intricate rhyming.

TO BE QUITE FRANK
UXOR PAUPERIS IBYCI
(Horace Ode 15, Book 3)

Your conduct naughty Chloris is
Not just exactly Horace's
Ideal of a lady
At the shady
Time of life.
You mustn't throw your soul away
On foolishness, like Pholoë
Her days are folly laden—
She's a maiden—
You're a wife.

Your daughter, with propriety,
May look for male society,
Do one thing and another
In which mother
Shouldn't mix.
But revels Bacchanalian
Are—or should be—quite alien
To you, a married person
Something worse'n
Forty six!

Yes, Chloris, you cut up too much,
You love the dance and cup too much,
Your years are quickly flitting,
To your knitting
Right about.
Forget the incidental things,
That keep you from parental things.
The World, the Flesh, the Devil,
On the level,
Cut 'em out.

281

It was Frank Adams who wrote one of baseball's few immortal lyrics—

> These are the saddest of possible words—
> Tinker and Evers and Chance.
> Pricking forever our gonfalon bubble,
> Causing a Giant to hit into a double,
> Words that are heavy with nothing but trouble,
> Tinker to Evers to Chance.

I was at the *Evening Mail* in 1912 when Mr. Miles, the managing editor, called me to his office. He showed me the verse Adams had just turned in. "Frank may write a better piece of verse than this," Niles said, "but this is one he will be remembered by." He was right.

One of the finest columnists I ever read was Hugh E. Keogh, who conducted a sporting page composium in verse and paragraphs. Keogh had but a short burst. He began his column in 1905 and died in 1911. A master, a fine verse writer and a brilliant paragrapher, Hughey had the most interesting sporting column I ever read. Here are a few examples of his one line masterpieces.

"The race is not to the swift—but that is where to look."
"The art of self defense—100 yards in 10 seconds."
"Throw your bread upon the waters and a carp will beat you to it."
"You can't pay off people in the square set with technicalities."
"The rules of sport are all founded upon fair play."

Whatever happened, the Peglers and the Winchells, the Brouns and the Ed Sullivans drove off the rhymers and paragraphers from most newspapers to the sorrow of many, many readers.

I think one reason the papers switched from verse to prose is this—good poets suddenly disappeared and readers for some reason lost the old poetic zest. I know that I started keeping a poetry scrapbook around 1905. I kept this up for 25 years. I have many rare things in it.

Suddenly, around 1930, I quit collecting. The reason—I found little worth pasting in my treasured book.

This is a much more serious age than the old days ever were. There was a lightheartedness that the world knew before the first World War that has never been worn since. Thank God for H. I. Phillips! There has been war or the shadow of war for the past 40 years and the dark shadow hasn't ever been absent from the scene in that time. Most of the true singers have had little heart with which to sing.

No newspaper man hits the road more often than the writer assigned to a major-league baseball team—or the one who enjoys syndication and can hunt at large in search of game. Sports writers, as a group, tend to be nomads, gypsies. If they weren't of that basic cut, they wouldn't be in that field.

It was in Bill Corum's drawing room aboard the train returning to New York from Cincinnati following the Detroit-Cincinnati World Series in 1940, that I heard a wise sum-up of a sports writer's approach to his job. Joe Williams was there and so were Tom Meany, Garry Schumacher, and Tommy Laird, the sage of San Francisco. The talk—over juleps—got around to jobs. Laird mentioned that Lefty O'Doul, as manager of the San Francisco Seals, was happier than he had ever been in the majors.

We were all sounding off on what we'd do if given another whirl at Fate's old wheel.

"As for me," said Corum, "I don't want to be a millionaire; I just want to live like one . . . or a sports writer."

Toots Shor put it another way. Watching a group of baseball writers carving their initials in his bar at 3 A.M. after a Baseball Writers' party, Toots said, "Grant, there's not a millionaire in that bunch. They just live like 'em!"

While stopping over for a brief stand, "We who are travelers for the night at this old wayside inn called Earth," we meet many people—few of them alike, and Toots Shor, a fellow who runs a great restaurant is strictly himself. There hasn't been and there won't be anybody like him. He is the only world-wide man I know. I was sitting with Toots recently at lunch when he lifted the phone and called Ben Hogan at Fort Worth to cheer Ben up after he'd been beaten by Sammy Snead in the '54 Masters. Ten minutes later he called up Ford Frick, the baseball commissioner to discuss some knotty problem that had come up in baseball. Five minutes later he was on the line to two close friends, Ernest and Mary Hemingway in South Africa. He found that Hemingway had been much more severely injured in that plane wreck than he had let anyone know. Then Toots called Gene Fowler in Los Angeles to see how Gene felt. "Heard he wasn't so good," Toots said.

Jimmy Cannon tells a true story from Louisville at the '53 Derby—when Dark Star upset Native Dancer's applecart. Before a certain race Toots told his bunch he would get the right tip from his old friend Horatio Luro, the Argentine pill muncher and horse trainer. Toots left, got the tip, and the horse was out of the money.

"Can you imagine an old friend double crossing you like that?" Toots howled.

"Is Luro a close friend of yours?" Cannon asked.

"I met him yesterday," replied Toots.

Shor is a friend of the world at large, barring all communists and hypocrites. In turn he is respected and loved by those that know him. A close friend of the athlete, sports writer and columnist, Toots and "Baby" his bride are tops in my little old book.

Certainly my most exciting days—and nights—have been spent on the road. There is a fresh outlook when you move out on the trail that takes you around the map —Los Angeles, Chicago, Miami, New Orleans, Louisville, Dallas, St. Louis, Atlanta, Philadelphia, Boston, Shelby, St. Petersburg, wherever there's a big sports story, that's where the compass points.

Since 1901, years of work and travel, I've enjoyed meeting and knowing so many stars and champions. But I don't think this feeling quite reaches the deeper glow that has come from my more affectionate connections with the writers and friends I've made along this almost endless trail.

In the earlier days a lot of us were often broke or next to it. But one thing about The Greatest Profession, a little thing like money or the lack of it never gave us much concern. I remember it was the night before the Willard-Dempsey fight in Toledo. There was a big party in the outskirts. It was on the house and nearly all the writers covering the show went. A good looking girl was checking them in. "Ring Lardner," "Damon Runyon," "H. C. Witwer," "Gene Fowler," "Heywood Broun," "Percy Hammond," "Rube Goldberg," great trade names were given, one by one. The hostess, thinking it was all a fake was getting sore. Finally another came up to sign in. She hardly looked at him but blurted, "And you, you big bum . . . I suppose you are Irvin Cobb." It was.

One of the livelier additions down the long journey has been Tom Meany, a fine writer, a keen story teller and a high-grade wit. One night after a World Series game in New York, Meany was the victim of a fellow who meant well but bored deep. Tom couldn't get rid of him. He wasn't a bad fellow but you know the type. He hung on like a leech. Finally Tom decided to leave the party.

His loquacious friend said, "I'll drive you home, Tom."

"You already have," replied Meany.

Writer-pals I've known go back to Bozeman Bulger of the Birmingham *Age-Herald* and Ren Mulford, Jr. of the Cincinnati *Enquirer* in 1901. That first wave consisted also of Hugh Fullerton, Sr. and Hugh E. Keogh (HEK) of the Chicago *Tribune;* Sid Mercer of St. Louis and the New York *Globe;* Ed Camp of the Atlanta *Journal;* Don Marquis and Frank L. Stanton of Atlanta; Charley Dryden of the Philadelphia *North American;* and Bob Edgren of the old New York *World*.

The second wave, starting around 1910, would include such writers as Ring Lardner of Chicago, Francis Albert-anti and F. P. Adams of the old *Evening Mail*. Harry Salsinger (Detroit *News*), Bill Hanna (N.Y. *Tribune*), Bill Phelon (Cincinnati *Times Star*), lovable O. B. Keeler

(Atlanta *Journal*), and Clyde McBride (Kansas City *Star*).

And coming strong in the third wave would be: Damon Runyon (N.Y. *American*), Heywood Broun (N.Y. *Tribune* and *Telegram*), Westbrook Pegler (Chicago *Tribune, N.Y. Post, World-Telegram, Journal American*), W. O. McGeehan (*Herald Tribune*), Harry Cross (N.Y. *Times, Herald Tribune*), Gene Fowler and Bill Corum (N.Y. *American*), Bob Kelley and John Kieran (N.Y. *Times*), Frank Graham (N.Y. *Sun, Journal American*), Fred Digby and Bill Keefe of New Orleans, Braven Dyer (Los Angeles *Times*), Bill Cunningham (Boston *Herald*), Dan Parker (New York *Mirror*), Stanley Woodward and Red Smith (N.Y. *Herald Tribune*), Freddie Russell (Nashville *Banner*), Ray Johnson (Nashville *Tennessean*), Joe Williams (N.Y. *World Telegram*), Henry McLemore (U.P., McAdams Syndicate), Harry Grayson (N.E.A.), Jimmy Cannon (N.Y. *Post*), and such comparative moderns as Tim Cohane and Vincent X. Flaherty.

Perhaps the finest group to grace American journalism flourished from 1910 to 1925. This list included Runyon, Lardner, Broun, Fowler, McGeehan, Pegler, Salsinger, McBride, Danforth and some others. With that pack sweeping down the field, how could this era miss?

Writing men necessarily are creative men and, as such, run to no set formula. There were odd varieties among the tops. As odd as a Chinese puzzle was Bill Phelon, the Cincinnati sage who could write, and well, about anything. He would write you 5,000 words for ten dollars and not junk. He neither smoked nor drank. It was different with women, art and other details. Built and clothed like great shaggy dogs, Phelon and Heywood Broun were as rare a pair of clothes horses as ever condescended to wear shoe leather.

Bill was an animal collector of sorts. One day in the Polo Grounds press box I was sitting with Phelon and me—punctured with many holes. I was leaning on it.

"By the way," Phelon said, "I was down at the wharf Harry Salsinger. There was a white cigar box in front of

286

this morning and I bought a young fer-de-lance. Most poisonous snake in South America—a slender snake who strikes quick. I got him cheap."

"Where is he?" I asked.

"In that box you are leaning on," Bill said. I covered 20 yards in a second. Salsinger beat that. The openings in the cigar box were bigger than the fer-de-lance.

In the Cincinnati press box another day Bill asked me if I would like to make $250.

"For that amount," I said, "I would rob a bank. What's the idea?"

"Well, it's this way," Phelon said. "I have a six-foot alligator living in my apartment." (He also had, I knew, a Gila monster, a squirrel, and a rattlesnake sharing the room.) "Now there's a Dutchman down the block who has a big bulldog. He wants to bet me five hundred bucks his bulldog can lick my alligator."

"What makes you think the bulldog can't win?" I asked.

"I know he can't win," he said. "I'll tell you why. I got a pit and I matched my alligator against three bulldogs at different times. He sheared the legs off all three dogs."

I bowed out. And yet, as I said, Phelon was a brilliant writer on almost any subject. Like Julius Caesar, he could talk to you on some outside subject and write a forceful story at the same time about the game.

William B. Hanna was one of my closest friends. He wrote perfect English and was an expert on football and baseball reporting. He was with the old New York *Sun* first, then the *Herald Tribune*. When you read one of Bill's stories, you knew that's the way it happened. He was a brilliant writer and a perfect reporter. A small fellow, he seemed a trifle shriveled.

Hanna was an eccentric. He would never stop above the fifth floor of a hotel. Twice on the same night he had been caught in hotel fires. Also, he hated number 13. One day, in making a reservation in Florida, I got the top floor for Hanna and myself.

Hanna almost fainted. "No higher than the fifth," he shouted at me.

287

I got another room. Bill had another fit. "You got fifty-eight," he called.

"That's the fifth floor," I said.

"But five and eight adds up to thirteen!" he said.

One afternoon, Phelon passed Hanna headed down Broadway in New York. "Hello, Bill," he said.

"Hello, Phelon," Bill responded.

A practical joker who knew Bill's eccentricities, Phelon hopped a southbound cab, got out a block below the oncoming Hanna and greeted him again with "Hello, Bill!"

A surprised Hanna returned the greeting. Phelon did this three or four more times. At the fourth "Hello, Bill!" Hanna started for the river and was barely prevented from diving in.

But for all his strange and at times brooding characteristics, Bill was a lovable fellow with a wonderfully keen, direct mind.

In the earlier years of my wandering about in the sporting domain, Westbrook Pegler was one of my closest companions. Later, Peg left our field flat to shoot at bigger game, in politics. He was a fine sports columnist, usually working in the role of offering bitter protests against various people and conditions. In his social connections, however, Peg could lay aside his protesting role and have more fun than most.

One summer at East Hampton we attended a big fancy dress party. The ladies took charge of Pegler and dressed him up as Sadie Thompson, the famous heroine of *Rain*. Sadie was the hit of the evening. But, as a rule, Peg remains a serious and, in some ways, the most fearless writer I have known. Nothing can keep him off the critical course when he feels criticism is in order. He was the same in writing about sport as he is in writing of politics and politicians, including union labor leaders. He usually has a hot target and rarely misses his aim. Such outspoken critics as Westbrook Pegler and Dan Parker, for two examples, are badly needed.

To Peg, "The Golden Age of Sport" was "The Era of

Wonderful Nonsense." Some years ago when he was covering both politics and a World Series in New York, the game was postponed on account of rain. We came back to my apartment. Peg was restless. He couldn't see any "off day" baseball story. So he began scanning the library ranged around the room. He got up from his chair and finally picked out a book.

"How big is a giant panda?" Pegler asked. He was scanning a book written by General Theodore Roosevelt about his year's search for the beast and how he had brought one home.

"He is about as big as a collie dog, although he weighs more," I said.

"Is he ferocious?" Peg asked.

"I don't think so," I said.

No more was said on the subject as Peg went back to work.

Next day there appeared a terrific blast at Teddy, Jr. for capturing what was believed to be a dangerous animal that, in reality, was as docile as a kitten or a puppy. A good friend of Peg's, Roosevelt took the column as a joke.

For 40 years and more, Frank L. Stanton turned out a column of verse and paragraphs for the Atlanta *Constitution*. By all odds the finest poet I ever met, he was like a mocking bird singing in a Georgia oak which happened to be flooded with moonlight.

Don Marquis, a far better judge of poetry than I, rated James Whitcomb Riley first and Stanton second among American poets. "Mighty Lak A Rose," "Just a Wearyin' for You," and hundreds of other remembered songs in his more than 40 years of service are pure Stanton.

One year, 1903, Marquis and I lived at the Aragon Hotel in Atlanta. Stanton liked a nightcap or two before the bar closed at 10:00 P.M. So did Don and I. Stanton had to escape to make port and he was frequently late. I remember the bartender one night saying, "Sorry, but time's up, Mr. Stanton."

"I will write thee a verse for a drink," Stanton said. He

immediately dashed off a verse beginning "Time's up for love and laughter." It was a beautiful thing and later on it appeared in *Judge* or *Puck*. The bartender received 25 dollars for sending it along.

Another night, with Don and me peering over his shoulder, Frank wrote the following lines on a piece of wrapping paper:

Hasten not, O traveler, to yonder distant town,
Where shadows shut the stars out and the dead leaves
    tumble down.
Tarry at life's tavern—one more cup they'll fill,
They'll light no lamps to guide you to that distant town
    and still.

But there is one who dwells there, in the night's embrace,
Love in life's sweet morning dreamed in her dear face,
The lilies are her altars where the winds kneel down to
    pray,
But all the violets loved her so they hid her face away

I brought on Frank's deep displeasure once—a peeve that lasted several weeks. He had written a short piece of verse that went—

> This old world we're living in
> Is mighty hard to beat.
> We find a thorn with every rose
> But ain't the roses sweet.

This verse was widely quoted at the time. I was with Marquis one day when we ran across Mr. Stanton.

"I have just written a verse," I told him. "I think you'll like it. It goes—

> "This old world we're living in
> I think is on the blink.
> You find a thorn with every rose
> And don't the roses stink."

We barely escaped with our lives.

Many good writers have tried to put together a book

about Ring Lardner but none has as yet succeeded. To contain Ring would be like wrapping up a wraith. I lived side by side or house by house with him for many years and yet I never quite knew that I knew him.

Ring was closer to being a genius than anyone I've known. He had a sense of humor that was at times beyond this world. He was tall, dark and slender and was never what you'd call loquacious.

Charley Van Loan was appointed by George Horace Lorimer to go to Chicago and get Ring to write for the *Saturday Evening Post*. Van could get nothing from Ring, not a word, as he marched from saloon to saloon. Van Loan himself was on the wagon.

Finally, about two in the morning, Van Loan said, "Say, I can't walk all night on water."

"Christ did!" retorted Ring.

I was with him one Mardi Gras night in New Orleans. We were surrounding a bar when an 80-year-old Southerner stepped up to Ring.

"You probably don't know who I am," he drawled. "My grandfather was General so-and-so on Napoleon's staff. My father was Count so-and-so of France. I was a general in the Confederate Army and, suh, I wear the Legion of Honor."

Ring spoke. "I was born in Niles, Michigan, of colored parents," he said. The general fled into the night.

Ring was a fine baseball writer and equally good at football. He was a magnificent comedy writer but the savage bitterness of his best work was his main feature. I never knew anyone who hated a phony more than Ring.

I took him to Washington with me for a golf match with President Harding. Harding said at the meeting—"Rice is here to get a story. Why did you come?"

"I had a good reason," Ring said. "I want to be appointed Ambassador to Greece."

"Why?" Harding asked.

"My wife doesn't like Great Neck," Lardner said.

"That's a better reason than most of these people have," replied Harding.

291

Following a luncheon of highballs and sandwiches, Harding told the secret service men assigned to him to take the day off and we went out to Burning Tree.

Harding had a way of driving and then walking from the tee, on ahead. Ring followed him on one drive and called "Fore" about three times. Harding had walked about 40 yards and was now under an apple tree. Ring drove, hitting a lusty ball with a slight slice. The ball struck a thick branch just over Harding's head. The branch fell on Harding's shoulder. He was startled and waited for Ring to come up and apologize.

"I did all I could to make Coolidge president," was all Ring said. Harding dropped his club and roared with laughter.

Harding was a poor President but he was quite a fellow and, I think, an honest man.

After Harding's death I decided to go back to Washington when Mr. Coolidge was in the White House to dig up another presidential story. The President was making a talk that day before a press gathering. When he was through, I was introduced to him. The party was very short.

"The last time I was in Washington," I said to President Coolidge, "I played golf with President Harding. Do you happen to play golf or tennis?" I asked him.

"No," he said, "but I have my game."

"What is it?" I questioned.

"Walking," he said.

"I couldn't write much about that," I said.

"No," he answered.

I found later that he had two other sports. One was fishing with worms. The other was wild turkey shooting.

Mr. Coolidge went turkey hunting with a South Carolina guide. He was hidden away under thick cover. The guide said to him, "When I nudge you, shoot."

The guide called the turkey up to about 20 yards. He nudged. The President shook his head. He tried again when the gobbler stopped about six yards away. This time the President let him have both barrels. The turkey disappeared. It was a massacre. But there was no turkey left.

Mr. Coolidge practically took no chances on anything.

My earlier traveling mates inside the profession were Westbrook Pegler, Ring Lardner and Bill McGeehan. They made any trip worth while, although it usually took some time to wipe out their initial annoyance with me. This trio had the habit of making a train by an hour. I had the habit of just making a train—several times after it had started moving. This habit—also shared by Babe Ruth—annoyed my traveling mates.

I soon discovered, however, that Peg, Ring and Bill were seldom covering the same event. So I sought other mates. I soon settled on three men willing to leave home and roam, now and then. They were Clarence Budington Kelland, the late Frank Craven, and Bruce Barton. In different fashions, all were ideal company.

Top man, perhaps because he "suffered" more, was Bud Kelland, noted novelist, short-story writer, elder statesman, after-dinner speaker, famous wit—with at times the tongue of a cobra. Kelland, who always took time off from some 80 or perhaps 90 novels to get away, required advance notice—from two hours to one week. I could count on Bud to be at Grand Central or at Pennsylvania Station at 7:00 P.M. on any given date. Bud never seemed to care where we went or what sport we were covering. At least he never cared to be bothered with these unessential details. He always knew there was some adventure waiting.

There was the week end we traveled to Columbus, Ohio, to see Jock Sutherland's Pittsburgh Panthers meet Ohio State. At the press gate I presented our two tickets.

"No good," the ticket taker said.

"What's the matter with them?" I asked.

"Look," he said, handing them back. They happened to be for the International Polo Matches at Meadowbrook. Fortunately at that moment I spotted Sutherland and his team entering another gate. I rushed over.

"Jock," I said, "today I am your assistant coach and Mr. Kelland is assistant team doctor." That's how we covered the game.

One morning at breakfast in Philadelphia, Bud looked terrible. He began cursing me. I discovered that around midnight I had ordered up two ice cold watermelons and had inadvertently left half a watermelon in Bud's bed. He hadn't closed an eye, with first his right foot then his left entangled with the iced melon. His genius, however, hadn't prompted Bud to remove the foot warmer.

One night I heard a soliloquy delivered by Mr. Kelland, who thought no one was listening.

"Why do I do it? Why am I here? I didn't have to come. Nothing but drunks and bums. I don't drink, but I rarely see a glass of water. No sleep—no nothing that makes any sense. Never again."

The reason Bud kept taking these trips for 25 or 30 years was his love for sport—also, he loved meeting people. He became a friend of every coach we ever met. They all wanted him around, especially Sutherland.

Down the trail of many years, and up to the Open Golf Tournament at Merion in 1951, Bud covered the map— golf tournaments, fights, football games. He didn't care so long as he heard the tocsin sounding from the tower. From New York to Los Angeles—from Minneapolis to St. Pete—we hit all stops.

Occasionally, I was prodded into getting Bud to say a few words at some dinner or function. Usually, it was a sad mistake. Annoyed at something that had happened or by someone present, Bud would take the toastmaster, club president, mayor or whatever, completely apart with a devastating attack that was totally unexpected. His rancor was and remains no light matter, and at times it's easily aroused. Yes, with Bud everything took place except the peace and quiet and orderly action which Kelland thought he sought.

Trips without Bud, who has retired from expeditions and safaris after a long and tumultuous experience, never have seemed quite the same.

294

Frank Craven, the superb actor who died in 1945, was another grand trouper. A keen fan, Frank knew all sports, especially baseball, football and golf. He was one of the most entertaining men I ever knew. He also had a keen sense of humor and a ready Irish wit.

Once, on a visit to London, he was stopped by some butler while trying to visit an English friend.

"Step aside," Frank ordered. "I've played a thousand of you."

In addition to being a great actor, he was a fine playwright. *The First Year* was one of his contributions. Frank and John Golden, one of the great men of the theater, worked together for many seasons.

In golf, Craven rarely varied from an 80 score. At Lakeside, in California, he played many rounds with Henry McLemore, winning almost every match. Finally McLemore had to go away for a week. When he returned, Frank sent him a bill for 45 dollars.

"What's this for?" Henry asked.

"For the money I would have won if you had not left," Frank said.

"That's right," Henry replied as he shelled out 45 dollars. "You couldn't have missed."

Since Craven died I have missed him heavily many times. No one could take his place on the golf course, on a trip, or standing bravely in front of a dry martini. He was one of the immortals—beyond all price.

Bruce Barton showed better judgment than Kelland or Craven. He suddenly realized he didn't have to take such beatings, like grabbing my typewriter and dashing for trains. However, during the few short years that Bruce accompanied me, he was a valuable blocking back. He swung a wicked portable through crowds, clearing the way like an icebreaker. A bristling conversationalist, decisive in action, he was a remarkable companion. The combinations of Kelland, Craven, Barton, Pegler, McGeehan, Lardner, Frankie Graham and Red Smith have been vital factors in holding the road.

Graham and Smith—both lovable guys—came along as a star team when most of the others had died or quit. Both are superb columnists—for the New York *Journal American* and the New York *Herald Tribune,* respectively. Marvelous companions in every detail, they are also experts whose opinions have been useful on many occasions. I hope they will be around at the last march.

There is another I always hope to see. His name is Gene Fowler. He writes movies for money, and books for his soul. He is the only one I know who would greet me now and then with a special column.

"I know you're tired after the trip," he would say. "This might help."

It happens that Gene, meanwhile, was probably the busiest of all the writers. He sent me the first hilarious story ever written on the highly-scented Gorgeous George, the marcelled wrestler, which started George toward considerable notoriety and cash.

For some reason, there are only two men in history I think of in terms of the word "gallant." They are the Gallant Fowler and the Gallant Stuart, meaning Jeb. Gene Fowler is certainly worth traveling across country to California for—even for a brief hello.

One night in the late 1930's I ran into two of my all-time favorites—both Army men. Their names were Rosie O'Donnell and Blondie Saunders, two of West Point's immortals. Saunders, a fine Army tackle in '28, became a one-star general in the Air Force and lost a leg in the Far East during World War II. Rosie was in a class alone. Among his minor acts he flew over Tokyo dropping bombs as he went.

But this is a different story. That night I ran into Rosie and Blondie and we took in New York. We called on Bob Neyland as well as the night spots. I arrived home about 7 A.M. Naturally Kit wanted to know a few details of this all-night pilgrimage. I had only one answer.

"Everything's all right," I muttered sleepily. "I've had a great time. Been out with Rosie and Blondie."

It took me a week to square myself . . . before I could

explain that Rosie and Blondie in my book are two of the finest fighting men who ever lived.

Sporting writers have their particular idols—some whom they cherished from boyhood, others whom they helped create in the headlines. San Francisco's Tommy Laird, archon of the Coast writing fraternity for so many years, chronicled most of Stanley Ketchel's bouts when Ketchel ruled the middleweights in 1908 and 1909. In Tommy's world, Ketchel was the greatest, period.

It was in 1939 that I decided to make my young confrere, Henry McLemore, aware of the facts of life, at least concerning Laird. We were covering a golf tournament in San Francisco. Gene Fowler, who had hung the questionable halo of "Dean" on my snow-flaked brow, an appellation he still uses, had mentioned that we ought to be on the lookout for a "Junior Dean." Perhaps McLemore, then writing for the United Press, might be our man. An indefatigable person, the Georgia-born McLemore is a hard man to down, either with refreshing drink or at charades. His mind has been known to fire as rapidly as a string of Chinese firecrackes. Fowler appraised Henry of our plans for him but informed him that he would be judged for his role through "a series of tests." Henry did not flinch.

This particular night, I was having dinner at the St. Francis Hotel with Laird and McLemore. Things were unusually sedate. I quietly suggested to Henry that he tell Laird that Stanley Ketchel was no good. Grabbing the bait like a tiger shark, Henry leaned across my bows and facing Laird, crackled, "Ketchel was a lousy bum."

That did it. Turning a horrible crimson, Laird screamed, "What!" . . . grabbed the completely baffled McLemore by the shirt collar and whacked him. As he was trying to escape from the ruckus with his life, Henry's head was bashed by a woman swinging a loaded handbag.

I had to flunk McLemore on this, his opening test, but gave him an "A" shortly after. The San Francisco Press Club, which owns its own building just a few blocks from the St. Francis, is well known for its annual dinners, at which all comments by the speakers are "behind the cat" or off the record. Arriving with Pat O'Brien, Guy Kibbee, Fowler and McLemore, I was worried over their condition to render a fit talk on anything to a gathering of perhaps 500.

I had to literally drag Henry from the washroom and sit him down. Following the introduction, Henry rose from his seat—in stocking feet—stepped upon the table, and strode through the asparagus to the microphone.

"Ladies and gentlemen," he intoned. "I would like to give you my recipe for apple butter. . . ."

He did, too, in one of the most lucid, most pristine, informative and certainly the most humorous of speeches I ever heard.

McLemore was just about "in" as Junior Dean when we arrived at Detroit the following September to cover the Joe Louis-Bob Pastor fight. We were staying at the Detroit Athletic Club. Our suite became a crossroads. In our corner was Hunk Anderson, Rockne's all-time guard and, I repeat, pound-for-pound the roughest human being, when aroused, I've ever known. At one time or another during the evening prior to the fight it seemed we had everybody including Louis and Pastor in our rooms and Hunk was prepared to engage them all—singly or in pairs.

"This should be a good test for you, Henry," I said. "Why not say a few words to Hunk?" Game to the core, Henry mentioned something about Hunk's bark being worse than his bite. The next thing I knew my little friend was being bounced on the floor as if he were a tennis ball. That night Henry resigned as Junior Dean.

There's another night I won't forget, the eve of the World Series between the Tigers and the Cubs in '45. Charley Hughes, manager of the Detroit A.C., decided to toss a quiet little party for me. "Bring four or five," he said. I may have told a half dozen but between 40 and 50 showed up. It was a lovely dinner. Over the brandy, Harry Grayson asked McLemore to say a few words. Still in uniform following three solid years in Service, including a long hitch in the Pacific, Henry was happy to oblige. He told us of his early Georgia upbringing: how he was the son of a Methodist minister, who, when Henry went north to write, said, "Henry, when you're up there, beware of The Killer."

In the course of time, Henry said he met The Killer. He then ran through a list of writers who had died during the past 20 years. It was a very long list of people like Lardner, McGeehan, MacBeth, Broun, and so many others.

"The Killer's intended victim, before me," continued Henry, "was Clarence Budington Kelland. Kelland, thank God, succeeded in breaking away from him just in time. For nearly five years now he's been in Arizona trying to regain a semblance of his health. It took a near physical breakdown to save Kelland. It took a second World War to save me! Gentlemen, I give you Grantland Rice."

Next to Brutus', that was the most unkindest cut.

* * *

From *OVER THE BORDER* (To those who have gone before)

All that we bring to the inn is this—the travelers' cloak
    we wear,
All that we take from the inn is this—wherever the road
    may fare;
All that we get from the inn is this—the friends that we
    know are true,
Shoulder to shoulder and blood to blood—till the call of
    the road comes through.

What new road does the rover fear, when someone
    knocks at the inn,
And leads the way to an untrod trail, as far as the
    comets spin?
On with the travelers' cloak again, as we call from the
    restless throng,
"Good luck, old friend, till we find the way that leads to
    another song."

INDEX

301

302

303

Holland, Jerome, 200, 203, 204, 205
Hoop, Jr., 249
Hoppe, Willie, 149
Hornsby, Rogers, 229
"House That Ruth Built, The", 81, 87
Hoyt, Waite, 137-141
Hubble Bubble, 250
Hughes, Charley, 298
Humphreys, Joe, 62
Hutchinson, Johnny, 107

I Will, 250
Illinois-Ohio State football game—1925, 125-131

Jackson, Joe, 13, 14, 15, 21, 77, 239, 240
Jacobs, Mike, 49
Jennings, Hughie, 13
Jet Pilot, 250
Johnson, Jack, 35, 36
Johnson, Martin, 58
Johnson, Ray, 286
Johnson, Walter, 13
Johnstown, 248, 251
Jones, Ben, 250
Jones, "Biff", 105, 109, 202
Jones, Colonel Bob, 176, 177
Jones, Bobby, 43, 67-73, 84, 85, 165, 169, 173-184, 220, 221, 244, 263, 264
Jones, Bobby III, 85, 221
Jones, Casey, 166, 167
Jones, Ernest, 221
Jones, Howard, 109
Jones, Jimmy, 266
Jones, "Soldier", 158
Jones, Tad, 23, 26, 30, 31, 32, 109

"Just A Wearyin' For You", 289

Kane, Eddie, 53
Karcis, Bull, 148, 150-156
Kearns, Jack (Doc), 48, 49, 53, 54, 55, 163, 259, 260, 269
Keefe, Bill, 286
Keeler, O. B., 285
Kelland, Clarence Budding-ton, 293, 294, 295, 299
Keller, Charlie, 212, 213
Kelley, Robert F. (Bob), 2, 286
Kelly, George (High Pock-ets), 158
Kennedy, Colonel, 42
Kent, Frank, 280
Kentucky Derby, 247-251
Kentucky Derby Winter Book, 250
Keogh, Hugh E. (HEK), 282, 285
Kerr, Dickie, 80
Ketchel, Stanley, 297
Kibbee, Guy, 298
Kieran, John, 1, 255, 286
King Ranch, 250
Koenig, Mark, 82, 137, 138, 139
Kurtsinger, Charley, 211

Lacoste, Rene, 165
Laird, Tommy, 283, 297
Lajoie, Napoleon (Larry), 13, 257
Lambeau, Curley, 103
Landis, Judge, 278
Lardner, Ring, 3, 5, 79, 80, 100, 162, 163, 168, 185,

305

306

307

Salsinger, Harry, 285, 286, 287
Sande, Earl, 89, 90, 91, 244
Sanford, Foster, 233
Santa Anita Derby, 250
Santa Anita Handicap, 250
Sarazen, Gene, 69, 70, 173, 174, 175, 183, 227, 228
Saunders, Blondie, 296, 297
Schmeling, Max, 268
Schulz, Germany, 234
Schumacher, Garry, 283
Schwartz, Marchmont, 112
Scott, Everett, 42, 43, 44
Seabiscuit, 209, 210, 211, 248
Seminole Indians, 255
Sharkey, Jack, 60, 61, 62, 63, 65, 169, 171, 268
Shim Malone, 250
Shocker, Urban, 44
Shor, Toots, 283, 284
Shor, Mrs. Toots (Baby), 284
Simmons, Al, 191, 192, 193
Sims, P. Hal, 18, 19, 214, 229, 230
Sinkwich, Frank, 219
Sir Barton, 247, 251
Sisler, George, 13
Skene, Don, 65
Slaughter, Enos (Country), 11, 229
Smith, Clipper, 202
Smith, Horton, 174, 181, 183, 263
Smith, MacDonald, 174
Smith, Red, 3, 286, 295, 296
Smits, Larry, 63
Snakes (various), 254
Snead, Sam, 58, 183, 284
Snider, Duke, 10

Snow, Neil, 233
"Soldier of the Legion, The" (excerpt from), 213
Speaker, Tris, 10, 13, 240
"Sporting Philosophy, A", 114
Sportlight, The (columns), 39-44, 74, 75, 92, 132, 133, 134, 135, 187-199, 209-216, 218, 219, 220, 221, 222, 224-234, 238-246, 253-270
Sprague, Bud, 107
Stagehand, 250
Stagg, Alonzo, 109
Stallings, George, 9
Stanton, Frank L., 280, 285, 289, 290
Staton, Harry, 64, 65
Stepfather, 250
Stephens, Helen, 198
Stoddard, John, 7
Stoneham, Charles, 82
Stranahan, Bob, 227
Stranahan, Frank, 227, 228
Stribling, Young, 63, 65, 66
Strong, Ken, 146-156
Stuhldreher, Harry, 94-99, 101, 103, 104, 113, 188
Stymie, 248
Sullivan, John L., 168
Sutherland, Jock, 109, 204, 293, 294
Swing On, 209

"Tarawa", 217
Taylor, Bert Leston (B.L.T.), 280
Thevenow, Tommy, 137, 139, 140
Thomas, Frank, 109

309